# MUIRHEAD LIBRARY OF PHILOSOPHY

An admirable statement of the aims of the Library of Philosophy was provided by the first editor, the late Professor J. H. Muirhead, in his description of the original programme printed in Erdmann's *History of Philosophy* under the date 1890. This was slightly modified in subsequent volumes to take the form of the following statement:

'The Muirhead Library of Philosophy was designed as a contribution to the History of Modern Philosophy under the heads: first of Different Schools of Thought—Sensationalist, Realist, Idealist, Intuitivist; secondly of different Subjects—Psychology, Ethics, Aesthetics, Political Philosophy, Theology. While much had been done in England in tracing the course of evolution in nature, history, economics, morals and religion little had been done in tracing the development of thought on these subjects. Yet "the evolution of opinion is part of the whole evolution".

'By the co-operation of different writers in carrying out this plan it was hoped that a thoroughness and completeness of treatment, otherwise unattainable, might be secured. It was believed also that from writers mainly British and American fuller consideration of English Philosophy than it had hitherto received might be looked for. In the earlier series of books containing, among others, Bosanquet's *History of Aesthetic*, Pfleiderer's *Rational Theology since Kant*, Albee's *History of English Utilitarianism*, Bonar's *Philosophy and Political Economy*, Brett's *History of Psychology*, Ritchie's *Natural Rights*, these objects were to a large extent effected.

'In the meantime original work of a high order was being produced both in England and America by such writers as Bradley, Stout, Bertrand Russell, Baldwin, Urban, Montague, and others, and a new interest in foreign works, German, French and Italian, which had either become classical or were attracting public attention, had developed. The scope of the Library thus became extended into something more international, and it is entering on the fifth decade of its existence in the hope that it may contribute to that mutual understanding between countries which is so pressing a need of the present time.'

The need which Professor Muirhead stressed is no less pressing today, and few will deny that philosophy has much to do with enabling us to meet it, although no one, least of all Muirhead himself, would regard that as the sole, or even the main, object of philosophy. As Professor Muirhead continues to lend the distinction of his name to the Library of Philosophy it seemed not inappropriate to allow him to recall us to these aims in his own words. The emphasis on the history of thought also seemed to me very timely; and the number of important works promised for the Library in the very near future augur well for the continued fulfilment, in this and other ways, of the expectations of the original editor.

H. D. LEWIS

# MUIRHEAD LIBRARY OF PHILOSOPHY

## General Editor: H. D. Lewis
*Professor of History and Philosophy of Religion in the University of London*

𝔐uirbead 𝕷ibrary of 𝔓bilosophy

EDITED BY H. D. LEWIS

# ETHICS AND CHRISTIANITY

# ETHICS AND CHRISTIANITY

KEITH WARD

*Lecturer in Moral Philosophy*
*at the University of St Andrews*

LONDON · GEORGE ALLEN & UNWIN LTD
NEW YORK · HUMANITIES PRESS INC

FIRST PUBLISHED IN 1970

© *George Allen & Unwin Ltd., 1970*

BRITISH ISBN 0 04 241001 0

USA SBN 391 00047 0

PRINTED IN GREAT BRITAIN
*in 11 on 12 pt Imprint*
BY UNWIN BROTHERS LIMITED
WOKING AND LONDON

TO MARIAN

# ACKNOWLEDGEMENTS

Many people have helped in the formulation of the ideas expounded in this book, and I would particularly like to thank the Rt Rev. I. T. Ramsey, Professor R. S. Downie and the Rev. E. H. Pyle for their inspiration and encouragement. I also owe a special debt, as do all who have worked with him, to Professor W. G. Maclagan, whose painstaking comments on the text were invaluable and whose personal influence has been considerable.

I am grateful to the following for permission to use extracts from published papers: the Editor of *Philosophy* for an extract from 'Moral Seriousness' (April, 1970); the Editor of *Religious Studies* for an extract from 'Existence, Transcendence and God' (April, 1968); the Editor of the *Scottish Journal of Theology* for an extract from 'Christian Ethics and the Being of God' (March, 1969); and the Editor of the *Journal of Theological Studies* for an extract from 'Freedom and the Irenaean Theodicy' (April, 1969).

Finally, I am indebted to Mr P. D. Shaw and Professor H. D. Lewis, who kindly read the manuscript and made valuable suggestions.

St Andrews, 1969                                    KEITH WARD

# CONTENTS

# CONTENTS

# INTRODUCTION

In this book I have tried to elucidate the fundamental characteristics of Christian ethics. I have not been concerned with particular problems of the application of Christian ethical principles in specific situations, nor with an attempt to expound in detail the substantive content of Christian ethics—what is meant by 'agape' and how this compares or contrasts with other alleged supreme principles of morality. Thus the problems with which I have been concerned have not perhaps been usually considered as central parts of courses offered on Christian ethics in the past.

My concern has been with what is of most vital concern to the moral philosopher—the exposition of the formal characteristics of a system of morality rather than with the detail of its content and application. But this is a foundational study for any treatment of ethics; it is precisely on such matters of the general character of a moral system that the deepest divisions between secular and religious interpretations arise. Thus, if they are not exposed and brought into the open, such divisions work unnoticed below the surface of all ethical discussion and make real communication impossible, even when it may seem superficially that some sort of understanding is being achieved.

This situation is commonplace at the present time, when it is fashionable for both secular humanists and liberal Christians to speak of commitment to love as the basis of their respective creeds; and it is difficult to see what it is that divides them. The divisions are indeed present, however, though confused by a failure to render them explicit; and so discussions proceed without any real understanding being achieved on either side. What I have tried to do is to render explicit those presuppositions of a Christian interpretation of the moral life which are often taken for granted, or very often overlooked by Christians and secularists alike. And, though this is not primarily a book of Christian apologetic, I have tried to put the Christian interpretation in as favourable a light as I can.

To put my conclusions in what may be a conveniently summary form, I hold that the Christian system of ethics is:

(1) *Objective*: it claims to state moral truths which are made true by certain objective facts (ultimately, as I argue, by the being of God).

(2) *Authoritative*: its moral truths derive from some authoritative experient of the ultimate moral facts.

(3) *Attitudinal*: it calls for the pursuit of personal perfection in the adoption of specific attitudes.

(4) *Teleological*: it speaks of a final moral end to be realized by individual moral actions here and now.

(5) *Charismatic*: it actually offers a power to begin to realize the new quality of life (or attitude) which it authoritatively demands.

All these characteristic claims are subject to dispute by moral philosophers, and some attempt must be made to defend them against attack. But not only do they need to be defended from attack by secularists; for there are Christian philosophers, too, who seem prepared to deny them. Thus it must also be established that they are indeed essential characteristics of a Christian approach to morality; and I try to establish this by showing how their absence would lead to conclusions which would not be generally acceptable to Christians.

My general thesis, then, is that, though an 'autonomous ethic'—one that does not depend on adherence to any religious beliefs—is quite possible, it is also possible to have an essentially religious conception of the moral life; and Christianity possesses one such conception. I would also hold that the Christian conception is a more adequate one than any secular conceptions of morality; but it does not follow from this that Christians will be morally better than non-Christians; for religious morality, like any other, can become an oppressive and relentless task-master. I would agree with the opponents of Christianity in thinking that there can be few things more abhorrent than a fanatical and intolerant pursuit of religious dogma; but no systems of morality are immune from the perversity of their adherents. The Christian conception in itself seems to me both more adequate to the moral situation of men and also more morally desirable. Ultimately, however, the choice between a Christian and a secular morality must be faced by each individual in the light of his own experience and reflection. What I have tried to do is to present the distinctiveness of Christian morality as clearly as possible, and perhaps thereby to make the factors involved in such a decision more apparent.

# PART ONE
# DUTY AND THE WILL OF GOD

# THE CASE AGAINST
# THEISTIC MORALITY

1. It used to be considered perfectly obvious that human morality depends essentially upon religious belief; so much so that even John Locke, in his famous essay on 'Toleration', decided that atheists were not to be trusted; for, lacking belief in a supreme being, they were presumed to be liable to break their word with impunity.[1] This sort of thinking persists among many if not most ordinary men, who at least expect believers in God to profess higher moral standards than professed atheists, and who associate atheism with immorality and depravity. Thus many people in Britain send their children to Church or Sunday School in order to teach them to be good; they tend not to be so concerned about the truth of the specifically religious doctrines they are taught. And there are even many Christians who believe that the central core of their faith is simply love for their fellow-men rather than belief in certain supernatural facts.

In recent years, however, there has been a rising tide of influential opinion which rejects any such essential connection between morality and religion, which denies that love for others is a specifically religious or Christian virtue, and which advocates the observance of high moral standards without belief in any religious doctrines whatsoever.

The very fact that this can be done at all seems to show that there cannot, indeed, be an essential connection between religion and morality. For there are highly moral individuals who profess no religious belief. If it is said that atheists are people who tend to break their promises, then one should be asked to compare the conduct of theists and atheists in this respect and see which class of men is more trustworthy. It might even be claimed by an impartial observer that the history of the Christian Church leaves little to be said in favour of the trustworthiness of Christians. One rejoinder to this charge might be to say that all who are in the

Church are not Christians; but this raises the difficulty of how one can find out who the 'real' Christians are. Presumably it will be said that they are those who sincerely avow Christ as their Lord and Master; but, once again, how can one sort out the sincere from the insincere? The answer, of a sort, is given in the Biblical text, 'By their fruits you shall know them'.[2] But this means that we call those Christians sincere who show, by their behaviour, that they are trustworthy—and so on. Now if our reason for calling people 'real' Christians is that they are trustworthy, it becomes ludicrous to claim that real Christians tend to be more trustworthy than non-Christians. For the game has been won by definition; one can reply in like manner by defining 'really sincere' atheists as the trustworthy atheists, and then claiming that such atheists also tend to be very trustworthy!

2.  But not only do many people claim to be moral, or at least have high moral standards, without having any religious beliefs; it might also be said that attempting to make morality depend upon religion is itself an immoral procedure, and one calculated to undermine rather than support the practice of morality. For such attempts seem to imply that men would not keep their promises unless they could be sure that it would pay them to do so in the long run. They would not be good unless they thought that they would be rewarded for their pains by God; they would not refrain from evil-doing unless they feared the punishment that God would inevitably allot to them. Thus morality is founded on fear and buttressed by intolerance; without fear of punishment no man would strive to do good; without intolerance of atheism the moral fabric of society would collapse.

It is a possible belief that all human morality is based on fear and repression, but I think most people would agree that this is a cynical and warped belief. In the history of mankind there are, fortunately, countless examples of men who have renounced riches, position, comfort or life itself, in order to do what is right, not for hope of reward but just because it *is* right. And there are countless men who would agree with Immanuel Kant when he said that to do what is right for hope of reward, or fear of punishment, or for any other reason than simply that it is right, degrades morality into prudence and cannot be counted as morally good in any real sense.[3] On this view, if a man throughout the whole course of his life does right actions, but only because he hopes to be rewarded by God, then he is not a good man at all. The good man does what is right even if it conflicts with all prudential considerations of his own welfare, both now and in the long run. This is the essence of morality; and since the theory that morality depends on religion seems to undermine it, it undermines morality itself by subsuming it under an appeal to one's own self-interest.

3. However, even if one could accept such a reduction of morality to rational self-interest, it is still not true that the rational self-interested man would not be moral at all without belief in a Divine Judge. On the contrary, it has been a constant theme of political philosophers throughout the centuries that a rational man will, at least on the whole, be moral because it pays him, not in heaven but now on earth, in terms of security and protection from others.

As Thomas Hobbes maintained, the life of a man who is not protected by the laws of a particular society is 'poor, nasty, brutish and short'[4]. He is continually at the mercy of ruthless enemies; and, even if he himself is strong, he must live in constant fear that the weak will band together to strike him down. So it is in man's own interest to accept the rule of law, which provides security at a moderate cost to himself. In other words, it is in the best interests of all men, atheists as well as theists, to support social regulations. If the support of morality is to be prudence, all that is needed is not belief in God, but recognition that social order provides security.

It is true that a man of this opinion will probably have a more restricted view of morality than a theist. He will respect life and property, keep promises and, in general, obey those laws necessary to the preservation of society; but he will not consider it necessary to abstain from lustful thoughts or to refuse to use the law for his own ends as a prudent theist might. For, whereas God is all-knowing and all-powerful and thus punishes even our most secret wrongs, human law has its blind spots and its loopholes which can be taken advantage of.

But the point is that the prudent atheist will not be devoid of all morality. He will always support the existence of law, and advocate that others conform to it, in the interests of his own security—even if he secretly hopes to break the law undiscovered. Under these conditions, the simple concern for social cohesion will suffice to ensure the existence of a large law-abiding body of citizens, even though it will probably also necessitate the existence of an effective law-enforcement organization and of a criminal class.

This, it may be said, is just how things stand with human society and, so far as can be seen, how they have always stood. Belief or disbelief in God is evidently not a sufficient motivating force to affect human morality in noticeable respects.

4. What I have said is that if morality cannot be reduced to prudence, but is a matter of doing right acts simply because they are right and for no other reason, then morality cannot depend upon belief in God. For it cannot depend upon anything except a recognition that certain things are right.

But if one takes a cynical view and asserts that human morality must be founded on prudence, then again belief in God is not necessary for the existence of some social morality, even though this morality may be a restricted and rather makeshift enterprise by theistic standards.

Of course, one may still say that if God does exist, conformity to this social morality will not be good enough to preserve one from the punishments God will later visit on men. And this may be true. But now the argument has shifted its ground slightly. Whereas it began by saying that the existence of morality *at all* depends upon belief in God, it is now saying that one cannot justify a very rigorous sort of morality on prudential grounds unless God exists. And to this amended argument the atheist can reply, first, that it is not a settled question that we ought to have such a rigorous morality; second, that one would have to be absolutely sure that God exists before one could accept that to obey such a morality was the prudent thing; and third, that since there is no *moral* worth in doing something because it is prudent, it is a strange, even monstrous, sort of God who will reward us for being prudent and punish us for being imprudent, even when we were not sure that we were being imprudent since we were not sure at the time that God existed.

The point of these objections is that if it were possible to be certain that God existed, and was a scrupulous Judge, then it would be prudent to obey his commands. But since it is generally agreed that one cannot be certain of God's existence, it follows that one cannot be certain that obeying his supposed commands is prudent. We must act in necessary ignorance, and where God has left us in ignorance of what it is prudent to do, it cannot be supposed that he will then proceed to punish us for being imprudent. It would be as though God said: 'I am not going to tell you what you must do. But if you fail to do it I will punish you'.

It is usually agreed that it is just to punish a man only if he does something knowing it to be wrong. But on the view here being considered, 'wrong' just means 'imprudent'; a man cannot know his acts are imprudent unless he already knows that God exists; since he does not know this, it follows that to try to make moral conduct depend upon belief in God undermines the very foundations of morality in at least two ways. First, by turning it into prudence; and second, by making it intrinsically uncertain. For whether or not we act morally on any occasion will depend upon our belief in God—a belief which may vary in strength from one time to another, which never possesses complete certainty, and which often vanishes altogether. Thus the argument that morality depends upon religion, when considered rationally by anyone at the present time, can only produce a continual tension arising from trying to found one's actions on a question of fact—the existence of God—which can never be established with certainty. Far from providing morality with a strong foundation, it will consequently tend to make men less sure of what is right, and less prepared to make a present sacrifice for the sake of an uncertain reward.

5. Moreover, it might even be said that religious belief itself, far from being the foundation of morality, is positively immoral. For it advocates the firm adherence to factual beliefs for which there can be in the nature of the case no sufficient evidence. Since one of the basic moral values is concern for truth for its own sake, wherever it may lead, the advocacy of beliefs which are to be held with a conviction greater than that which the evidence would warrant must be directly opposed to this value, and must therefore be itself immoral. It is indeed not at all difficult to find many instances in which religious leaders have attempted to condemn scientific discoveries on the sole basis that they have been alleged to conflict with Biblical revelation. Such instances display very well the sort of tension that can arise between religious belief and scientific evidence. And they raise the general question of how far

considerations of empirical evidence can be allowed, by the believer, to count against his belief.

This question is perhaps the key question of modern theology; for Christians preach that belief in the Lordship of Christ is necessary for man's eternal salvation, and so it is naturally, they believe, of greater importance than any other item of human knowledge or belief. But it is precisely because religious belief has this importance in the life of the believer that a tension can and, it may be held, even *must* arise in the minds of all scientifically educated Christians. For the basic axiom of scientific method is that one must always seek to test one's beliefs by attempting to find empirical evidence for their falsity. That is not to say that all great scientists spend their time trying to prove their theories false; there is a place for obstinacy and recalcitrance in science as in other spheres of life. But it is to say that the test of a scientific theory is whether it fits all the empirical facts it ought to cover; and that if it finally becomes apparent that it does not, it must be rejected or, at best, amended.

Must not the Christian, then, always bear in some part of his mind the knowledge that one day his religious beliefs—those beliefs which are more important to him than anything else on earth—might be shown to be false? Might it not be shown, for instance by some historical discovery, that Jesus was a political agitator, or that his body was secretly hidden by the disciples, or that Paul was a lunatic? Or in different scientific fields, might it not be shown, by molecular biologists for example, that life can be completely accounted for on mechanical principles, or that survival of bodily death is impossible, or that there is life on other planets with no religious beliefs or with different ones? What would the Christian then say—that Jesus died for all the Universe or only for the earth?

These are certainly the sorts of questions, however hypothetical, which must be borne in mind in assessing the truth of the Christian claims; and yet it must be admitted that we just have not got the evidence to give a firm answer to them. In such a situation doubt is the only possible option for a man whose concern is wholeheartedly for the truth, whatever it is. Does it not follow then that the Christian who makes a total, unconditional commitment to the truth of his faith does something which is unreasonable? More than that, does he not do something which is fundamentally immoral, because it must undermine his commitment to seek truth by putting preconceived opinions in place of unbiased investigation? The Christian in a scientific age, it might be said, must be either schizophrenic or immoral. For he must either unconditionally affirm some facts which he knows with another part of his mind to be inadequately evidenced; or he must simply refuse to accept evidence as counting against revelation, and thereby set his face against all possibility of finding the truth about the nature of the Universe.

6. This extremely weighty argument does not count against purely moral commitment, of course, because it is generally agreed that empirical evidence about what is the case cannot be used to count against statements about what ought to be the case. Some restriction needs to be put on this formulation, it is true; for one might have to know what it is possible to do before one can assert that something ought to be done. Nevertheless, the fact remains that one can quite reasonably undertake an unconditional commitment to telling the truth, for example; and there can be no fear that the subsequent discovery of new factual evidence about the world could threaten to undermine one's commitment; for it is just not a commitment as to the facts.

In the nature of the case, then, it seems that it is quite possible, reasonable, and desirable to undertake unconditional moral commitments and to be perfectly certain about what one ought to do. So, as far as the logic of the situation is concerned, one must say that moral beliefs are logically more certain than religious beliefs. That is to say, whatever the conviction of the person who holds the beliefs there must always remain a logical possibility of showing religious beliefs to be false, whereas there seems to be no logical possibility of showing moral beliefs to be false. To seek to base morality on religion, therefore, is to attempt to base the more certain on the less certain; and to try to found human duty on the declared will of God is to found what we can be sure of upon what we can never be sure that we know.

7. Faced with such formidable objections as these, some Christians have attempted to deny that Christianity does consist in the acceptance of factual propositions about the nature of the Universe.

The very requirement it makes for unconditional acceptance, they say, shows that it is not a set of facts to be believed on authority, but a particular sort of morality or way of life. To be a Christian, on this sort of interpretation, is to commit oneself unreservedly to love as the supreme value. If this move could be accomplished, it would indeed remove the logical difficulties inherent in the claim of religion to unconditional belief in matters of fact. But it also seems to remove religion itself; for why should an atheist not commit himself unreservedly to a life of love?

Again, it seems that, since commitment to a loving way of life is solely the decision to live in a certain manner, it entails or depends upon no factual statements whatsoever—except that such a manner of life is a human possibility. So there is no reason why a person who makes such a self-commitment should call himself a Christian at all.

Two Christian thinkers who have tried to interpret Christianity solely as calling for commitment to a certain way of life are Professors Braithwaite and van Buren,[5] who agree in specifying this 'way of life' as one of love, or freedom from fear and anxiety, to live wholly for others. But when they attempt to say why such a commitment should be called 'Christian', all Braithwaite suggests is that the Biblical stories about Jesus, whether or not they are true, have a psychological efficacy in helping one to adopt the 'agapeistic' life; while van Buren supposes that the 'agapeistic' life is 'caught' from Jesus or his present-day disciples rather like a psychological infection. In both cases the connection between stories (not even regarded as true by Braithwaite) about Jesus and the present way of life which they recommend is alleged to be some form of psychological causation.

As Braithwaite writes, 'A religious belief is an intention to behave in a certain way (a moral belief) together with the entertainment of certain stories . . . in the mind of the believer.'[6] Any such view, however, that religious stories are just psychological aids to a previously selected policy of life, is incompatible with any claim by the Christian religion to a final or unique revelation in Jesus. For there is nothing to be 'revealed' except a way of life; and Jesus can only be, at best, a perfect *example* of the morally good man. He may exemplify the good life; but there is no guarantee that he is the only example. Indeed, if his life presents a real human possibility there is no reason why many men should not achieve it, and no reason to suppose that any who do are more than ordinarily human. Moreover, there is no logical reason why the story of the life of a morally good man should help us to live morally good lives. For as long as it does, it could well be said that we have failed to come to moral maturity when we still need fairy-tales to encourage us in well-doing.

But Christians often treat Jesus not just as the perfect example of a previously known morality, but as the one who authoritatively reveals that morality to them. Braithwaite himself appears to waver on this point. For he says that the agapeistic way of life can only be specified adequately by the whole religious scheme; a main function of the stories is actually to outline the policy. Yet if these stories actually tell one what the right policy is by the examples they provide, it is hard to see how one can be free to interpret or discard them in the way one finds most helpful. It is quite a different thing from saying that religious stories are crutches for moral invalids, to say that they provide an authoritative standard for human morality.

On the other hand, how can the life of one man provide an authoritative revelation of morality? It is clear that no authoritative declaration could *make* something right; at most it can declare something to *be* right in itself. Now it does seem true that a morally perceptive individual can come to see something as right which is not so regarded by others—the abolition of slavery, for example. And in this sense a man can 'reveal' a higher moral code than any hitherto accepted. So Jesus might be said to reveal the ethic of love, or concern for individual human worth, as higher than that of, for example, obeying a certain code of laws, human or divine. But even supposing this to be so there seems to be nothing specifically 'religious' about such a moral code, however revealed. Even if Jesus was the first man to advocate loving concern for others (which he was not), if this is the right principle of action for all men, then it is right for Christians and non-Christians alike, and it is right whether God exists or not or whether Jesus said it or not. There can be nothing distinctively Christian about the principle of concern for others; anyone, Christian or not, can adhere to it, all men ought to, whatever their religious beliefs, and many non-Christians do. Nor is there any reason why, once stated, this principle should retain any connection with its historical exponent. If agapeistic life is the right moral code, then it does not matter who first said that it was so. It is, one might say, the moral commands which are important, not the commander. So it could certainly not be the case that one accepted a certain moral code as right *because* Jesus (or anyone else) first promulgated it. Any such reason would only undermine morality by subordinating it to some non-moral principle. Thus there can be no appeal to authority on this interpretation of Christianity.

What is left is a form of belief in which Jesus cannot function as a unique or final authority, and in which there is no dependence upon any special revelation through or by him. In other words, it fails to retain any significant connection with the historical Jesus, and therefore must fail to be distinctively—that is, uniquely and solely—Christian.

It seems, then, that no plausible case can be made out for calling a moral code of 'agapeism' or 'freedom from anxiety, and for others', a specifically *Christian* code. And, *a fortiori*, there is no case for calling it a 'theistic' morality, since the notion of 'God' has been dropped, quietly or noisily, from such accounts as an unduly metaphysical concept. Atheists, therefore, need have nothing to say against the recommendation of an agapeistic life; nor need they object if some who adopt such an attitude decide that they will call themselves 'Christian'; they will reject only the mistaken theory that such an attitude can *only* be adopted by people who call themselves Christians.

However, it may be noted that it would not be unreasonable for them to point out that Jesus, whom the 'agapeists' select as their supreme example of total devotion to others, would rather seem to be, on their own assumptions, deluded, arrogant and intolerant. His reported utterances about God and life-after-death must, such agapeists say, be false; his alleged claims to supreme authority and knowledge of God are not signs of undue humility; and his remarks about the Pharisees are not expressions of unbounded tolerance. If one grants the existence of God and the unique status of Jesus in relation to him, these characteristics of his reported life become quite natural and appropriate; but to those who reject such suppositions and seek only an example of a perfectly moral but completely ordinary human being, Jesus would seem to be one of the last men on earth to qualify as an ideal. The atheist may therefore be forgiven if he evinces incredulity upon being informed that some men find their devotion to agapeism heightened by meditation on the life of a deluded fanatic; and if he therefore claims that the agapeistic life belongs more properly to atheistic humanism than to the Christian religion.

8. From the arguments of this chapter it appears that religion, so far from being the necessary support of all morality, actually undermines morality by introducing prudential considerations—which are in any case largely ineffective in governing conduct—and by rendering the foundations of morality uncertain; it is itself immoral in that it calls for total commitment to factual beliefs without adequate evidence; and even in its most lofty moral doctrines it can add nothing distinctive to a non-religious morality. This constitutes what I consider to be the most powerful part of the case against basing morality in general on religion, or against any particular sort of morality which is based upon religious beliefs and therefore against theistic morality.[7]

In attempting to answer this argument, in attempting to show why the Christian system of ethics does not fall to these powerful criticisms—and how, in fact, it can be the fulfilment of various strands in secular systems of ethics which, as it were, point beyond themselves—the whole nature and framework of ethics itself will have to be examined and clarified. This is a large enterprise, calling for a total reconstruction rather than a series of piecemeal attacks and rejoinders. Accordingly, the first task is to distinguish the various sorts of questions which may be asked about human morality, and how the Christian will answer them. In this way the points of difference between a Christian and a non-religious system of ethics may be located with some precision, and it will become clearer what reply the Christian is able to make to the charges laid against him in the preceding paragraph.

# II

## THE BASIC QUESTIONS
## OF ETHICS

1. In setting out the case against theistic morality it has been assumed that it is quite clear what morality is. It has been assumed, for example, that the concern of morality is with the actions of men in the world, and with the general principles under which those actions can be brought; that some acts should be performed simply because it is right to perform them, regardless of the consequences to oneself; and that the 'rightness' of an act cannot be established by appeal to matters of fact. It was also noted that a rational and prudent man could construct a moral code—a set of general principles as to how men should act—by considering what classes of action must be enjoined or forbidden if peace and security were to be attained in society. Of course, such a man must ultimately say that it is right to aim at peace and security, either for their own sake or as a means to attaining further goals such as personal happiness, which it is right to aim at.

Morality, then, is concerned with establishing what sorts of things men should do and what sorts of things they should aim at in life. And this is quite different from asking what sorts of things they actually do, or wish they could do, or want to do. Some recent philosophers have said that it is not their concern to say what men should do or aim at, at least *qua* philosophers. Nevertheless they do, as men, give their assent to certain moral principles. And since their moral philosophizing is usually about the moral principles to which they assent, it is important at least to know what are those principles which their analyses are supposed to elucidate.

When a man asks what it is right for him to do, there are at least three different things he might have in mind. First, he may be asking on a quite particular occasion, 'Which of the actions now open to me is it right to perform?' The answer to this question, if it could be provided, would be to specify some particular act as right. But this answer only raises a further question, which is the second thing a man may have in mind; namely, 'Which general principles of action is it right for me to adopt?' For if one says of any particular act that it is right, there is usually some general principle under which the act falls which is held to be right. For example, if I say, 'You ought now to give Fred the money', this raises the question 'Why ought I to do so?', to which a possible answer would be, 'Because it would be an instance of promise-keeping; and the principle that promises should be kept is right'. Thus if one accepts particular acts as right, one thereby accepts also that the general principles under which they fall are right. But the question can be pushed yet further back to ask, 'Why are these moral principles accepted as right?' or 'What makes these principles right?'; and this is the third thing a man may have in mind. One may, indeed, reject this question as inappropriate—just as one may, logically, reject as inappropriate the suggestion that particular acts can be right only if they fall under general principles which are accepted as right. One may say, that is, 'It is just *right* to keep promises; and there is nothing more to be said' (just as one may say, 'It is just *right* to hit John, but not because "hitting Johns" is an acceptable moral principle'). But there is a human urge to seek one ultimate principle of morality, or at least no more than two or three principles, under which all the other general moral principles fall. Moral philosophers have not been slow in suggesting such ultimate principles; and some candidates for that position, phrased in an over-simple but not grossly inaccurate way, are: 'the greatest happiness of the greatest number' (Mill); 'the fact that a principle can be willed by all men, everywhere' (Kant); 'the pursuit of happiness' (Epicurus); 'the fulfilment of one's distinctively human capacities' (Bradley); 'the completely disinterested love of others' (possibly Jesus); and 'obedience to Conscience' (Butler, at least at times). As putative ultimate principles of morality, these are suggested clauses to complete the expression, 'Any act is right if it satisfies this principle. . .'.

In this way it is possible to construct lists of acts, principles and ultimate principles which various communities of men, our own among them, hold to be morally right. These lists will differ in many respects; some communities may have no ultimate principles; others may have a plurality of them; some may contain quite different principles from others, and so on. It may be said that the compilation of such lists is a job for sociology, not philosophy. That may be the case where what is in question is simply the formulation of other people's explicit beliefs; but in the case of one's own beliefs, and even of the implicit beliefs of others, reflection of a type which may properly be called philosophical is at least desirable. For it needs reflection to decide what moral beliefs one really wishes to espouse when they are explicitly put before one; to decide whether such beliefs fall under more general principles; whether all one's beliefs are consistent; and whether certain principles need to be revised or discarded when one sees the nature of the consequences which their consistent application would have. In all these, and perhaps in other ways, reflective thinking is a desirable factor in any attempt to construct a list of all the moral beliefs to which one is prepared to give assent.

2. When one has such a list of moral principles, however, one can proceed to press the fundamental philosophical question 'Why?' even further back, and ask, 'Why does one accept just these principles as the right ones?' One cannot answer by offering a further, higher-order principle; there must be at least one principle which is ultimate in that it cannot be subsumed under any other principle. So much is plain. What sort of answer can be given to this 'Why?' question, then?

All that can be done is to make clear just what one *means* by saying that an act is 'right', or a thing is 'good', and to make clear the grounds upon which assertions of 'rightness' or 'goodness' can justifiably be made. For example, an intuitionist in ethics will say that when he says an act is right he means, perhaps, that it (or the principle under which it can be subsumed) possesses an actual property of 'rightness'. In a similar way, when one says that a proposition is true, one may mean that it possesses the property of 'truth'. What these properties of 'rightness' and 'truth' are, is very difficult to determine, but it is generally agreed that they do not depend for their existence upon their apprehension by any human mind and that they are, in this sense, objective. For an intuitionist, then, the answer to the question 'Why accept these principles as right?' is simply that they objectively possess the property of 'rightness'—just as the best answer to the analogous question 'Why accept this proposition as true?' is simply that it *is* true.

Of course, this immediately invites the question, 'How do you know it is true?' And for the intuitionist a distinct area of moral philosophy is the attempt to show how one knows moral truths (whether by reason or moral sense, for example) and just what it is that one thus knows (a property, relation or proposition, for example).

Many other philosophers, however, need not explore this sort of question since they do not admit that moral truths are *known* at all. Thus, emotivists hold that when they say an act is right they mean that they are apt to express approval of it—not that it has any particular objective property. And prescriptivists maintain that the expression 'This act is right' means that they recommend or prescribe it to themselves and others. For such philosophers their ultimate answer to the question 'Why accept these principles as right?' must lie in an appeal to behavioural facts about human beings. Even in one's own case one must say either 'I just do approve that sort of act' or 'I just do commit myself to this principle of action'; and these are both statements of fact about human behaviour. It is incumbent upon even such philosophers, however, to give some sort of answer to the question, 'Why accept a given set of principles?' And the way in which they can do this is to give an account of what it is in the facts of human existence which makes the use of moral terms appropriate. Such an analysis will not, of course, provide the reasons for accepting any particular set of moral principles (though it may naturally suggest or exclude some principles); but it will, in stating the sorts of context in which moral language arises and is normally used, make clear the sorts of consideration which would be relevant in assessing, promulgating and justifying such principles. The 'Why?' question is answered by showing how moral language is used, and what features of the human situation generate moral discourse. It is answered, as perhaps all ultimate 'Why?' questions must be, simply by showing how things are, by articulating in a clear and orderly way the complex and various modes of moral thought and belief, the relations between them and other areas of human thought, the similarities and dissimilarities between them. Such an enterprise has sometimes been denigrated as a mere concern with words and their meanings; perhaps more of its importance is suggested if it is seen as an analysis of a fundamental area of human thought, in the context of those features of the human situation which it exists to articulate and explore. With this

C

proviso one can then say that a second main philosophical concern with morality, in addition to the construction of a list of moral beliefs, consists in an analysis of the meanings of the terms used in ethical discourse.

3. Such investigation into the meaning of ethical terms and the contexts of human activity in which such terms find their proper use may, by a natural extension, lead to what may be called a study of the metaphysical foundations of morality. The sorts of question which will arise for such a study will be those concerned to relate the whole complex of moral activity to the other main sorts of human concern—for example, in art, science and religion. And one may attempt to construct a synoptic vision of human existence within which morality has a specific place or function; one's conception of what morality is will then be presented as intelligible in the light of one's broader conception of what man is.

To take an example: if one believes, for whatever reasons, that man in all aspects of his behaviour is made up of nothing more than sets of fundamental physical particles, governed in their interaction by a few physical laws, one will tend to view the phenomenon of morality in a specific light—intuitionism will almost certainly be excluded, for instance; and one's views on such topics as responsibility and punishment will inevitably be coloured by one's basic belief about man's nature.

The influence of metaphysical views on moral views is not a one-way relation, however. For one does not first decide what the nature of man is and then adopt a certain set of moral beliefs. The moral beliefs one inevitably starts from are one of the most powerful sets of considerations which help to form a metaphysical view of man; and in the example just cited one may say that it is only because the theorist is prepared to adopt a broadly naturalistic view of morals that he is able to assent to the materialistic view to which his reflections on other aspects of human knowledge and experience lead him. One could, like Kant, maintain that the awareness of moral obligation was so overriding that it alone provided a sufficient ground for refuting a materialist view of man. But even (or especially) in Kant's case the matter is exceedingly complex; for it is true that he could not have said this of morality if his theoretical investigations had not left open the possibility that materialism was false, or even if they had not positively suggested (in the demands of Reason) a transcendent ground of human knowledge, even though knowledge of such a ground was denied to Theoretical Reason.[1]

The influence and interaction of one's reflections on morality and on the other aspects of human knowledge and experience is thus a mutual and constantly developing one. And if one does adopt a general metaphysical view of the nature of man, it will be largely shaped by the constant and complex interplay of considerations drawn from all the major areas of human concern as they adjust, coalesce and unify into a more or less coherent 'picture' of man's nature.

The question of the metaphysical foundations of morality is of special importance in any consideration of Christian ethics, for—as I hope to show, but as is possibly obvious in any case—Christian ethics is essentially metaphysical in nature. It embodies, and depends upon, a certain view of human existence. What I think it is important to say is that the Christian view of existence cannot be conceived of as something which simply precedes ethical questions, and from which ethical beliefs can be derived afterwards—as though one first had to have a theoretical belief in God, and subsequently could decide that it was one's duty to do God's will. It is truer to the nature of Christian belief to say that assent to the existence of God is itself a matter of evaluation, of being disposed to conceive of the moral life as obedience to a Divine intention. But of course this is not a straightforward moral decision like saying, 'It is right to respect persons'. It arises out of a reflection on one's practice of the moral life in relation to the other distinctively human activities in which one engages.

Just how theoretical belief and ethical evaluation are related in the development of a distinctively Christian system of ethics is a question I shall pursue in the first part of this book. But, as a preliminary remark to the secular moralist of the first chapter, one can say that the integral relation of metaphysics and morality is not peculiar to theists or Christians. Some (like Camus) see human life as a heroic gesture of nobility in an uncaring universe, others (like Nietzsche) see it as the survival of the strongest; as the theatre of ephemeral happiness or the predetermined interplay of atoms. All such visions of life offer a particular metaphysical interpretation of morality. One may refuse to adopt any such vision; but that can be seen as the denial of one of reason's most insistent demands, to 'see life whole'. It may even be seen as a moral failure; for it is in such metaphysical visions that the ultimate ground of morality is to be found, since it is metaphysics which ultimately attempts to show how things are. And so one may say that the failure to pursue such ultimate metaphysical grounds as rigorously and sincerely as one can is a failure to think through one's ethical beliefs as clearly as possible. That would naturally be so only of one who had the ability, the time and the inclination to devote himself to such an end; but of such a one it might plausibly be said that the analysis of morality is not complete until it is able to present a coherent account of the nature of man, within which a specific conception of morality has an intelligible place.

4. There are probably other questions than these with which moral philosophers concern themselves; but I think that any attempt to distinguish the various sorts of question which may be asked about human morality must include at least these distinctions. To summarize them briefly, I have claimed that the moral philosopher must:

(i) state what acts or principles are right, and what things are good;

(ii) say what moral terms like 'right' and 'good' mean, and how they relate to each other;

(iii) if 'moral knowledge' is admitted, say how one can know what is right or good;

(iv) give some account of how the moral life is to be conceived in the context of the general nature of man and his world.

To these questions one may add one more, which I have not yet discussed:

(v) suggest how goodness or the moral end can be achieved.

I have omitted discussion of this question because it may seem to be one for psychology to answer. However, though the moral philosopher does not in his philosophizing give advice in particular cases, there are probably certain general rubrics which he can lay down, defining the appropriate methods in general, for achieving goodness. One might, for instance, say that it must be achieved simply by exertion of the will or by the cultivation of good habits, by asceticism or by a moderate indulgence in pleasures. By a natural extension, such means to achieving goodness come to be spoken of as themselves things which are good;

they are not, however, good in themselves but only as means to the achievement of ends which are good in themselves. This sort of question, then, is concerned with means rather than ends; and it suffers from the practical difficulty of constructing test-conditions and the uncertainty of generalizations derived from such partial results which make it, at least for the moment—and perhaps for ever—a subject of philosophical as well as of psychological investigation.

To each of these questions Christian ethics has a distinctive answer, and the main purpose of this work is to expound and defend those answers. Though some non-religious systems of morality may agree with Christianity in some of the answers, I think that agreement with all five answers would be a sufficient condition of making a system of morality Christian. In going on to attempt a Christian answer to each of the questions listed above, I hope to make clear that there is a distinctively Christian ethic; that it is different in fundamental and important respects from secular ethics; and that where the two differ the Christian ethic has at least a good claim to be the fulfilment and corrective of the secular.

# III

## OBJECTIVITY IN MORALS

1. The first characteristic which Christian morality must possess is that it must be objective. This is a remark not about what things are good but about what moral terms mean, and consequently also about how one can know that particular things are good. To say that morality is subjective is to give general assent to the adage, 'Goodness is in the eye of the beholder'. It is to say, that is, that nothing is good unless and until someone says it is, and then it is only good for him and for others who happen to agree with him.

All those moral philosophers who find the ultimate basis of morality in man's psychological constitution, in his basic desires or emotions or dispositions, are subjectivists, on this criterion. A more restrictive definition of subjectivism would be that a subjectivist is one who, whenever he says 'X is good', means 'I like (or approve of, or desire) X'. But I think that one can say of many other views than this, that they propound a subjective basis for morality. Emotivism, for example, which alleges that sentences of the form 'X is good' cannot be translated into sentences of the form 'I like X', nevertheless maintains that such sentences only express or seek to evoke feelings. This is a subjective theory of morality, not in the sense that it analyses moral statements as statements about the speaker's subjective states, but in the wider sense that moral statements are said to be solely founded upon men's subjective feelings. That is, what makes the statement 'X is good' correct in a certain society is not anything about X as an independently existing object, but something about all the members of the society who accept it—about their feelings towards X.

An objective theory of morality, on the other hand, would have to maintain that what makes the statement 'X is good' correct is not something about men's feelings for X but something about X itself, or at least something independent of any human mind. One way of putting this is to say that the statement 'X is good' is capable of being true or false, and what determines its truth or falsity is not any fact about any human mind. This is, first, an assertion about the meaning of moral terms—that they possess a truth-value—and second, an assertion about the conditions which determine this truth-value—that they are objective, or not facts about any human mind or minds.

2. Why must Christian morality be objective? There are Christians who have held that it need not be. Professor R. M. Hare, for instance, holds that moral assertions are prescriptive in character— they prescribe courses of action and do not refer to 'moral facts'. But he places restrictions on the sorts of action which can be prescribed; if a prescription is to be 'moral', he claims, it must be universalizable, or capable of being adopted by any moral agent in relevantly similar circumstances.[1]

This view is, of course, very similar to that of Kant, who rejected any theory of morality as based upon moral sense or feelings, and also any view that moral truths could be directly intuited. The basic reason for Kant's rejection was that any such dependence of moral judgements upon psychological dispositions or *a posteriori* knowledge would make them contingent; and Kant held that the absolute bindingness of the moral 'ought' could only be assured if it was universal and necessary. Consonantly with the rest of his philosophical architectonic, Kant believed that only *a priori* knowledge could possess such features; and thus the moral law had to be *a priori* and thus mind-legislated. Moreover, since it was consequently a purely formal law, devoid of empirical, *a posteriori* content, it had to be binding on all, in every situation and at all times. The test of universalizability, for the Kantian ethic, is simply a consequence of the fact that morality must be legislated *a priori* by practical reason; which itself is alleged to follow from the moral fact that the bindingness of moral obligations cannot be taken to depend upon any contingent empirical fact—such as a moral sense would be—which may or may not be present.[2]

Professor Hare's de-mythologized version of the Kantian criterion does not possess the advantage (if such it is) of this metaphysical foundation. He cannot justify the principle of universalizability by the sort of transcendental deduction that Kant provides—that 'ought' statements can be categorically binding *only if* they are *a priori*, and *consequently* universalizable. Why, then, should one think that one *ought* only to accept and prescribe those principles which could be universalized? The reply might be that one would not call principles 'moral' unless the were universalizable—but that would seem to be an unduly restrictive stipulation. Why should one accept it? Again the answer might be advanced that it is just a matter of logic that any word must be applicable in all similar situations. But it seems to be something more like a substantive principle of 'fair play' that is really being employed. For what is being suggested is that when I say 'X is right', I am commending the performance of X, and doing so on the basis of a certain criterion—that the action and its context can be appropriately described in a specific way, and, wherever that description is applicable, the performance of X is also, *ipso facto*, being commended. As a matter of logic, whenever I prescribe a specific action I am prescribing all and any acts which fall under that description; I am prescribing, one might say, an action-universal.

But is it really a matter of logic that this is so? Suppose that a confirmed egoist affirmed that he believes that he ought to aim always at his own happiness, however much he caused others to suffer—that is, he prescribed the principle 'Always seek your own happiness' to *himself*, but refused to prescribe it to others. Is there anything *logically* wrong with such a procedure? The peculiarity of this situation lies in the egocentric reference of the noun 'myself'. It uniquely refers to one individual agent in space and time; namely, the agent who exists *here* and *now*. There is thus nothing logically wrong, or even peculiar, in saying that *this* uniquely identified individual should do X, but no other individual should do X, even if similarly placed. For the egoist does not simply say 'X is right', he insists on saying 'X is right *for me*'; and he will oppose any attempt to eliminate these words—for all he means by 'is right' is 'will be done if possible'.

There is nothing logically odd about prescriptions directed only to particular individuals on particular occasions—most commands, for example in the Army, are such prescriptions. Why then should one insist that *moral* prescriptions must be addressed to classes of people in general? An appeal may be made to language; not this time to logical criteria of consistency, but to the facts of ordinary usage, which does so use the word 'right' that it is general in scope, that it does not require, and even excludes, the addition of the words 'for me'. I cannot think that such an appeal would seriously trouble the egoist. For, he might say, it is true that a society of avowed egoists would be a very shaky, dangerous and insecure affair. Certainly, the only foundation for a stable society is the existence of a set of universally applied rules, whether they are freely submitted to by all or are imposed by force from above. These rules will be sanctioned as 'right' in any society; and here they will be 'right' for everyone without exception. In this sense the existence of morality, a set of rules universal in scope and uniformly enforced, is the condition of a stable society, which in turn is the condition of having any sort of life worth living. The story is a familiar one; moral rules are established by a social contract between the members of a society and obedience to them is enforced by the governing body.

The egoist would not deny the existence of such universal moral rules nor the desirability of their general enforcement; it is even conceivable that he might accept them in general. But he would almost certainly insist upon one or both of two sorts of restriction on them.

First, he might restrict their *scope*. That is, he might positively endorse the enforcement of the rules on others or on a large class of people in his society, and yet himself claim exemption from their claims. Such exemption is in practice claimed by most monarchs who are 'above the law', and has often been claimed by men of a particular élite or ruling class. There is nothing inconsistent, again, in believing that the enforcement of morality over most members of society is necessary and desirable while claiming exemption from its dictates for oneself. The defender of a 'social contract' morality might protest, 'But what if *everyone* felt as you do? Surely society would then collapse.' But the egoist could say, 'Not everyone feels as I do—and, if they did, they must be *compelled* to obey the law'. 'Then you also must be compelled', the social contractor may expostulate; to which the reply is merely, 'Compel me if you can'. Faced with this naked appeal to power, the contractor may try another tack. 'But what if you had been born weak? Or what if you lose your power? What when you grow old and feeble? Would it not be safer to insure your future by cultivating friends now, obeying the laws and thus ensuring that others will respect you when you are weak?' It must be confessed that this is an extremely weighty considera-tion; perhaps it is the one which chiefly causes men in power to abide by the law. But it is far from decisive; the egoist may well be prepared to take that risk for the sake of present eminence, and he may consider that he can insure his future in other ways; by surrounding himself with a small, privileged class or family, by instituting a series of checks and balances that only his continued existence preserves, and so on. It is undoubtedly true that sufficiently cunning and powerful men can live above the moral law and never suffer for it. And, on a prescriptivist view of morality, it would not make sense to say that such a course was morally wrong, except in so far as this meant that one did not prescribe it oneself.

Second, the egoist might restrict the *range* of the moral laws; he might accept some of them as universally binding, but only on a very minimal and easily kept level—such as not killing. Above that minimal level he may practise egoism: and then he would be committed to two sorts of moral principles; first, a class of universally applicable principles, minimal in the range of actions they restrict; and second, a class of egoistic, individually applicable principles which do not take other agents into account. On this second level it would not be true that what is right for me must be right for all men, or even for any other man whatsoever.

3. Are there, then, two uses of the word 'right' here? There are: but I find nothing extraordinary in that. The first use of 'right' may be called the 'conventional' use: and in this use, saying 'X is right' may or may not commit one to prescribing it to oneself as an action to be performed. One may mean that it is an act which is sanctioned in a certain society; or that it ought to be so sanctioned; or that most people should perform it, though it is not necessary that one should believe all three of these things. 'Right' in its second use does involve a personal commitment as to what one believes one should do *oneself*. But in this use there is no commitment to the belief that *everyone* should do it, or that anyone other than oneself should.

What is termed the 'ordinary use' of 'right' is probably the first use; which is strengthened by the fact that most egoists think it best to conceal their real principles on prudential grounds, and thus pretend to commit themselves to moral principles, conceived in this way as universally enforced rules. But to conclude from this that the real basic principles which guide the lives of egoists are not *moral* principles at all is to propagate the worst sort of verbal chicanery, and to fall into the hands of egoists themselves by taking their hypocritical avowals for the genuine article. Now if it is said that any egoist who governs his conduct by egoistic principles really knows that he is being immoral, what is the justification for such a claim? It cannot be, I hope it is clear, simply that his principles are not universally applicable, as if there was something *logically* wrong with that. It can only be the belief that moral principles *ought* to be universal in scope. And this is not an analytic truth about when principles are to be called 'moral'; it is a substantive claim that principles which I prescribe to myself I *ought* to be prepared to ascribe equally to others. Why so? Logic will not tell me; the suggestion that it can may derive, however, from the fact that logic itself employs and depends upon the basic values which are here in question—the values, namely, of *impartiality* and *equality*. The difference is that, in logic, what one treats impartially are merely symbols; in morality, they are human beings.

Thus the foundational principle of Hare's ethics is in reality the principle, 'Treat people impartially and equitably'. But that is just one possible prescription amongst others, and it cannot be inflated into a criterion of morality. Why should one prescribe and commend this principle? At this point Hare may say that one must stop somewhere with some principle. That is undoubtedly true; but what is in question is not 'What is the most basic principle in your system?' but 'Is it possible for you, in your system, to say that *this* is a principle which all men *ought* to accept?' On a purely prescriptivist theory it is not possible. For saying 'All men ought to accept principle X' would mean something like 'I prescribe X to all men'. If one then asked, '*Ought* I to prescribe X?', the answer 'yes' would again mean '(I prescribe that) you prescribe X'. At each stage there is only the fact of my free prescription which is offered; and such a fact can never justify the assertion that all men really *ought* to do X, *whether or not I prescribe it*. This is to say, of course, that I refuse the proffered translation of 'You ought to X' into 'I prescribe X', or even into 'I prescribe X universally, to all'. My objection is not that the translation founds the moral 'ought' on a fact, but that it founds it on the *wrong* fact. It is, I believe, a fact (for example) that I ought to do X, but this is not identical with the fact that I prescribe X to all men.

It is interesting, in this connection, to construct an imaginative account of how Kant might have dealt with this point. He would, I am certain, have said that judgements of the form 'You ought to X' are true (or false)—it is precisely because he believed that, that he could not accept that morality depends on feeling, which varies from person to person. But, if asked what makes them true or false, what determines their truth-value, his answer would be more difficult to guess. Certainly, like Hare, he thought that what made them binding was their universalizability; but this was because they had to be legislated *a priori* by Practical Reason. Thus what makes a moral principle true is the fact that it is legislated by Reason, *a priori*.

The 'moral fact', for Kant, may not be the will of God; but it is the dictate of Practical Reason. It would not be right to call this a 'subjective' fact; for, on Kant's view, Reason is the same everywhere and in all men and is independent of the particular subjective constitution of human individuals. So it seems that Kant may perhaps be correctly interpreted as an objectivist in morals; but his conception of the moral fact, as Practical Reason, needs to be carefully compared to and, I think, contrasted with the Christian conception.

The important element which a belief in the objectivity of morals attempts to preserve is the belief that it is true that one ought to do X. Such a belief cannot be preserved by a prescriptivist theory which translates 'ought' into 'I prescribe', and thus invites the question, 'ought I to prescribe?'; or by a subjectivist or emotive theory which founds one's belief explicitly or implicitly on the contingent occurrence of some feeling, and thus invites the question, 'Ought I to express that feeling?' Supposing that one has any control over one's feelings at all, one has to decide how to control them; and if there is nothing to guide this decision except the strength of those feelings themselves, it is senseless to talk of controlling them at all. This is the strength of the prescriptivist case, which at least provides for human decision-making and freedom. But, like existentialism, it provides in the last resort no criteria of what sort of decision to make. Human freedom is thus secured, but it becomes wholly arbitrary. Paradoxically, therefore, the philosophy of total freedom ends at the same place as the philosophy of determinism; for whereas one affirms that one cannot help what one does, the other affirms that there is no final criterion of what one should do; and so both deprive moral freedom of importance by making it either illusory or arbitrary.

4. It may be said, nevertheless, that moral statements are truth-valued and that what ultimately determines their truth or falsity is some fact about the approvals or desires of men. For, it may be claimed, all moral statements have their ultimate justifying reason in the very general human passions of self-interest and benevolence; and there is no sense in asking whether one ought to have such passions. On such a doctrine there cannot be an irreducibly categorical 'ought'—a moral claim which cannot be resolved into some natural fact about human behaviour. This theory therefore agrees with views which deny truth-value to moral statements, in that it makes morality conditional on one's free decision, or one's social role, or one's feelings and dispositions—any of which might be different and which therefore cannot be the ground of absolutely binding obligations.

Now the acceptance of such a view seems to commit one to moral relativism. If each man's morality simply expresses the overriding desires which he happens, as a contingent matter of fact, to have, there is no way of assessing different moral codes as good or bad, correct or incorrect. So a plurality of diverse moral codes may exist, and there can be no reason for choosing one rather than another. Where there is nothing to choose between two moralities it is hard to see how one could think it reasonable to have an ultimately serious commitment, even at the cost of suffering, deprivation or death, to one particular view.

A recent exponent of a non-objectivist theory of ethics, D. H. Monro, accepts that the denial of objectivism involves the acceptance of relativism.[3] But he tries to defend a relativist theory by arguing that the objectivist claim that moral codes other than one's own are mistaken does not in fact make serious moral commitment more reasonable. For, he says, it is no less justifiable to condemn those who do not share one's own moral attitudes, simply for that reason, than it is to condemn others because they differ from oneself in beliefs about (moral) matters of fact. Thus, he claims, the objection that relativism leaves the choice between diverse moral codes indifferent fails because, in the first place, I do condemn your moral attitudes just because I do not share them and, in the second place, to condemn a man simply for differing in moral belief, and therefore for intellectual error is, if anything, more morally objectionable than to condemn him because he differs in emotional attitude. Thus, Monro claims, the objectivist neither succeeds in adding anything significant to the relativist account, nor in escaping the very sort of moral objection he is making to it.

There are two things wrong with this defence. First, an objectivist does not morally condemn a man who sincerely differs from himself, but he would wish to convict him of intellectual error. A man is *morally* condemned only for doing what he himself believes to be wrong; and in this respect the objectivist is not just condemning a belief because he does not share it, for he may share the belief of the man he condemns, and thus be condemning himself too. The objectivist would say that it is important to distinguish moral condemnation—which lies in failure to implement one's *own* moral principles—from the accusation of mistaken belief; and it is difficult to see how a relativist can make such a distinction, when he construes moral condemnation as being made solely because a man's attitude differs from one's own: he has no usage for an 'incorrect' moral code, just different ones.

Second, 'not sharing one's attitude or belief' is so far from being a sufficient reason for rejecting a moral code that it is not a reason at all; it is unintelligible to say that one rejects a moral code *because* it differs from one's own, for that is just to say that one does not hold a code because one does not hold it. Thus Monro's position must really be that there is no reason for choosing one code rather than another, not that the reason is 'because one code is mine'. And here the objectivist will assert that it is important to maintain that there is a reason for accepting a particular moral code, other than that I, or my society, or anyone else, accepts or desires it; this is an irreducibly moral reason; that is, that it is right.

So one does not morally condemn a man for sincere intellectual error, and one would not reject his opinion simply for the reason that he differs from oneself either about matters of fact or in emotional attitude. The objectivist would reject a moral opinion for the reason that it is false—which is not a fact about human psychological states—and he would morally condemn only where he believed that a man had freely chosen to disregard the moral principles the man himself espoused. The case is complicated by the extreme difficulty, if not impossibility, of knowing when a moral belief is sincerely held or when a man is free to implement or disregard it; nevertheless, there is here in principle a rationale for distinguishing moral attitudes which provide grounds for moral condemnation and those which do not. It is not clear that a relativist could provide any such rationale. Thus moral codes whose upholders are not condemned must be rejected; and one's own code, if it is taken seriously, must be affirmed unconditionally. Such a rejection and such an affirmation is expressed by asserting that one's own moral code is 'true'.

One thereby excludes the possibility that what a man *says* is right, *is* right. And though there is nothing observable by the senses to decide the issue, one can say that where moral standards differ there is something which decides the issue in favour of one (even though this cannot be an independently knowable standard of assessment). While this may be taken merely to reaffirm one's own commitment—and it does—one may say that it also affirms that one's commitment is, in some sense, about matters of fact, that it is favoured by the way things are, though not by the sort of things one can measure or manhandle. In this sense it is a commitment to 'something more', beyond but not unrelated to the empirical facts. Such a view—and only, I think, some such view—excludes the possibility of a plurality of independent moral standards; and it licenses the sort of moral discourse which employs such concepts as 'claim', 'demand', 'insight', 'development' and 'mistake' or 'blindness' with regard to matters of moral conduct. These concepts are typical of and central to Christian morality, which speaks of 'doing the will of God', 'disobeying God', 'coming to see God's will' and being 'called by God'. Here morality is seen, at least in part, as a cognitive enterprise in which there is something (God) which wills, calls, whose will can be 'seen' and disobeyed. Indeed, the moral life of the Christian is often expressed as one of learning to know and love God more fully. If objectivism were rejected this vocabulary would seem to be both misleading and misguided.

5. It is possible, however, that a non-objectivist interpretation of Christian ethics might still be proposed, and this could be done in two ways. First, it might be said that the concept of 'God' is itself non-objective—that is, it expresses certain emotions or practical commitments. I have argued against such an interpretation elsewhere;[4] but it seems clear that such views would require a revision of much traditional Christian talk about God, and to that extent are inadequate accounts of actual Christian belief. Second, one might suggest that our ethical beliefs, founded upon our

emotions and desires, just happen to coincide with the will or the desires of a supernatural being, God. The being of God would then be strictly irrelevant to ethical belief; it would not have a central place in one's view of the moral life. Moreover, the problem would arise of the relation of the being of God to his own ethical beliefs; are they just expressions of the overriding desires he happens to have? As I shall argue later, such a concept of 'God' is altogether too anthropomorphic to withstand criticism —it makes God too much like an empirically observable being, for which the evidence is then lamentably inadequate. Both these views seem unable to express the intimate relation of the concepts of 'God' and 'duty' in Christian language. Perhaps it is worth adding, too, that if one believes in God then the argument against objectivism which depends on using Occam's Razor to shave off non-empirical facts loses its force; for the non-empirical facts are already admitted, and it might seem very peculiar, then, if one's basic moral beliefs were not in some way essentially related to them. Thus Christianity is committed to objectivism in a special way. For it must relate morality to God; and any non-objectivist view of the sources and motives of moral action seems to make the concept of 'God' as superfluous to practical life as he now is for scientific speculation. A Christian must view ethics as objective —interpreting his moral experience in terms of the concept of 'God'—even if he can find no independently convincing reasons for doing so; it is not, after all, necessary or possible to find justifying arguments for all one's beliefs. However, while allowing this possibility, I do think that objectivism in ethics can be defended apart from any question of theistic belief; and such a defence will try to make clear why the moral objectivist speaks as he does.[5] I shall present two related considerations which seem to me decisive in this regard: one elucidating the sense of moral necessitation which many men, and certainly Christians, feel to be phenomenologically central to morality; and one attempting to bring out the conceptual connection between assertions of 'importance' and of 'truth' in morality. Thus I wish to argue in favour of accepting the view that a commitment to moral seriousness involves a certain metaphysical assertion about how things are.

6. Suppose, first, that there is an altruist who thinks the keeping

of promises, development of talents, truth-telling and concern for others to be ultimately important; activities which, in cases of conflict, ought always to overrule other possible acts for everyone whether they think so or not. As a non-objectivist moral theorist, however, he might think that assessments of 'ultimate importance' are received standards of which there are many alternatives, not jointly assessable. But could one believe both these things together? Well, is this a psychological 'could'? No; for psychologically almost anything is possible. What is it, then? Not just logical consistency, for any view that X is important is consistent with any view of what 'importance' is; these propositions cannot contradict for they are talking about different things.

But suppose the altruist believes—as he probably would—that not only he but all men ought to be (for example) benevolent. And suppose the moral theorist believes—as he probably would— that no moral standard is universally agreed. Then it is at least clear that the standards of an altruist and an egoist will contradict each other—one entailing 'P (the egoist) ought to be benevolent', and the other stating 'P ought to be selfish'. As an altruist one would assent to the former proposition of this contradictory pair; but, as a moral theorist, one would be committed to neutrality. One would say, 'these are incompatible beliefs; there is no question of comparing or assessing them since each depends on its own ultimate standards'. Now it is a paradoxical position to say that there is no question of comparing two incompatible propositions, and yet to assent to one and reject the other. Well, it may be said that one must have one and cannot have both; all that is being said is that one cannot explain why one assents as one does (even if one is apathetic, that assent is inexplicable).

Yet it must be remarked that there is a difference between saying that one cannot explain why one believes what one does, and saying that there is no question of one's belief being more correct than an incompatible alternative. Does the altruist not think, however inexplicably, that his view is more correct than that of the egoist (and vice versa)? Indeed, is this not analytically entailed in the notion of assenting to one of two incompatible propositions? It would certainly be incomprehensible to say that one assented to one proposition because it was less correct. And if one says that correctness is not in question, what way is there of choosing?

One must be careful here—one cannot say why one affirms one's

D

moral principles as one does; this entails that one cannot say that they are affirmed because they are known to be correct by some independent test. Nevertheless, when they are affirmed are they not affirmed *as* correct? If one says not, one is saying not only that one does not know why one chooses, but also that there is nothing to choose between them—that it does not matter what one chooses. If the altruist held that view, then he would have to affirm both 'It is most important that you are benevolent' and 'It does not matter whether you or I think it important that you are benevolent'. In saying benevolence is important one is expressing the necessity of a strong commitment to it. But in saying that it doesn't matter whether that, or something else, or even nothing, is important, one is saying that strong commitments are optional— that is, not necessary. In this way the altruist who, in his first-order moral utterances, prescribes the moral necessity of strong commitments to (for example) benevolence, for others as well as himself, contradicts the moral theorist whose meta-ethical theory leads him to assert the morally optional character of any particular, and even of all, commitments.

Perhaps there is nothing logically wrong with saying both that sets of moral principles are in principle incomparable and that some member(s) of such a set ought to be adopted by everyone— for the former may be taken as a descriptive, the latter as a prescriptive, utterance. Yet something is lost on this account; and that is the distinctive sense of 'moral necessity' which Kant accepted as the unquestionable foundation of his ethics ('If a law is to have moral force . . . it must carry with it absolute necessity').[6] There is certainly a distinction between an agent committing himself to or prescribing to others a certain course of action in general and a *moral* commitment or prescription. And one main ground of this distinction is that non-moral commitments (to a particular job, perhaps) are seen as chosen alternatives, in the same sense that one can choose between right and wrong. But the commitment to a certain principle as morally right does not seem in the same way a matter of open alternatives; on the contrary, the moral agent is unable to conceive that an incompatible principle could be right, and accepted as such by him. The foundation of the claim to necessity is in the agent's refusal to envisage other possibilities as real possibilities, not only for him but for any man. Thus he refuses to found morality on any contingent fact (including the facts of feeling and prescribing).

He may indeed claim to understand what makes others differ from him morally, but he cannot conceive their position as an alternative for him, and so he cannot conceive it as a real alternative at all. On this interpretation (which I think is firmly founded on moral experience) the thesis that there are alternative, incomparable sets of moral principles must entail that particular members of those sets are incomparable, and this contradicts the assertion that some particular moral principle is morally necessary for all men.

The notion of 'necessity' is a particularly perplexing one; and a fashionable practice has been to make all necessity disappear into the language; according to this practice, moral necessity simply lies in the prescribed principle of action, and it is senseless to ask whether that in turn is necessary. It is clear, however, that such a view cannot be an adequate descriptive account of a form of language which insists that only one moral view is finally acceptable, that men are mistaken and possibly even blameworthy—if self-deception is suspected—for failing to uphold it, however sincere they may think themselves, and that there are irreducibly moral reasons for action which are believed to have a necessity not compatible with being dependent on any contingent fact. Such views embody a substantive view of human life, in which to be morally serious is to commit oneself to a view of human existence as confronted by necessary and undeniable moral constraints. They express and specify a particular form of life, a way of seeing and living in the world, which cannot be attacked on the basis of a descriptive analysis of moral language; indeed, Nowell-Smith clearly sees this when he attacks what he calls 'objectivism' precisely because it leads to what he regards as intolerant attitudes.[7] At the least, then, one can point to these ways of speaking about morality, and the reactive attitudes and practices in which they find their place, as data which the descriptive analyst must accept as given. More strongly, one may reasonably claim to see an integral relation between serious moral commitment and the refusal to allow that what is seen as good or obligatory could be otherwise—the sense of 'moral necessity'—which induces one to posit an objective basis for morality.

7. One can make the same point from another direction. Consider the man who sees his moral life as a constant warfare against the passions, a battle always arduous, often lost, and never finally

won. Of course, he takes the goals he aims at to be important. But suppose he also sees that 'what people take as important' varies, and that moderately egoistic views are neither morally nor rationally nor in any other way inferior to his own (or, of course, superior either). Well, if he has no choice, he will have to continue taking as important what he does so take. But suppose that he has some choice. One may object to the notion of 'choice' on the grounds that it would have to be criterionless—and so would be simply random—as well as on the phenomenological ground that we do not seem to 'choose' our standards. Nevertheless, if a man thinks his 'choice' is entirely random, but may be changed, there is nothing to stop him opting for a more pleasant standard. One is here appealing to the criterion of pleasure as a criterion of choice, in fact; but it can be plausibly argued that such a criterion is common to all men, and though it is often overruled it is never entirely obliterated by moral standards. So it may be said that there is a fundamental contrast between pleasurable states of the agent and things which one might take to be morally important, whether or not they were pleasant (whether or not men are, as cynics suggest, mistaken about their altruistic motivations). In such a situation, conflicts of desire (where desire is construed as being for pleasure) and moral importance will almost inevitably arise. And when they do the altruist may say, 'I think X important. If I did not, then I would implement my desires'—that is, unless desires are overruled, it is rational to implement them; that is, there is no reason not to do so, and they provide *ipso facto* a reason for acting. (I eschew the consideration that a person may intelligibly be said to desire another's good or pleasure, since for my argument I only need a clear case in which one does not desire to do one's duty.)

If one says, 'I think X important; if I did not, then I could do what I want (not-X)', and also, 'It does not matter whether I think X important', then one has no motivation to sustain a belief in the importance of X; and one has a motivation (one's desires) for giving it up. Now no doubt one cannot choose to believe or disbelieve X in a moment; nevertheless, one's beliefs can come to change, over a period of time, as one's attention is concentrated on particular aspects of experience, or as one adopts a pattern of behaviour which exemplifies and reinforces specific preferences; and in this sense one can be said to choose one's beliefs. Naturally, one will only do so if one has the (unchosen) belief that evaluations are relative and that fulfilling one's desires is pleasant. But this belief may be said to be compelled by the facts, by one's knowledge of how things are. Of course, an altruist will say that his motivation to continue the pursuit of X is simply that X is his duty; and to concede the possibility that this is not a sufficient motivation is already to begin to lose that motivation. That is, even to question whether it is sufficient, to raise the doubt—in a real and not an idle sense—is to undermine its sufficiency, which rests on its inviolability to rational questioning. Thus the altruist seems to be committed to a disagreement about the facts with the relativist moral theorist; for his belief in the sufficiency of the moral motive commits him to denying that there is nothing to choose between various discrepant views of the moral life. There is nothing he can call upon to justify his vision of life as a real and difficult warfare of good and evil, except the strength of the moral motive itself. If he feels (and I think he would rightly feel) that this is put in question by the view that there is no rational criterion of choice between competing moral standards, then he is committed to rejecting that view, or to raising a question about his own moral standards which already weakens his motivation to accept them. That is not to say that he will give them up; but he may, and could be called neither irrational nor immoral for doing so. There are, however, many morally serious men who would insist that it is just such a choice which is of the utmost moral significance; which is, indeed, the final most awesome moral temptation. To this extent, a philosophy which does not allow objectivity to morals is inconsistent with certain strongly held moral views.

So the question I would put to the non-objectivist is this: Why, supposing you have free choice, should you choose moral principles which often oppose your own best interests, which are hard to live up to and which sometimes call for positive sacrifice? To this, he may consistently reply that since his choice is criterionless, there is no reason why he shouldn't choose such principles, even though there is no positive reason why he should; he may or he may not choose to. He may, indeed, take it as a presumption of the objectivist to assume that he would naturally choose to be self-interested; there is no reason why the very opposite should not be the case. Why, he might ask, should self-interest be considered to be more 'natural' than altruism? This must, I think, be granted to him; yet it remains true that, if he does choose self-interest, no blame can be attached to him; it might be just as 'reasonable' to live a life of service to others as to live a life of egoism, but there is, at any rate, no moral reason why one should not be an egoist.

Moreover, though one can well choose principles as difficult as may be, it remains true that altruistic moral principles are generally much more difficult to practice than egoistic, or at least than benevolent though prudentially based principles. And where there is no particular point in choosing the more difficult of various alternatives, it seems fairly obvious that most people would opt for the less arduous way. In the case of Christianity, the moral principles are so extremely difficult—even impossible, as we shall see—of fulfilment, it would even seem foolish to choose such principles, which one could never constantly fulfil. So non-objectivist theories of ethics do pose a very real threat to the acceptance of Christian ethics and, consequently, to the Christian faith itself.

8. Non-objectivists have, however, produced a *tu quoque* argument in answer to this charge that their ethical theories tend to undermine morality. In fact, they would say, it is objectivism which causes most harm in practice. For objectivists think that they possess the ultimate ethical truth; and they are consequently opposed to all change in moral standards and to any spirit of compromise which they interpret as a sign of weakness of purpose. Thus their concern for a certain set of moral standards leads them to repressive measures against those who differ with them, and a resolute opposition to any attempt to meet their opponents half-way.

Now a relativist or non-objectivist will not be intolerant in this way, it may be said. Since he knows that all moral standards are just matters of choice he will in many cases be prepared for a little moral give and take—just as, if I want kipper and you want porridge, we may compromise and have a boiled egg. Compromise, he will say, is a great virtue; to lack it is to be bigoted and, indeed, to assume infallibility. And so non-objectivists are, paradoxical as it may seem, less dangerous to the maintenance of morality than objectivists.[8]

There is more than a grain of truth in this charge so far as the actual conduct of Christians, for example, is concerned. It does seem to be true that where men adhere to firmly held moral beliefs they tend to be intolerant of those who, however sincerely, oppose them. On the other hand, it does not seem that an objectivist is necessarily committed to intolerance—and, in the case of Christianity, there are specific moral rules enjoining the virtue of tolerance.

The first thing to be remarked upon—and it is a point which will be developed at a later stage—is that an objectivist is not committed to saying that all the moral principles which he accepts are known by him, with certainty, to be true. He may, indeed, quite consistently maintain a belief in the objectivity of morals while denying that he is in a position to know the truth of any moral principle. Even if he does suppose that the truth of some principles is known to him, he will almost certainly differentiate between those principles he is certain of (perhaps 'love for one's fellows') and those which he might be prepared to amend if circumstances suggest amendment (for example, the economic institution of slavery). Furthermore, even those principles of which he is certain may be of such a generality that they are capable of many different interpretations in specific circumstances; and though, no doubt, one interpretation is the objectively right one, the objectivist need not claim any certain knowledge about it. Indeed, as I hope to elucidate later, an essential part of the Christian doctrine of ethics is that, because of 'sin', no man can be certain that what he thinks is right really does reflect the objective truth, even though men can be certain of the rightness of very general principles—such as that of 'love for God and men'. For what that principle entails in particular circumstances is by no means clear (though that is not to say that it is not worth trying to find out).

The Christian conception of objectivity, then, allows for a great deal of tolerance and compromise of different views, in principle, however little individual Christians live up to their principles. And it is perhaps worth pointing out that whether a non-objectivist is tolerant at all is not a function of non-objectivism as such but of the particular views, attitudes or dispositions of the person concerned. It is surely not inconceivable that a man who believes his moral views simply express his attitudes may nevertheless have very intolerant and restricted attitudes. One cannot guarantee tolerance by withdrawing claims to truth; nor, I have suggested, does the claim to truth disallow tolerance and compromise in many areas of moral concern. But it must be pointed out that there are limits to tolerance and compromise. Whereas one can perhaps be tolerant of opposed views on the desirability of contraception or abortion, and may compromise on the subject of whether one should eat 'meat offered to idols', one could not tolerate or seek compromise with a policy of genocide or racial imperialism. It is in such extreme situations that the importance of a belief in an ultimate 'objective rightness' becomes apparent. At such points the objectivist will want to assert that it is not just a matter of preference as to which principles one supports. So while he strives for humility in his search for truth in morals, and for tolerance wherever there is a reasonable diversity of particular views on what is good, the objectivist will hold it to be of supreme importance to assert that there is a moral truth to be found which, even though dimly discerned at best, claims his whole being absolutely and which, at least in its most fundamental principles, can never be compromised. This I think is the Christian view of morality; and it can only be supported by a doctrine of moral objectivity.

# MORAL FACTS

1. Given, then, that Christian ethics must be objectivist, how is one to conceive such objectivism? In other words, what does determine the truth-value of moral judgements? The truth of an empirical statement—for example, 'That is a table'—is determined by a fact—that it *is* a table. So it seems that there must be facts which determine the truth of moral statements also. But must not these facts be very different from the sorts of fact which make empirical statements true? Some philosophers, whom one may call naturalists in ethics, hold that the truth of moral judgements is determined by straightforward matters of fact—for example, that it is relevance to human flourishing (or good and harm) which determines truth in morality, and what counts as 'human flourishing' can be established on ordinary empirical criteria. This sort of theory hardly seems able to get off the ground. First, it has been an almost universal moral belief of mankind, whether one agrees with it or not, that considerations of justice override considerations of human good or ill. Kant quotes as proverbial and true the phrase *Fiat justitia, pereat mundus*—let justice reign, though the world perish.[1] The traditional doctrine of Hell also values justice above Divine benevolence; so it is not at all plausible to hold that all moral terms are defined in terms of 'human flourishing'. Even apart from this clear case, human morality is such a complex, unsystematic and many-stranded thing that it is quite unrealistic to suppose that it is so neatly rational as the naturalists suppose; so if they are talking about what morality actually is, rather than what it ought to be, they seem wide of the mark.

Second, there seem to be very different evaluations of what 'human good' consists in, and men do differ about what final happiness or well-being consists in. Third, it is not totally clear that human well-being is the point of morality, in any case; it is certainly true that many moralists have rigorously opposed moral considerations to those of prudence, and would regard as perverse any attempts to found moral codes on an ultimate appeal to prudence. Fourth, one may well have to introduce irreducibly moral considerations before one would admit some otherwise desired state to be a 'human good'; for it may be that the things which an evil man desires may yet be things for which he ought not to strive. And fifth, the force of Hume's point remains undiminished, in the case of empirical facts at least—that no mere statement of existence can entail a statement about what ought to be done.[2]

Modern naturalist arguments often try to counter this point by appealing to the fact that words like 'courageous' and, greedy' have clear criteria for application in a given society; thus in the application of these terms, factual and evaluative considerations cannot be distinguished; the facts already have moral import.[3] But, after all, this is only to say that one builds the values one has—the ways in which one values things—into the terminology for describing those things. This does not by any means show that there is no distinction here between facts—which are taken to exist independently of human minds—and values—which are, for subjectivist views, imputed by human minds; for a man in the very same culture may choose a different word for the very same fact, simply because he evaluates it differently. Thus one may say, 'That was not courageous; it was foolhardy.' One thereby accepts the evaluative implications of these terms, but differs over their application. Equally, one may doubt whether 'courage' is a good thing, even though one accepts that a man is indisputably courageous on the agreed social criteria. Here one accepts the empirical criteria for applying the concept but disputes the commendation of the disposition in question. In a complex, plural society, differences of desire and evaluation are so marked that one seems forced to say that, in such cases, while the factual criteria cannot be in dispute, the application of partially evaluative terms will vary widely; and this in itself corroborates the distinguishing of factual and evaluative considerations. Naturalism inevitably leads back to the subjective relativism it was attempting to escape, for the facts are simply not determined regardless of human approvals and evaluations.

Moreover, if one holds that there is a range of considerations to do with human welfare, which in some central cases may entail a moral conclusion (for example, pointless suffering is objectively wrong), one can still ask what *makes* (for example) suffering wrong. Here the naturalist can only appeal to the desires of men to avoid this sort of fact, and thus once again moral assertions are founded solely on very general facts about human desires. One may distinguish this view from subjectivism, since a subjectivist holds that moral predicates are not founded in an object itself, but in one's feelings (of desire or approval) about the object. But the naturalist is maintaining that human wants or needs *are* the objects of moral concern, so in this case moral predicates are founded in the object itself. Nevertheless, the truth of moral judgements is determined solely by the empirical occurrence of human desires which, though they may be very widespread, are still contingent and relative. Naturalistic views only seem to avoid relativism—if they do—because welfare, flourishing, happiness or interest may seem at first sight to be confirmable facts apart from matters of human desire. But on closer inspection it becomes apparent that such terms can only be applied where the desires of the agent concerned are taken into account and presumed to be fulfilled. And the view that moral truth is determined by the occurrence of desires or aversions which men, as a matter of fact, happen to have, is akin to subjectivism in founding morality on human desires—albeit those of others—and entails the sort of relativism which has already been considered and rejected in the previous chapter. Here the objectivist would probably want to agree that pointless suffering is always and necessarily wrong; but he could not accept (or perhaps even understand) the contention that it is simply the fact of human aversion which makes it wrong (whether the aversion is one's own, that of society, or that of the patient).


2. So one cannot say that moral statements are determined in truth-value by empirical facts. It seems, then, that the objectivist is compelled to introduce a set of non-empirical facts to do the job. In seeking to determine more precisely the nature of such facts, I will confine my attention to statements of the form 'P ought to X'—statements of obligation. There are, of course, many complexities of moral terminology which I do not particularly wish to explore now—the many different ways of evaluating and commending, and in particular the relation of the central terms 'good' and 'right'. It seems to me, however, that the distinctive character of morality, if not its complexities, can

be brought out by concentrating on what I would term a primitive, undefinable and non-exponible moral sense of 'ought'. This term is primitive, in the logical sense that it cannot be translated without change of meaning or defined in terms of any other concepts; and it is non-exponible in that it cannot be eliminated without change of meaning. Other moral concepts, however, may be defined in terms of 'ought', so understood; thus 'X is good' may be rendered as 'This thing or state *ought* to exist'; and 'X is right' would become 'This act *ought* to be performed', and so on.

It has been said that there is, or should be, no such distinctively moral sense of 'ought'. Thus, Professor Anscombe writes, 'the concepts of obligation and duty . . . of the *moral* sense of "ought", ought to be jettisoned'.[4] This is a very revealing statement, for it does bring into the open one of the consequences of naturalistic or relativist views of ethics. On such views there is simply no place for a logically primitive, irreducibly moral sense of 'ought' at the foundation of human conduct and evaluation. One must therefore say of them that, when their proponents speak of morality, they are not speaking of the same thing as the objectivist; the divergent accounts spring from different ways of apprehending human existence and action; they differ as to what the facts are, what human life is, though not in an uncomplicated, straightforwardly disputable way.

The vocabulary of moral constraint, with its accompanying urge to assert the objective existence of obligations, thus expresses a particular sort of practical commitment. It is, one might say, a different language for the same facts. But are the facts the same? The acceptability of the language in shaping one's experience adequately ensures that 'the facts' are not precisely the same as they might have been seen to be. We see the world in our reaction to it; and how we see it shapes our actions in it. Apprehension and action are here not separable, without erecting clear lines of division where none exist. It is not just that belief is a disposition to act in a certain way in the very same world as someone else; the world of action is not the same, because what counts as a world is seen differently. There are many ways of understanding the world of human experience; and though, no doubt, the one perfectly adequate understanding is a mere dream, the objectivist, and particularly the Christian, will certainly claim that his insistence on a distinctively moral 'ought' and his conceptualization of the moral life in the terminology of 'claim' and 'demand' is part of a wider understanding of reality which is more adequate, in the long run, than its alternatives, and expresses an ultimate importance about moral commitment of which he feels more certain than of the truth of any philosophical theory about the foundations of morality.

Now if the distinctiveness of the moral 'ought' is to be preserved, it would seem that what must determine the truth of a moral statement that 'P ought to X' is simply a distinctively moral fact—that P *ought* to X.

Immediately, however, the basic difficulty of moral objectivism emerges. When we say that a table is, we mean that one identifiable particular exists among others in space and time. But when we say that 'P ought to X' is a fact, we can hardly be referring to one spatio-temporal particular among others. Indeed, because of the occurrence of 'ought' in the statement it seems very strange to say that anything called 'ought' exists at all; for such 'oughts' refer to prospective actions and thus to the future, the not-yet-existent; how then can they be said to exist? Perhaps it may be thought that a nearer parallel can be found with future-tense inductive sentences. The sentence 'The world will explode at $T^2$' may be said to be true at $T^1$ if, at $T^2$, the world does explode, though nothing actually exists at $T^1$ which determines its truth. So one may argue that statements may be truth-valued though this value is not determined by anything existing at the time.

Nevertheless, the truth-determining event does exist at some time; and it is still hard to see how 'P ought to X' can be made true by any existent event at any time. For it may be true whether or not P ever does, did or will do X—that is, whatever the facts. Of course, that is just to say that 'P ought to X' is not a statement *about* the actual behaviour of P; but it also implies that it is not a statement about any *empirical* fact whatsoever. The situation is that at a certain moment T, person P is faced with two or more courses of action, between which he is free to choose. One of these possible acts is the one he *ought* to choose; it is binding on P absolutely; it is like a claim laid upon him. The fact that makes 'P ought to X' true, then, is the fact that there is a claim which binds him to a certain possible action at a given time. The fact that 'P ought to do X' is identical with the fact that a certain non-empirical claim exists; that is, therefore, what 'P ought to X' *means*.

The objection may at this point be made that the existence of a claim does not entail that P ought to obey it; even supposing a claim of that sort does exist at T, that fact does not entail that P must (ought to) obey the claim. So in addition to the claim there is still required acceptance of the further proposition 'P ought to obey the claim'; and one must ask what fact makes this true. On the formula, another non-empirical claim must be introduced as the referent of the moral 'ought'; but again the same objection arises, that the mere existence of a claim, and even its cognition, cannot be the ground of a commitment to act. Thus appeal to 'non-empirical claims' does not solve the problem of the objectivity of obligation, but only generates an infinite and surely vicious regress.

But if apprehension of a certain fact must always be distinguished from commitment to act, and so cannot *ipso facto* bind one to a course of action, there seems to be no possible way in which one can move from the existence of a certain fact (even a 'non-empirical claim') to the undertaking of a moral commitment. And if this is so, moral objectivism—which must attempt to base obligations on matters of objective fact—however desirable, would be impossible.[5]


3. It may be supposed, however, that one can be an objectivist in morals without having to postulate non-empirical facts. For all that is required is assent to specifically moral *propositions* which are seen to be self-evidently true. Here a comparison of the basic propositions of morals with the fundamental truths of logic is being suggested. Such truths of logic—for example, 'A thing cannot have incompatible properties at the same time'—are propositional in form; but assent to them is, at the same time, a practical commitment, a commitment to think or to manipulate verbal symbols in a certain manner according to those rules. This is because what one *means* by 'assent', in such cases, is acceptance of a rule of action which one can and will implement. In a similar way, assent to moral propositions may be taken as acceptance of a rule of action; and in that case the alleged distinction between apprehension of the proposition and practical commitment would be undermined.

But, it may be asked, does it make sense to ask whether propositions which express rules of action could be true or false? Surely truth and falsity are not values which are properly applicable to mere rules of procedure. The thought behind this objection is that rules can be properly expressed as indefinite sets of hypothetical propositions; thus the rule of non-contradiction unfolds into an indefinite set of statements of the form, 'If I ascribe $\phi$ to something, then I will not ascribe not-$\phi$ to it at the same time.' And though in propositional logic hypothetical statements may be regarded as true or false, in ordinary language there is some peculiarity in saying that something which is purely hypothetical is actually true. It may be true of a certain person that he accepts such a rule; but the rule itself, when not uttered or assented to by anyone, can rarely if ever be called true.

What can be spoken of as true, however, is a further statement of the form, 'One ought to keep rule R'; that is, certain rules ought to be assented to. But that means that one cannot speak of such statements, in turn, simply as rules of action; otherwise one merely raises the same question one stage further back, '*ought* I to keep this rule?' Consequently it is not possible to interpret assent to moral propositions just as an assent to certain rules of action. For one cannot avoid the ultimate question, 'Ought one to keep these rules?', which is a demand for truth.

Nor is it possible to say that one simply knows certain moral propositions to be self-evidently true in the way that some logicians have claimed that the fundamental truths of logic are indeed true, but are self-evidently so. For even such a logician, who upholds the truth of his basic rules, would have to find some factual ground for this truth, some fact or facts that made it true. And I think it would have to be found somehow in the structure of the world: the propositional functions $\sim(p . \sim p)$ and $(p \vee \sim p)$ and $(p . q) \supset (p)$ will have truth-values in virtue of the fact that things are identical with themselves, are distinguishable and exclude their opposites, and are divisible: that is, it is correct to think according to the rules (if one is thinking about things in a very broad sense of 'thing') because this is how things in fact are structured. Failing to think logically is stupid but not immoral, because it is thinking not in accordance with the structure of the facts, and is not directed to its proper end—but there is no *moral* obligation to achieve that end. Thus an objectivist in logic would have to appeal to facts about the structure of reality to justify his logical intuitions (I am not here defending *logical* objectivism, but only saying what a logical objectivist must believe). It is not enough to say that one intuits the truth of propositions. Whether or not one knows it, if they are true propositions there must be something in the facts which makes them true.

The difference between logical and moral rules is that those of logic are conditional—one ought to think thus, *if* one wishes to think in accordance with the facts. But moral rules are unconditional—one just *ought* to act thus. What this means is that whereas logical rules can be grounded in straightforward matters of fact about the world (for those facts bind *only if* one has a certain wish—to think rationally about them), moral rules still require to be grounded in specifically *moral* (that is, binding) facts; for they must be facts which obligate of themselves, whether or not one has the wish to be obligated. So it seems that the objectivist must conclude not just that he intuits certain moral propositions, but that the world is so structured that it contains morally binding, non-empirical facts.

4. I have spoken of these moral facts as 'claims' which impose a particular course of action upon a man and which are binding. And the objection raised to this was that it does not follow from the fact that a claim is made upon a man—by an order of the courts, for example—that a man acknowledges the claim as his duty. So, it was said, there still remains a gap between the apprehension of any moral fact and one's acknowledgement of it as binding on one.

This sort of objection seems to rest upon the assumption that cognitive apprehension is necessarily a neutral, detached activity, which finds its paradigm in the experimental approach of the natural sciences. To apprehend a fact correctly one must simply register it as a neutral datum, as a machine might. However, most people would probably concede that there are some common items of human knowledge which are not, and perhaps even cannot be, apprehended in a detached way. Among the most obvious of these are bodily sensations, whether pleasant or painful. I think it is quite proper to say that one does apprehend bodily sensations; though some philosophers have denied this, the denial seems to contradict the plain facts of experience. But if one apprehends a pain, this is not something which can be apprehended by others, or which can be measured by scientific instruments—all they can measure is the neuro-physiological data associated with the felt pain. The experience of pain is something which involves us uniquely and essentially; I do not think that one can separate the quality of the sensation from one's subjective pain-reaction to it; it is the sensation itself which is intrinsically painful.

Now I am not suggesting that moral claims are like pains; I am only pointing out that, in areas of human experience other than morality, most of us are prepared to admit private objects of apprehension which involve intrinsically a specific personal reaction on our part. There are, however, at least two significant differences between sensations and moral claims. First, the sensation *in fact* evokes a personal response in us; whereas a moral claim *demands* a response. That is, just as the apprehension of a painful sensation is not separable from pain-response, so the apprehension of a moral claim is not separable from acknowledgement of it as a claim; but whereas the sensation naturally produces pain-avoiding behaviour, the claim demands—but does not produce—the behaviour which it demands. Second, it might be said that pains are purely subjective existents, for sensations do not exist apart from our apprehensions of them. Now a moral claim could perhaps not exist as a claim unless apprehended as such by someone. But if it is objective it must have some sort of unapprehended existence. What must be said is that something exists which, when apprehended by a man, is *ipso facto* acknowledged as demanding (but not necessarily receiving) a certain course of action from him.

I am suggesting that a clear distinction cannot always be made between 'apprehension' and 'acknowledgement'; to apprehend a painful sensation is *ipso facto* to acknowledge it as painful—the feeling of pain is not just a response to something apprehended in a logically prior way; and to apprehend a moral claim is *ipso facto* to acknowledge it as binding—to acknowledge oneself as being bound by a principle is not to respond to a previously cognized fact in a specific way. One reason why some philosophers have been loath to admit this may be a confusion between acknowledging a moral principle and actually committing oneself to act in accordance with one. Indeed, Professor Hare suggests that to acknowledge a principle simply is to commit oneself to act according to it.[6] Many if not most people, however, would acknowledge moral principles which they rarely and sometimes never manage to implement. For example, a man might agree that he ought to be more sympathetic to others; and yet he might continue to be brusque and off-hand. To save himself continual guilt, this would probably mean that he would not put that

E

particular moral principle at the forefront of his mind, that he would seldom if ever remind himself of it, that he might even attempt to disavow it on occasion. But none of these things is incompatible with saying that, in a cool moment, he may in quite an intelligible sense acknowledge that he ought to be other than he is, or even tries to be. It is one of the characteristic features of the human situation that men can deceive themselves about their moral principles—they can avoid situations in which those principles would clearly place a strong claim upon them; but that does not mean that they do not acknowledge those principles at all.

Thus, to acknowledge that one ought to do something is not necessarily to commit oneself to do it. The apprehension of a moral claim, therefore—though it is naturally unique and different from empirical facts—is not radically different from other kinds of knowledge in being synonymous with a certain sort of acknowledgement. After all, even the apprehension of a chair is also the acknowledgement that it exists. The gap between moral perception and moral commitment comes precisely between acknowledgement of a principle and actual implementation of it; not between apprehension and acknowledgement.

Why some men should choose to implement the principles they acknowledge, and others should not, is a question which brings one up against the mystery of human freedom. But it is not an epistemological problem; as far as epistemology goes the objectivist is only committed to saying that there exist non-empirical facts which can be apprehended by men; and that they impose a certain course of action on men as right, as a future possibility which it is incumbent upon men to bring about. This relation of 'binding-ness' must simply be asserted to be unique and not further analysable; but it is a relation which obtains between a moral fact and its apprehender; and it is this which makes it a *moral* fact.

5. One must say, then, that there is something which exists which for particular men at particular times appears as a future possibility for them, but which they are free to bring about or not; and when they apprehend it it 'binds' them to bring it about, as their essential possibility.

That this existent can take the form of a future possibility for particular men suggests three things—first, that it is conceptual or at least quasi-conceptual in nature. For possibilities plainly cannot be actualities; one cannot say that a possibility exists at a certain place; but one can say that a possibility is conceived by a certain mind. In other words, if one grants a possibility any sort of existence, one seems compelled to give it conceptual status, whether or not one thinks that all concepts must be conceived by minds. If it is true that one ought to do X, whatever X may be, then the fact which makes this judgement true must be an existent which binds one to do X; and 'what one is thus bound to do' can only exist as a concept or set of concepts; it cannot be a state of affairs, since what one has to do is precisely to bring it about—to make it a state of affairs. I am not suggesting that 'what one must do' exists as a concept in just the way that concepts exist in human minds; my suggestion is the more tentative one that it must have some sort of existence, and that it will be more analogous to conceptual existence than material existence.

Second, there are good reasons for thinking that moral facts must have the character of universals, rather than of particulars. For suppose that there is an infinite, or indefinitely large, number of moral facts coming into being and passing away at particular times. Then large numbers of these facts would be qualitatively identical; for propositions like 'You ought to respect others' are true perhaps for all men everywhere, and so there must exist moral facts at every time at which they are true. But how is one to tell whether different moral facts exist at different times, or whether it is not the same fact for everyone?

In attempting to answer this question, one of the first things to consider is that there is a hierarchy of moral obligations, of different orders of generality. One may place at the lower end of this hierarchy such propositions as 'You (John Smith) now (at 2 p.m. on June 3rd) ought to pay your bus fare', which are quite particular in their reference. And one may say that the existent which makes that proposition true (which I call the 'moral fact' for brevity even though, strictly speaking, I mean 'that which makes the proposition true; that is, which makes it a fact') has only a momentary existence. But what about general principles of the form, 'Bus fares ought to be paid'? Well, one may say that these are just universal generalizations from many qualitatively identical moral facts—that all situations of bus fare paying are accompanied by such moral facts as these. The difficulty with that assertion is that of knowing how one can be sure that the same qualitatively identical obligations will always attend the same situations. For it is logically possible that on some occasion one's obligation might turn out to be quite the reverse—and then the general moral principle would be falsified! To admit such a possibility would contradict our actual attitude to moral principles; for we do not regard them as falsifiable hypotheses; we regard them as at least *prima facie* obligations. That is, we want to say that it is not just a matter of contingent fact that all instances of non-fare-paying are wrong; that some of them could just as easily be right; we want to say that they are necessarily wrong just because they are instances of non-fare-paying.

Such a consideration is the basis of the doctrine of Sir David Ross that moral claims are connected in a synthetic but *a priori*—universal and necessary—way to certain empirical characteristics of acts.[7] Wherever those characteristics, and only those, occur, there necessarily follows from them the non-empirical characteristic of 'rightness' or 'wrongness' as the case may be. However, this doctrine does not really succeed in answering the query as to how one can know the truth of general moral principles. All it does is to say that they are true because of certain necessary connections between empirical facts and moral facts; this necessary connection must simply be intuited, in addition to the intuition of the moral facts themselves. Thus the facts which make general principles true, for Ross, are not moral facts but epistemological facts about necessary connections. Again, this thesis seems to contravene our normal attitudes to moral principles. It implies that the principle 'One ought to love God and men' can be analysed into some such statement as 'All instances of loving God and men are necessarily accompanied by moral obligations'. As a matter of experience it seems to me extremely implausible to say that one apprehends obligations on every such occasion; that is, one might assent to the principle in general without feeling the obligation to act on every occasion that can be subsumed under the principle. Further, I cannot see how one could be justified in asserting the sort of necessary connection that Ross's translation requires; unless, indeed, the justification was simply that one intuited the truth of the general moral principle itself; but that would make the suggested analysis redundant. This means that the moral fact underlying a general moral principle must be considered as a universal rather than as a particular—that is, the fact that all men ought at all times to love their fellows is made true by the existence not of many particular moral facts but of one universal moral fact which determines the truth of all particular cases falling under it. The admission of universals may seem an extreme metaphysical step; but it is the only way in which the necessary connection of empirical facts and obligations can be rendered intelligible. Once one admits universals one has decided the question of whether there is one or many moral facts in favour of unity. That is to say, one believes that the fact which makes any proposition expressing a general moral principle true is just one fact, existing unchanged throughout all the times at which that proposition is or could be apprehended. There may still, of course, be as many moral facts as there are general moral principles. But those who believe that there is just one ultimate principle of morality seem to be committed to asserting that there is just one ultimate moral fact which exists timelessly and determines the truth of the many various moral propositions which, in various ways, fall under it.

6. Third, the account of the moral fact I have given suggests that it is intimately bound up with whatever cosmic forces constitute the nature of men. For it does not seem possible that the connection between the objective demand and the possibilities of human life could be just a contingent matter—that is, that it is a fortunate coincidence that one can do what is objectively demanded by the moral fact. I have said that 'what one ought to do' has a conceptual, universal existence; but it is also a possible future for particular men at particular times. But how can one be sure that it really is a *possible* future? So long as one maintains a belief in the objectivity of morals, it does seem logically possible that an existent moral claim could demand the performance of a physically impossible act—whatever men felt, or said they felt, the claim could exist.

Such a possibility is delusory, however. For a 'moral claim' is not just a sort of discrete entity which enters into contingent relations with certain empirical facts. It must be conceived as a relation, triadic in form, which holds between moral facts, moral agents, and possible actions, such that it may be represented schematically thus: '(claim A) binds (P) to perform (X)', where A is a moral value, P a moral agent and X a possible action. It is because the relation of 'obligation' can only hold between values, persons, and possible acts that one can know *a priori* that one cannot be obliged to perform the impossible. If, *per impossibile*, one tried to suppose that a moral value gave rise to an 'obligation' on a person to perform an impossible act, one would simply have to say that it could not be represented by the concept of 'obligation' which we have. For it would lose all connection with action, even with endeavour to act, and thus with the activities of exhorting, prescribing, commending, praising and blaming, and with the sense of guilt for not doing what one could have done. Where none of these concepts is applicable—when so many strands of our present notion of morality have been swept aside— one would hardly wish to call what was left 'obligation', in any sense analogous to our present concept. One cannot make sense of the sentence, 'I have an obligation to do X', when conjoined with the sentence, 'I cannot do X'. So one might say, 'I have a feeling of obligation about X', in an attempt to remove all reference to possible action. Then, that would simply be a peculiar feeling attached to certain thoughts; it would not be our concept of 'obligation', which is essentially practical, in being connected with action.

What this brings out is that there could not logically exist an obligation to do the impossible—just as there could not be an obligation upon a tree or a rock. There might be some relation between a moral value, an inanimate object and an impossible act, but it could not be a relation of obligation; the nature of the relation is delimited by the nature of the objects it relates. Thus one can say *a priori* that it must be possible, in general, to realize the moral demands made upon us, because the concept of a 'moral demand' requires that it demand only sorts of act which are in general possible for men. It should be noted, however, that what I have just said is compatible with the Christian doctrine, to be examined later, that men cannot (because of 'original sin') do what they ought. For it is always possible for them, as men, to do the sorts of act in question; the impossibility has its source in the inherent infirmity of the human will in particular cases.

The objectivist must thus suppose the existence of a set of moral values which give rise to the triadic relation of 'obligation' if and whenever there exist moral agents with certain possible courses of action open to them, and at no other time. He must further suppose that the relation of 'obligation' is not just a contingent relation which may or may not hold between the referents of terms of the appropriate sort. Given the existence of moral agents and certain future possibilities, the agents are necessarily obliged to realize one of those possibilities. That is just to say that obligations are not arbitrary; if it was not so, objectivism would be in just the same position as relativism in that morality would ultimately depend on contingent facts. Now, a moral claim cannot necessarily follow from empirical facts about moral agents and their possible actions alone; to say that it did would be to re-assert a naturalistic theory. Yet moral claims do refer to particular persons in particular situations. So it seems that moral values must already contain the complete specification of all the empirical situations in which they will be applicable.

One may try to evade this conclusion by claiming that particular claims are deducible from higher-level claims like 'one ought to aim at the general happiness'. I think, as a matter of fact, that not all moral claims are thus deducible from general principles (cf. Chapter IX); but even if they were one must meet the difficulty that the more general one's principle, the less detailed it will be. So even if one knew all the facts in a specific situation one might still ask, for example, 'What does provide the greatest happiness—giving a lot of pleasure to a few, or a little to many, the application of a general rule or consideration of the particular case, concern for quality or quantity of happiness?', and so on. Many decisions which are not simply empirical have to be made in applying highly general moral principles before one can give the principle determinate meaning in a situation. Thus I do not think that one could remain satisfied with wholly general, highly indeterminate principles in morality; lower-level moral principles are required to determine their application in particular cases.

Even if one restricted consideration to very high-level principles, however, those principles cannot be stated apart from reference to some empirical facts. 'One ought to be benevolent', for example, intrinsically refers to a world in which moral agents are able to help each other. Thus the very statement of the claim specifies, however vaguely, a world of a determinate nature, including the features of 'moral agency', 'community' and 'aid' with all that they imply or presuppose. So moral values must antecedently specify a schema of a possible world in which the claims could be realized. Moreover, if the moral demand is taken to exist objectively, the specified world must be presupposed as actual. That is, if there exists a certain moral demand then it must be possible for moral agents to meet its requirements; the world must accordingly be such that what is objectively demanded of man is possible for him; that there is a necessary and not just a contingent connection between the moral demand and human possibilities.

So it seems that one must conceive the moral fact as somehow constituting, or at least helping to constitute, the essential possibilities of human being. One may think, in Platonic fashion, of a Divine Demiurge fashioning the empirical world in accordance with the eternal Forms; or one may think of the Forms themselves (those universal quasi-concepts which define the moral demand, what men ought to be) as being the exemplars and patterns of a world which shapes itself on them, in such a way that 'man as he is' has, as a necessarily determined possibility of his being, the possibility of being as he ought, of conforming to the universal exemplar of humanity. However one pictures it to oneself it seems that the moral objectivist must somehow assert that the empirical universe is necessarily so constituted that it could exemplify all the moral demands made upon it. And since this is a matter of necessity, not of brute fact, one must regard the moral fact as having the metaphysical status of an efficient cause in the world; as itself constituting (or being the pattern for constituting) those human possibilities, the realization of which it demands. Here it seems that Kant saw rightly in locating that Practical Reason which legislates the moral law in the sphere of *noumena*, the ground of the natures of things.[8] The fact in which our obligations are grounded is also the ground of its own possibility in the world.


7. However, this line of argument presupposes that the moral demand is actual, *qua* demand. Persuasive though it is to some, one can avoid the conclusions to which it leads by supposing that moral demands are hypothetical in character. Then if the world specified by the demand is not actual, the moral claim can have only hypothetical existence; it must be formulated as, 'Claim A *would* bind any P to perform X-type acts.' It is clear that hypothetical claims only give rise to actual moral demands if there exists a world of the sort specified in the claim. Thus one is not, after all, entitled to say, on the strength of a general doctrine of moral objectivism, that there is a moral goal which it must be possible for the universe to actualize. For there may not be a

universe; or, if there is, it may be impossible to actualize in it all, or some, or any of the existent moral values; or it may be possible to actualize them only in part or for a short time.

One must still conceive a set of necessary moral values. And for these to be stateable they must contain a set of exemplary possibilities, schemata of possible worlds and situations of the form 'If situation X then (necessarily) moral demand Y.' But the existence and actual nature of the universe is contingent. Thus one can never know *a priori* the nature or extent of one's moral obligations; it is only by inductive consideration of the possible acts in fact open to us that we can form an estimate of what the moral demand upon us is. Here we must always allow for the danger of either under- or over-estimating our capacities; but we can, in this way, form an idea of what the moral demands are which we must endeavour to realize, which are in general and *prima facie* possible, though not necessarily so in all circumstances, or in some specific way or to some specific degree. What is demanded of the universe will depend on what is possible in it; and yet moral values specify the range of acts which can, and indeed must, be duties in any possible world. One can therefore say that, as well as being conceptual and universal, moral facts are exemplary in character: they specify the range of possibilities within which duties can arise.

One may be content to leave the investigation there, with the postulation of ultimate moral facts which specify various hypothetical situations. But these hypotheticals must give rise to categorical claims if and whenever their protases are actualized. For the hypothetical is not merely a statement of what is the case; it is a statement of what will be the case, given certain conditions, at any future time. But this raises the problem of how such possible future states can be determined in advance with certainty. It is hardly enough to say simply that this is how things are: for it is also how they will, indeed must, be. The easiest way to render this situation intelligible is to posit a being which, on the analogy of human minds, is able to know when situation X arises and to determine that Y (the moral claim) will consequentially exist. That is, some analogon of 'knowledge' and 'will' may be conceived as constitutive of the moral fact, which ensures that its hypothetical specifications of moral claims are necessarily actualized on the proper occasions.

This analogy may be resisted on the grounds that here human

knowledge finds its limits, and we simply do not know what objectively determines that the hypothetical 'If X then Y' will always be applicable in the world. Such an appeal to agnosticism is justified; but it may be noted that the use of such analogies does render more intelligible the existence of moral facts, and that it is a natural development of objectivism, not the imposition of a doctrine of 'God' from elsewhere. Moreover, it must be remembered that Christians do not rely on a general doctrine of moral objectivity alone for their doctrine of 'God'; if they did, it could rightly be thought an insecure sort of belief which relied on such a tentative analogy as this.

Christians would also wish to call attention to the elements of intelligibility, causal necessity and purposiveness in the Universe as pointing to a necessary being with causal efficacy; to what they experience as a providential ordering of their lives, and a power of moral regeneration; to their view of morality as being essentially concerned with human fulfilment, and as presupposing the possibility of such fulfilment; to their belief in Incarnation, in which God causally and specifically interacts with the world; and to their faith, based on the Divine promise, that a moral purpose for the world will be achieved. All these features of Christian belief, here very briefly adumbrated, point towards the belief that the reality of God has causal power in the world; and they are factors which help to sustain the interpretation of moral objectivism in terms of a being with knowledge and will—an interpretation which is, I suggest, entirely natural but necessarily tentative on the basis of the doctrine of objectivity by itself.

If, as has been suggested (and as will be more fully developed in Chapter IX), particular moral claims are to be admitted in addition to very general ones, one must in any case speak of new moral facts which arise in accordance with new knowledge of contingent circumstances. So here again the concept of 'knowledge' must be introduced into the articulation of the doctrine of objectivity: 'God', the moral fact, does not only lay down a general moral goal for the world; he is concerned with individuals and their fulfilment, with the adaptation of demands to new particular situations, which requires an analagon of a knowing, responsive element in the realm of moral fact. Thus the general form of moral facts, 'If situation X then claim Y', requires that God should know, in any possible world, when X occurs, and thus that he should know exhaustively all possible worlds, that no possibility can be beyond his knowledge; God must not only be conceived as knowing, in other words, but as omniscient. And the fact of the generation of new moral demands in accordance with knowledge of contingent circumstances reinforces this claim.


8. Now I do not think one could ever be entitled to say that God is able as a matter of fact (which might have been otherwise) to know any possible universe. For how could one know that no possible but as yet unconceived, universe could be beyond God's knowledge? What is required is much more than that God should be able to know all the actually existent entities in the universe; he must know that he has knowledge of *all* actual beings, and this entails knowing that there exist no other beings than those which are known; and he must also know all possible beings. What one must consequently say is that it is not just a contingent matter of fact that God is omniscient. He is necessarily omniscient; and it is only if this necessity can be established that one could be justified in asserting in advance God's continued omniscience. But how can it be established that an actual being is necessarily omniscient? It does not seem that there could be any way of establishing this, if the actual being had no control over the coming into being of all possible beings. If this could not be assured, then it remains possible that there might come to be some being unknown to God. And, of course, if such a thing came about one could no longer exclude the possibility that one's moral experience might be delusory, the work of a powerful malignant demon. So one must maintain that all possible beings are known to, and under the causal power of, God; it is impossible that there could be anything beyond his causal power. The only way such a thing could be assured would be if God was himself the ground of all possibilities. As Kant says, perfect knowledge can only be ascribed to an 'intellective intuition', a knower which creates the objects of its knowing;[9] for as long as objects are considered as external to the knower, one cannot be sure that they are known fully and perfectly, or that all of them are known.

In this way the theist is inexorably driven away from the misleading notion of a spectator God, passively knowing a world external to himself, towards the more adequate but vastly more mysterious notion of a necessary infinite ground of all possibilities, the *Ens Realissimum*, the Creator God. God must himself be infinite or unlimited in the sense that, as the ground of all individualities, he is himself beyond individuality. He must be conceived not as one individual over against others but rather as the unlimited 'Place of Forms', the teleological parameter of the world which posits and calls man to his destiny. It is at this point that language, which is adjusted to a world of discrete particulars, to diversity and plurality, breaks under the strain of expressing an ultimate and all-inclusive unity; all it can do is to point very inadequately away from the finite and contingent and assert that, at a humanly unattainable distance in the direction of these linguistic gestures, there is something which we may designate, without comprehension, the infinite and necessary.

God cannot be limited; for where there is a limit there may be something beyond it; and a being thus limited could not claim to know everything beyond that limit, even less to be its necessary ground. Only by being unlimited can God be the ground of all finite possibilities. The theist must here steer a wary course between the Scylla of pantheism—saying that God is nothing but the totality of finite possibilities—and the Charybdis of anthropomorphism—saying that God is a personal individual rather like a supreme architect of the cosmos. God, *qua* ground of possibility, should not be conceived as just a sum of all possible perfections, a sort of impossible combination of all incompatible predicates, but as that necessary being which allows certain possibilities to develop and excludes others, which sets limits to what is finitely possible.

Talk of 'possibilities' is extremely complex and fraught with logical difficulties; and this is not the appropriate place to probe the subject in detail. But it should be said that there seem to be at least two alternative conceptions of 'possibility', which give rise to rather different concepts of God, as ground of possibility. One line of argument is that if anything ever will be possible then (analytically) it must always have been possible; therefore it is senseless to speak of 'new' possibilities coming into being; and therefore every possibility must really exist eternally and changelessly in the mind of God. Further, it makes no sense to talk of 'choosing possibilities' since choice is always between possibilities. Thus the exhaustive set of possibilities in the Divine mind is necessarily what it is. The problem for the theist is then to explain on what ground some of these possibilities are actualized in an empirical universe of fact; but he conceives God as changelessly omniscient in his knowledge of all possibilities, though perhaps as changing in respect of his knowledge of actualized possibilities in a world.

It might be maintained, however, that it is mistaken to speak in this way of 'possibilities' as really actualities, though of a quasi-conceptual order. And so one may wish to speak of continually new and changing situations in the Universe, bringing to light new possibilities of development by some sort of creative development. Even if this view is coherent, however—and it is one which has been proposed, notably by Professor Hartshorne,[10] as more adequate than the traditional view of a changeless universe of possibilities—the theist must still attribute to God the capacity of limiting the development of new possibilities in definite ways. It is not that God must, like the great architect, do the best he can with materials over the existence of which he has no control, for then whatever is beyond his control may be unknown to him. Rather, God is able to set limits to the actual existence of entities in the Universe in which his purpose is worked out. But although there are deep and perplexing problems involved in working out a coherent conception of God, that is not the task I have here set myself. And it is true of both the conceptions just mentioned that God is to be conceived as the creator, not the spectator or even the architect, of the universe; for the coming to be of events in the Universe, and not just their specific nature, must be conceived as under his control if one is to adopt an adequate conceptual basis for the necessary ominiscience of God.

Drawing together what has been said in this chapter, it seems that an acceptance of objectivism in ethics, when its implications and presuppositions are fully explored, naturally unfolds into a form of metaphysical teleology. A realm of universal conceptual values, or ideals, is taken to exist—values which contain exemplary schemata of possible world-structures and which are the ground of specific moral demands upon actual moral agents. One may simply leave the matter there. But further consideration of how such hypothetical demands can be conceived to be implemented in appropriate circumstances, and of how demands can come to exist in new and unforeseeable situations, taken together with considerations from various other contexts of human experience which lead the mind to posit an ultimate being with causal efficacy in the universe, makes it natural to conceive of the moral facts as being grounded in a creative power, working through understanding and will to bring the universe into being, to shape its specific character and to draw it to moral perfection. Thus the moral facts are given causal efficacy with regard to the physical universe, comprising the exemplary pattern upon which the world is founded, towards which it strives, and which it is the task and responsibility of men to implement. But men can refuse this task, refusing to shape what 'is' an accordance with what 'ought to be'; and this is a rejection of the value of the ideal, and the 'proper' structures of human being, in favour of the structure of the actual and imperfect. It is these ideals or moral facts, whether one or many, which, together with certain empirical data, determine the truth of certain moral propositions. With this view of the general nature of moral objectivity I shall now turn to examine more specifically how Christians conceive the moral demands which they believe to be made upon them; and this in turn will help to illuminate further the nature of the moral demand itself.

# V

## ATTITUDES, IDEALS
## AND GOD

1. In the previous chapter, the conception of a realm of universal
values or ideals as the exemplary patterns of human possibilities
was developed as the metaphysical implicate of moral objectivism.
This conception may be further articulated by an examination of
another major characteristic of theistic morality which I shall call
its *attitudinal* character. What I mean to imply by this term will,
I hope, become clear in the course of the exposition; briefly, it is
meant to signify that theistic morality is concerned with the
realization of a certain sort of character and attitude rather than
with external observance of moral rules, or even with the obedience
to moral rules for their own sake. It is concerned with what a
man must become in himself rather than with what specific acts
he must do. And it is sharply contrasted with any moral view
which maintains that it does not matter what sort of person one
is as long as one does what is right—one's duty.

These are remarks not about what moral words mean but about
what things are morally good, and thus they seek to develop the
theistic answer to the first of the basic moral questions distinguished in Chapter II (that is, 'What things are good?'). But
the connection between the question about what things are good
and the question about the meaning of 'good' can be seen in the
way in which the development of the concept of objectivity led to
the postulation of a realm of exemplary patterns of human being,
values which may be said to constitute a specific, 'proper' possibility of human living. For this development certainly suggests a
substantive morality according to which 'what is right' becomes
identified with what is implicit, in the structure of things, as their
'ideal' or final end (that is, the ground of their possibility which is
also the purpose or 'telos' of their actuality). And thus it becomes
natural to think of human life as aimed at the realization of a
certain ideal in oneself, as the imitation of and growth into those

exemplary forms which one acknowledges, the transformation in oneself of the actual into the ideal.

I do not wish to suggest that one can simply deduce a doctrine of what things are good from the mere doctrine of the objectivity of morals. In fact the content of one's morality must, at least in the main, precede the sort of reflection upon it that gives rise to a doctrine of objectivity. But, once attained, the notion of objectivity, by leading one to ask what sort of facts could make moral judgements true, does help to develop further one's general conception of the moral life, and thus may deepen or perhaps modify the actual content of one's moral beliefs. In the present instance, for example, any consideration of Christian ethics must start from the data of actual Christian moral beliefs. One can then form the general judgement that these beliefs appear to be mainly attitudinal in character—that they tend to be concerned with what may be called 'the life of the soul' rather than with social or political principles, for example. Then, in pursuing the question of objectivism, one may, in relative independence, develop a view of moral facts as being existent values which are conceptual, universal and exemplary in character. When these two lines of thought are brought together, one will be able to see more clearly in what the life of the soul consists, and what general conception of the moral life underlies an attitudinal morality—that it is the realization in one's own being of the exemplary ideals. And thus one will be helped in the interpretation of those data of Christian morality which seem obscure or even unintelligible (for example, the seemingly impossible demands of the Sermon on the Mount).[1] The doctrine of attitudinal morality will in turn help to articulate in more detail one's conception of the moral facts upon which one's morality is based. So, as in most philosophical thinking, the answer to one question naturally leads into another question; the answer to that leads one back to modify or extend the first answer; and out of this dialectical interplay there emerges, if one is fortunate, an overall view of the nature of that with which one is concerned, in which each element complements and balances another.

2. I shall first seek to develop the notion of attitudinal morality by distinguishing three importantly different kinds of 'duty'. There are probably more distinctions than these to be made, but I think

that these three would be generally admitted and will serve my purpose.

(*a*) There is the class of duties which accrue to me in virtue of my particular position in society. These are imposed on me as conditions of membership in certain groups—in my job, my family, my tennis club, my church, etc. Different groups of which I am a member may impose quite different duties on me; and my duties in these groups may change relative to their other members, or they may be changed by convention (by drafting a new constitution, for example). Within these groups I also have certain rights, and the understanding is that if I do my duty the group will guarantee those rights—for example to be paid, looked after, or allowed to play tennis. This class of duties may be called the class of *contractual duties*—one does not need to appeal to moral objectivity to justify their existence: the justification lies in one's own desires and needs for social intercourse and security.

Nevertheless, the objectivist will of course maintain that one objectively ought to perform one's contractual duties, other things being equal. My point is only that contractual duties and also the class of social duties which will be next distinguished, would remain even if moral objectivism was a false doctrine. But the way in which they are regarded, the ultimate justification given for them and the motive to moral obedience will be different for a non-objectivist; and these factors will emerge in more or less marked differences both in conduct and, more important perhaps, in attitude.

It may, I think, be plausibly argued that a view which founds morality solely on its utility to social life is, to the extent to which this foundation becomes known, actually self-defeating. For men are unlikely to be deterred from making exceptions in their own favour whenever possible, simply by the thought that honesty and justice are in general for the good of society. Where authority is not omnipresent and omniscient, only a morally founded respect for law and justice can preserve social cohesion. And thus, though a utilitarian view of the basis of morality may be the true one—the view that morality exists to preserve social cohesion—it may be able to fulfil its function only if most men are conditioned to accept a more absolute sense of moral authority which can motivate them to value society above their own deprivation. This consideration does not serve to establish an objectivist view of morality; but it does suggest that a pure utilitarianism, given that

F

human nature is as it is, may actually undermine the social stability it exists to preserve. Its success would perhaps depend upon there being sufficient men who were strongly conditioned to an unquestioning obedience to a 'moral' code, the foundations of which they left unexplored. Though a profoundly depressing view of man, that is no argument for its falsity; but it does throw doubt upon the ability of a purely contractual account of moral rules—for which each agent consciously and rationally enters a 'moral contract' with others—to serve as an adequate explanation of moral behaviour. And it suggests that the real alternative to an objectivist account of moral obligation must be a reliance on the strength of the unrationalized, instinctive feelings of unreflective men.

(b) There is a class of duties which are said to accrue to one not in any particular social capacity but simply as a man. Such duties might be those of being benevolent, sympathetic, trust-worthy and courageous. These too are primarily social virtues. Their existence can be—though need not be—justified by reference to the conditions necessary for the existence of a complex society; for they are virtues which conduce to the greater integration and security of society. Such *social duties* will be those which all men will reasonably require of their fellows; they will tend to be strictly universalizable within a given society—for granting exceptions may produce social disharmony—and they will tend to be roughly the same in all societies, since the conditions of social stability are roughly the same everywhere. Nevertheless, it would be unreasonable to regard them as absolute, in the sense of eternal or unchangeable laws; it is only reasonable to allow circumstances to modify them. For instance, it may be a social duty to preserve property; but in a communist state the specific ways in which this is done will naturally differ, for what will be preserved will not be private interests but the people's collective interests. Thus the specific application of the general duty may reasonably vary from time to time and in different places.

This class of social duties is often equated with the realm of Natural Law; the unchanging core of general presuppositions of social life is termed the 'primary law'; and its specific applications, modified by context, is the 'secondary law'.[2] This law is to be found by the consideration of what a reasonable and impartial judge would lay down as rules to govern the social conduct of men with diverse and often conflicting claims and interests in a relatively stable society. Its discovery is thus partly a matter of empirical induction, based on practical experience of men, and partly a matter of moral commitment to social stability (as a condition, perhaps, of security in pursuing one's own interests as freely as possible). It is thus a law based on *reason* (providing for impartiality) and on the *desire* to promote one's own interests (providing for the content of the law).

This equation between social duties and Natural Law would, however, be mistaken. For the justification of social duties provided above is a justification which is ultimately based on psychological facts about men (and is thus a subjectivist view), the facts that one has certain desires and drives; the only valuational commitment is to the fulfilment of one's own interests. Or if it is to the equitable fulfilment of all compossible interests one must ask whether this is objectively binding. If so, what facts make it true? It must be that everyone's interests ought to be furthered. And here the gap between this (utilitarian) concept of social duties and Natural Law theory begins to be seen. For the question must be posed: are any human interests, just as such, to be furthered, or only some of them? Does it matter what the interests are which are furthered, or may any interests be furthered which do not conflict unduly with others? This question brings to light the point at which the concept of 'social duties' must be transcended by the Christian.

According to the utilitarian conception (at least in its pure form, which Mill admittedly does not consistently maintain)[3] there are specifically moral principles, and these are to be found in the requirements of impartiality and equality. But the content—the things which are 'moralized' by being brought under such principles—are simply human desires or drives; and they are neither moral nor immoral in themselves. They will be constituted as immoral in a specific context only if they do, or tend to, produce social conflict or inequality; with the avoidance of such 'unfairness' they will be quite permissible. And virtues such as benevolence are good only because they tend to social cohesion: they are not binding in themselves.

(c) There is, accordingly, a third class of duties which not all men accept (classical utilitarians could not, though it appears that Mill to some extent could).[3] These consist of all those aspects of human being which *ought* to be furthered. They are thus distinguishable from interests, which are aspects one wishes to further; their furtherance is binding on all men in an absolute and unconditional sense. It is the existence of such aspects which is the distinctive claim of Natural Law theory; it gives what I termed the attitudinal character of Christian morality. And it must be distinguished, too, from Kant's ethics of disposition. Kant distinguished between the observance of social duties and their observance from the right disposition or motive—the 'good will'.[4] But I am not simply asserting that morality consists in doing whatever is one's duty with the motive simply that it is one's duty. I am asserting that there are some aspects of human being ('inner' aspects because they are characteristics of man's nature, not his external acts—though naturally these are related) which *ought* to be realized.

The question here, then, is what sort of being man should become, what nature he *ought* to have. And this nature is plainly not something which he just has; it is something he must himself choose to create: though, in so choosing, he chooses only that character which is objectively binding on him. This way of conceiving moral objectivity does not regard 'rightness' just as a quality synthetically *a priori* related to situations or acts of a certain type, as the British intuitionists did. It locates obligation in the nature of human being itself—a nature which is defined not only by its present being, but by a final end or goal implicit in it. What is obligatory is the cultivation of those specifically human excellences which are implicit in the constitution of man's nature. Acts are thus right not if they possess a supervenient quality of 'rightness' but if they conduce to the development or fulfilment of man's nature, or, secondarily, if they maintain a state of affairs in which such free development will be possible (this is the justification of social duties).

I am maintaining that what man apprehends, or could apprehend, as the factual core on which his moral principles are (if true) based is what one could call an 'ideal of human nature'; not just a set of ultimate moral principles—for they stand in need of truth-determining facts—nor a set of diverse distinguishable moral intuitions; but an ideal conception of what human being ought to be. Such ideals are the facts which make principles of duty true.

3. Now it may be agreed that some men have such ideals, and that Christians, in particular, do base their lives on an ideal of

human nature which is exemplified in Christ. But two things may be said—first, it is nonsense to talk of ideals as facts; one can choose to follow a certain ideal but it is senseless to say that the ideal *exists*; it is simply my conception of a possible future; and it does not matter to my following an ideal, whether it exists or not, in any case. Second, different men choose different ideals of life and may even change them from time to time, so one must talk of a plurality of ideals, none of them universally binding in the way duties are, but many of them morally laudable. Moreover, what we mean by an ideal is something that is not categorically binding as duties are: it is something to be aspired towards and perhaps never attained; and failure to achieve it is not something for which one is blameworthy.

To the first point, one might say that it is a typical affirmation of empiricism, and such a philosophy has already been transcended as soon as one begins to talk of moral facts of any sort. And it does matter whether ideals 'really exist' or not; for if they do not then they are just things which I *choose*; and the choice, being ultimate, must be criterionless, so I cannot be objectively claimed by such ideals. But the Christian wishes to say that he is objectively claimed by an ideal; consequently the ideal must exist.

But how does it exist? It cannot be actual, in a straightforward sense, or it would be an 'is', not an 'ought'; yet it must be actual if it really is objective. It exists, it seems, as a claim upon men, a possible future to be actualized, and therefore as a 'not yet'. And yet if this is an objective goal one must conceive it as somehow existing from the first moment of the world's existence; if it does not come into being until the end of world history then it could hardly be called a 'goal' at all; it would be a fortuitous product of many chance occurrences. There are two contrasting ways in which this ideal has been conceived in the Christian tradition. According to the Natural Law interpretation, prevalent in Catholic thinking, the goal is to be found simply in the 'essence' of humanity itself; for on the Aristotelian pattern of metaphysics it is the 'formal cause', as a timeless and universal concept, which forms matter to be an individual of a certain sort; and this formal cause is also the 'final cause' or perfect idea to which material things tend to conform, though always imperfectly, due to their admixture with matter. Basic to this interpretation is the whole Aristotelian metaphysics of form and matter, act and potency, essence and accidental attribute—the concept of a Universe interpenetrated by a teleological unity of Intelligible Forms which the empirical world shadows but does not manifest completely. The account I have given of a 'realm of values' possesses obvious similarities to this scheme, though I am not thereby committed to Aristotelian metaphysics.

In Reformation theology, however, this Greek system was largely rejected in favour of a more directly personalistic way of thinking about the relation of God and man. In this scheme it seems natural to speak of moral claims as arising out of a direct encounter of God and man, and so as being based on the sovereign will of God.[5] However, though these are contrasting views the difference between them is not as great as may be imagined.

One may oppose Natural Law and 'encounter' theology—one placing 'moral facts' in the nature of man itself (erecting an autonomous 'nature'), the other placing it solely in God's gracious encounter with man. But a mediating solution is possible—the final end of man's nature is not just *in him* as though he were quite autonomous; it is, *qua* ideal, an objective claim *on* him; he must become it, but only in *response* to it—and, at best, he can manifest only a part of the Ideal, a refraction of it into the world, even in the paradisal world. What man is, is to be defined only over against and in response to the being of the Ideal: the structure of human being is essentially structured-in-relation-to the objective Ideal.

There is indeed something peculiar in the notion of a 'natural end' if one is really thinking of this end as a sort of completely autonomous nature. For in nature itself what is 'natural' could easily be taken as what is demonic; the survival of the fittest is as 'natural' a principle as the development of embryos into the 'fullness' of animal life. Thus it is impossible to divorce the concept of a 'natural end' from the concept of that which is demanded of one. Indeed, a certain end is only called 'natural', 'essential', or 'proper' because it is the possibility which is morally demanded of men. Since this is the case it is not possible to speak of an 'autonomous' nature if by this is meant a purely natural phenomenon, not subject to the demands of the transcendent realm of values. The 'natural end' of man can only be defined in relation to the Ideal which claims a certain possibility as the right response by men to its existence.

It is for this reason that I have called theistic morality 'attitudinal', rather than by some term which would emphasize its concern with the realization of value in oneself. For such a realization is demanded by an existent value; and the demand takes the form of a claim made upon men to take up a specific responsive attitude to the Ideal. Now it may be said that the attitude is simply that of being prepared to bring about the value in question whenever possible. Thus one may say that there exists a certain value which may be designated by the term 'truthfulness'. The attitude which this value demands from men is simply that of being concerned to discover and promulgate the truth. Now to have such an attitude is certainly something other, and more, than assenting to a general moral principle that one should always tell the truth. The principle provides a general description ('telling the truth') which covers many different instances of human action; though often it is unclear whether it provides an adequate description of any given action or whether it needs to be supplemented by different or more general principles (such as 'telling a lie to save a life', for example). And it asserts that acts of this sort should be done as often as possible; or that at least no action directly contradicting it ('telling a lie') should be performed.

To have an attitude of 'concern for truthfulness', however, is to adopt a general policy of action and a general way of regarding things; so that one does not just refrain from lying, or tell the truth when asked; but one is actively concerned to discover the truth and make it known. It is not to accept a specific rule as one that is not to be broken; it is to adopt an emotional and practical stance towards the world, one that extends over the whole of one's conscious life. And it is the cultivation of this general attitude which is the attitudinal response to the value of 'truthfulness'. Further, it can be seen how the response to this value does constitute the fulfilment of human nature; for it enriches man's consciousness and reason and sets them on their 'proper' pursuit.

It must be denied, therefore, that talk of the 'final end' of man implies a belief in human autonomy in any sense that opposes the belief that man's existence is determined by a transcendent reality. For man's final end can only be realized by his own free response to the demands of the transcendent realm of values.


4. Even so, it may be said, the postulation of a realm of values to which man is called to respond still omits any mention of the

God who must be the ground and focus of all Christian morality. To speak of values and ideals, even to speak of one supreme ultimate Ideal, is to speak of something other than the personal God who calls the world into existence by Divine *fiat*. And, it may even be claimed, I have in fact derogated the being of God by supposing a realm of self-subsisting values over and above God's will. The Christian must just do God's will whatever it is; that is his sole concern.

On the other hand, it is strange to talk of the moral law being given *simply* by Divine command; this is an over-simplistic account of moral objectivity. Calvin did indeed, perhaps notoriously, maintain that moral principles were right simply and solely because God as all-powerful Will commanded them.[6] But such a view has never been accepted in the mainstream of Christian thinking about morality. The consequence has seemed to most to be too unpalatable to stomach—that if God commanded men to torture each other then torture would be right. But the real objection to the view is that, if 'what is right' is 'whatever God commands', then it no longer makes sense to say that what God commands is right, or that God is good. Like prescriptivism (of which it is a form), this view of morality founds rightness simply on the fact that certain orders are given; and, as with other forms of the doctrine, this is to found rightness on a fact which is not distinctively moral. Why ought one to obey God's will rather than our own, if its only distinctive characteristic is that it is more powerful than ours? The only reason which can be given is a prudential one—that if one does not, God's power will punish one in some way. Thus morality would be reduced to prudence, to what it pays to do—and if a Christian finds himself able to accept this, then and only then can he accept the view that morality is whatever God commands.

Some philosophers have attempted to argue that theists are compelled to base morality on the *de facto* Divine will, since otherwise God would be constrained by something external to his will—namely the Moral Law; and second, God would become quite extraneous to morality, since his espousal and promulgation of the Moral Law are quite unnecessary to its objective bindingness and supreme authority; the fact that God wills the Moral Law adds nothing to the logical character of that law.

The basic reply to these assertions is that moral principles, if they are to be regarded as Christians do regard them, as true, must be determined as true by moral facts; and 'willing', even if done by God, is not a moral fact. Thus the question to be asked is: do these moral facts constrain the will of an omnipotent being to obedience, so that God's will is necessarily good?

To put it in the classical form in which it is first found, in Plato's *Euthyphro*: does God love good things because they are good, or are things good because God loves (or wills) them?[7] Both alternatives seem equally unacceptable to the theist; for if God loves things because they are good then their 'goodness' becomes something independent of God—superior to him, even, to which his will must conform; while if whatever God wills is good then 'goodness' becomes consequent upon the decisions of a completely unconditioned and therefore arbitrary will. This will need not even be consistent; for 'consistency' is an intellectual good by which God is not bound, on the theory. So 'goodness' becomes dependent upon an arbitrary and incalculable Divine *fiat*, and one must find out that there is a God, and what he wills, before one can know what is good.

I think it must be said that the decision as to what things are good usually precedes any claim to know what God actually wills; indeed, the main test available of whether it is 'God' that wills something, rather than a demonic power, is the test of the moral goodness of what is willed. That is, we would not call anything 'God' unless it met, and perhaps fulfilled, the highest moral demands that we could conceive. However, if one does not wish to make the moral law dependent upon knowledge of God's will, neither does one wish to make it superior to God or even an independent entity on the same level as God.

The only escape from this dilemma is in fact to *identify* the will of God with the 'realm of values' which constitutes the goodness of things. As Professor W. G. Maclagan says, 'The moral experience is . . . one index of what we mean when we speak of "God".'[8] Thus we do not have a prior conception of a God, which must subsequently be brought into some sort of relation with our notion of the realm of values so that either they depend upon him or he is conditioned by them. Rather, it is by starting with and developing the notion of a realm of values that we come to gain some idea of part of what is meant by the term 'God'. It is not, of course, easy to relate the various parts of the concept of God into a coherent whole; but neither do I think that it is impossible. And the theist does need to explain why he speaks of what other men are perhaps content to call their 'duty' as 'the will of God'; what difference, if any, this phrase denotes in reality. But I think the only defensible position for a theist, on this whole question of the relation of God and morality, is that when one speaks of 'God's will' one means to speak simply of the Moral Fact which determines the truth of our value-judgements.

With this thesis in mind one must proceed to enquire why the moral facts which demand specific attitudes of men should be interpreted as elements of the 'will of God'; and what more there is to the concept of 'God' that moral theory cannot supply but which may be intelligibly related to the moral concept elucidated above.

# VI

# THE CHRISTIAN EXEMPLAR

1. In the last three chapters I have spoken somewhat indiscriminately of 'moral facts', 'values' and 'ideals', both in the singular and in the plural. When I have spoken of 'moral facts' I have been concerned to stress that there must be something existent which determines the truth-value of moral judgements; and I have remained agnostic on the question of whether each judgement has its corresponding fact, or whether there could be just one fact which determined the truth of all moral judgements. When I have spoken of 'values', however, moral facts have been interpreted pluralistically as discrete exemplary patterns of human conduct which have the character of universal quasi-concepts. It is as if there existed a realm of self-subsistent entities—such as 'truth', 'courage', 'love', 'wisdom', 'justice' and so on—which demanded specific policies of action and apprehension (specific attitudes) from men. And when I have spoken of 'ideals' I have had in mind men's conceptions of what they ought to become, the goal of their striving; and here I have inclined to a monistic interpretation of one objective Ideal towards which all men ought to strive, like the Aristotelian concept of God as that which moves all things by their desire for it.[1] The reason for this move towards monism lies in the teleological implication of the word 'ideal': that it is a purposive goal rather than the result of a mechanistic process. Then all men's individual ideals are seen as converging on the one objective teleology of the world, that which really is the moral purpose for all men.

One main problem of interpretation, in the analysis of what it may be in the facts which sustains a doctrine of moral objectivity, is thus the problem of unity and diversity; is the moral fact one or many? From one point of view it is obviously manifold; for there are many diverse obligations at different times and for different persons, more or less specific in their nature. Indeed different obligations, such as those to pursue freedom and equality, may conflict in certain situations; and this fact inclines one to stress the diversity of moral facts rather than their unity.

On the other hand, the manifoldness of values is not just that of a chance collection of quite disparate items. As was maintained in Chapter IV, each value is necessarily related to some human possibility as its exemplary form; and each was said to demand the actualization of a certain responsive attitude which fulfilled human nature. Further, since these values do not derive solely from already existent human possibilities, they were said to constitute an exemplary schema of such possibilities. But at this point a complication arises as to the difference between obligations on particular occasions and obligations to pursue policies of action in general. Exponents of moral objectivism very often assume that, on particular occasions, one intuits some specific course of action as binding on one; and that is one's duty in that situation. But it may be that one may intuit a general demand to adopt an attitude of, for example, truth-seeking, which is not limited to any specific sort of situation, though of course it will first occur in a specific situation. And it may be that the latter view more accurately represents that element of decision-making which plays so large a part in actual moral experience. For even though, as I have argued, it is important to maintain that we acknowledge values and do not just choose them, nevertheless there seems to be a fairly large area of free decision as between different and sometimes competing values in specific situations. One must, for example, decide whether a certain act could be subsumed under a description which most adequately expresses a demanded attitude; and one must decide whether that attitude itself, though in general demanded of us, is appropriate in the situation in question.

What I am suggesting is that though there is a place in the Christian life for special moral direction, the general situation of the Christian, as of other men, is that he feels himself bound to acknowledge and pursue specific values (such as 'love' or 'courage') in general; but he is not at all sure how he ought to go about pursuing them, or to what extent, or which take precedence in specific situations, or what, in detail, the pursuit of them implies for his particular decisions. Of course, Christians do pray for guidance about specific decisions, and sometimes some of them seem to receive definite promptings in some direction; but I do not doubt that most of the time and for most Christians particular moral decisions just have to be made to the best of one's ability with all the impartiality and practical wisdom one can muster, in the hope that at least God will take the intention for the deed and turn one's action to the true good. In other words, moral decisions remain *decisions* calling for thought and care and an element of risk; they are not turned into a sort of 'reading off' of moral rightness in every human situation so that all one has to do is to implement what one clearly 'sees' to be right.

2. Nevertheless, there is a distinctively Christian doctrine of the nature of those values which men ought to realize. That is, the Christian cannot just say that there exists an indefinitely large number of values, all of which demand realization by men; and that it is entirely up to the individual which values he chooses to realize, and when. For it is at this point that the great differences between the various ethical doctrines of humanity begin to appear. In Confucianism, for instance, the key-values—the realization of which constitute the ideal for man—are: benevolence, decorum, wisdom and sincerity. The ideal is that of the man of gravity, honour and reasonable charity—the 'gentleman'. In Buddhism the ideal is one of compassion, detachment and recollectedness— the 'knower of the truth'. By contrast, the Christian ideal is that of the man of unlimited charity, humility, courage and temperance—one who may be most aptly called the 'lover of God'. As Augustine put it, 'I hold virtue to be nothing else than perfect love of God'.[2] All the values which the Christian is concerned to realize are forms of Christian love, and arise from it as character-traits which naturally express and, in turn, help to sustain it.

In each of these ethical systems a certain group of values is selected as constituting an 'ideal' of human life; and this ideal is usually paradigmatically presented in the form of a perfect human exemplar of the ideal—Confucius, the Buddha or Jesus, in the examples just cited. As one examines these ideals, and the groups of values which they incorporate, the sense in which one may speak of values as unitary rather than as a simple diversity becomes clearer. To take the example of the Confucian ideal, it is not that a certain, rather arbitrary, selection is made from a whole realm of logically independent values, and that the selected items are then placed side by side as elements of an ideal human life. It is rather the case that each of the values in question is modified and developed by its juxtaposition with the other values in the ideal; the ideal—of a whole human person—itself controls and unifies the various component values and adjusts them to their proper role in the total pattern of life.

Thus the benevolence of the Confucian ideal can only be understood in its characteristic quality when it is supplemented by the values of decorum and reasonableness; then it becomes clear that what is meant is not an immoderate concern for others, at one's own expense, but something more like a recognition of one's proper place in society with an acceptance of the obligations as well as of the rights of that position. So, too, the value of decorum would be misunderstood if it was interpreted as a legalistic concern with ritual for its own sake. Again, one can see it for what it is only in the total context of the values of benevolence, wisdom, sincerity and so forth, which reveal the underlying notion of 'good order', of the measured and harmonious life both in society and in oneself.[3] Thus each value which goes to constitute a specific ideal is itself given its distinctive character only by the controlling unity of an ideal conception of what human life, as such, ought to be, which shapes the values it selects as 'forms' of one controlling unitary conception. Although one may say, then, that there is a great number of diverse values, nevertheless various groups of them are unified by ideal conceptions of human life and can then properly be spoken of as elements in, or forms of, the unitary ideal which they express.

It thus transpires that it is not sufficient, in speaking of the moral life, to speak of a realm of self-subsistent values, any or all of which one may choose to realize at various times. For from such a realm of values one could select an indefinitely large set of ideal patterns of human life, each governed by a dominant character according to the ultimate principle governing the selection of values. The existence of such a controlling principle does seem to be an essential component of the moral life; for in setting the predominant tone of a pattern of life it modifies the way in which values themselves are interpreted. It gives unity and direction to the individual life, so that one seeks to develop the realization of values in a certain direction with that consistency which only a dominant principle can give. Those who devote their lives to the pursuit of such ideals, and those exemplars who present them paradigmatically in themselves, do not envisage them as optional possibilities only to be realized if they happen to fire one's imagination. And they do not regard diverse ideals of human life as all equally adequate. Their claim is usually that the ideal they espouse is binding on all men as such, and would be seen to be so were men only able to attain complete clarity of vision.

If one grants the existence of truth-determining moral facts at all, it does seem reasonable to suppose that it is ideals, rather than values, which are morally binding on men. For the various values must all supplement one another before they are capable of giving rise to a moral demand on man. The reason for this is the reason Kant gave for rejecting all moral values as good in themselves, with the one exception of the 'good will'[4]—an exception which at first seems trivial and indeed analytic (the 'good will' is made good by definition); but which is later developed into a complete ethical doctrine at the cost of reintroducing at least two of the values previously discarded; namely consistency and impartiality. Kant's reason was that though courage (for example) is a value it is not good in itself, for one may be a courageous robber. Similarly, one may be an intemperate lover, an unmerciful judge or a humble idiot. In other words, the realization of one moral value in an individual life does not make that life morally laudable. Thus one feels compelled to say that, though the response to one or two moral values may be all that can be desired in a given case, one may still wish to convict a man of moral inadequacy in his whole person and in the development of his character in general.

I do not, however, think that this sort of consideration should lead one, as it led Kant, to reject an ethic of values entirely, on behalf of something like a purely formalistic system of ethics. Rather it should lead one to uphold the necessary unity of diverse values in one total ideal of life, unifying a whole set of values in one coherent pattern. One ought to be, in other words, both courageous and benevolent, both just and merciful, both prudent and humble. It is only a commitment to the realization of all these values that deserves to be called an adequate response to the moral demand made on men. Furthermore, as has just been argued, the concept of a set of values is not just the concept of a collection of separately defined virtues; the relationship of the values within the set to one another subtly defines their character. Each human attitude and disposition can be considered as a separate value only in artificial and to some extent falsifying abstraction. For, in fact, all the dispositions of a man interrelate as dispositions of one unitary person; it is the whole person which imports its distinctive character to its constituent elements, and one can adequately interpret one disposition to virtue (for example, 'courage') only in the light of the whole of a man's acts and attitudes throughout a period of his life.

It is because of this integral interrelation of moral values as realized in human dispositions that religious morality tends to be, and Christian morality certainly is, *exemplary* in character. That is to say, it defines the attitudes and dispositions it requires not in terms of a list of abstract values but in an actual human life, by reference to which, in its total pattern, the various demanded values can be abstracted.

3. It seems, then, that the moral demand is conceived by the Christian not as a sum of demands made by a number of discrete values but as a unitary ground which demands the realization of a set of integrally related attitudes. It is this set of attitudes which can be abstractly defined as a list of 'Christian virtues', but which is in fact a total response of the human person to a unitary moral demand, a response of which the virtues are constituent forms or aspects. And the required attitude is embodied in the life of Christ, the exemplar of the perfect moral response. For Christ is more than the *example* of realized values which can be independently known in their true nature; he is the *exemplar* of those values, in that the particular forms of the adequate response to the total moral demand can only be rightly discerned in the pattern of a life which embodies that response, and so characterizes the various values within their integral relation to each other, a relation which cannot be known apart from its exemplification in such a life. This point, of course, would not be important if all men were able adequately to discern the true nature of the moral demand. For in that case one would not need a pattern for what was right other than the demand itself. It is because men cannot discern the moral demand in its true nature that some guide is needed as to just what attitudes are demanded. And it is at this point that lists of abstract values lack the unifying and coherent character of an exemplary life.

Thus when a Christian asks what sort of life he should, in general, pursue, it is not true to his conception of the moral life to say that he must devote himself to the realization of objective values. Nor is it fully true, though it is better, to say that he must pursue a specific set of values which are all grounded in and controlled by the ultimate value of love, or charity. What one must do, and what Christians usually do, is to recount the Gospel story of Jesus. It is in that life, as the writers of the gospels recall it, that one finds a concrete exemplification of the ideal pattern of life which all Christians must pursue. The Christian is called to be an imitator of Christ, not just in the minimal sense that he is to reproduce in himself those values which Jesus realized; but in the stronger sense that it is only by reflection on the life of Jesus that the Christian believes himself able to discern what the appropriate response to the moral demand is like, and thereby say what it means to realize all values as 'forms' of charity. Jesus remains, for the Christian, a living image of what charity means, because the Christian accepts Jesus as the one who was in an uniquely authoritative position to see what the moral demand is.

There are two features which are essential to this account of the exemplarity of Jesus; and without them a doctrine of exemplarity cannot be maintained. They are, first, that most or all men are unable to discern the moral demand truly for themselves; and second, that Jesus was unique in possessing that ability. I am not now concerned to defend these assertions—that will be attempted, at least in part, later. But it does seem that, if they are granted, it would be reasonable to accept the life of Jesus as exemplary—not an example of what can be known, in a logically prior way, to be right, but as the revelation of what is right. Yet if either assertion is rejected, then either Jesus becomes simply an example of what we can know for ourselves to be right, or there is no reason why one should select Jesus as defining the ideal for man.

There are some theologians who speak as though one could accept Jesus as one's moral ideal simply and solely by a sense of overwhelming admiration for his goodness. This view, however, attributes moral discernment to the wrong person; it supposes that we are discerning enough to see that Jesus is supremely good, but does not speak of the moral discernment of Jesus at all. If it is merely being supposed that we and Jesus discern the good equally well, and that the difference is only that he realizes it and we do not, then it must be said that the person of Jesus loses any distinctive significance for the moral life. He may be an inspiring example, but that is a matter of psychological efficacy;

G

as far as logic goes one could dispense altogether with Jesus and retain just the same moral discernments and practices. In order to retain the centrality of Jesus for the Christian life one must consequently maintain that he can be accepted as the moral exemplar only because he is credited with unique insight into the nature of the moral demand.


4. We are now in a better position to attempt to answer the question posed in the previous chapter, namely, why should one interpret the ultimate moral facts as elements of 'the will of God'? I have tried to show that it is not finally satisfactory to speak of 'moral facts' as though they were quite discrete existents making various and often contradictory demands on men. Rather, the particular values which Christians accept are to be seen as forms of one integrated response to a unitary moral demand. Thus whereas, at the close of the previous chapter, I acceded to Professor Maclagan's suggestion that the word 'God' was to be defined, in part, by reference to a realm of self-subsistent values, I would now like to suggest that this thesis needs to be amended—though not in very radical respects. The problem of defining 'God' as a realm of values was that of gaining any doctrine of the unity of the being of God, and of gaining any foothold at all for the anthropomorphic concept of 'the will' in relation to God. But now—at least, if the positions of this chapter are adopted—it can be seen that it may be misleading to speak of values as 'self-subsistent', if this is meant to imply that each value exists in isolation and in its own right. A more appropriate way of speaking of moral values may be to see them as attitudes and dispositions which express an integral response to a unitary demand. So instead of speaking of an existent value of (for example) 'courage', one would speak of a claimed response to X, which leads one to a policy of action and apprehension of maintaining one's beliefs in the face of danger and fear, of being 'steadfast in the truth'. The word 'courage' is properly applicable only to the human disposition, or virtue, which is thus demanded; it can be attributed to the demanding value only extrinsically—in somewhat the same way as one might speak of 'healthy' food, meaning only that it is food which produces health.

One can adopt this analysis for all the moral values one accepts; so, for instance, 'temperance' will be a response to X which binds one to a policy of moderation and discipline in the pursuit of the good; 'humility' will be a response to X which binds one to set one's own dignity at nothing; and so on. The general form for speaking of moral values is thus 'X binds one (to do $\phi$)', where $\phi$ is an attitudinal response to X and X itself cannot be further characterized except in terms of the attitudes which it demands. But one must regard 'X' as unitary, as being the same X which binds one to all these attitudes; and this is because they can only be adequately conceived as elements of one total response, as forms of that 'love of God' which is the basic theistic attitude.

It is X, the reality which binds one to pursue specific moral values in the realization of one fundamental moral response, which must be identified as 'God' by the theist. So one can more properly speak of 'God' as the *ground* of values than as those values themselves; and thereby the unity of the being of God is secured. God is that which demands the realization of various values as forms of one integral responsive attitude to his being. But what is the nature of God, and what is the response which he demands?

It has been suggested that the demanded response is exemplified in the life of Jesus and that this is because he had, whereas we have not, a clear vision of the moral demand. All we can say of God is that this is a being which does demand, or claim, a specific attitude from men, and which can evidently be more or less clearly discerned. Of course, the being of God must be *sui generis*; there is no real parallel to a moral fact in other realms of human experience. But one must speak of it in some way; and one must decide whether to speak of it as personal or impersonal. There are various features of the concept of 'God' which seem to imply a personalistic interpretation. In the first place, talk of 'claims' and 'demands' strongly suggests personal agency; for inorganic objects do not make claims or place demands on men. In Chapter IV, moral values were spoken of as conceptual, universal and exemplary in character; and it has been argued in the present chapter that they form the content of the bracketed clause in statements of the form 'X binds one (to do $\phi$)'. This suggests that moral values, or the moral claims made upon men, in their particular content exist as universal exemplary concepts in relation to God (X) who imposes them on men. It is very natural, then, to speak of them as concepts 'in the mind' of God— Aristotle, after all, defined the mind as 'the place of Forms'[5]—

and as imposed on men 'by the will' of God. Of course, one needs to discard a very anthropomorphic interpretation of this language—God does not apprehend a set of concepts which are independent of himself and then decide, by some arbitrary *fiat*, to impose them, or some of them, on men. For God is—indeed, as far as we are concerned, is *defined* as—the ground of values, the unity which binds them all as forms of a general responsive attitude. And those values, as they are apprehended by men, simply *are* his will; they comprise the Divine intention for man's being. The Divine intention is not, like human intentions, something which may be changed or retracted; it is the response demanded by the moral fact, of men, to its own unchanging being. Yet the language of 'intention' does express, in a way that impersonal concepts cannot, the fact that the moral response can be brought about as a future state, that it is enjoined on human beings to be brought about and that it is purposive, in so far as it is capable of determining human conduct by a conception rather than by a purely material cause. It therefore does not seem impossible to claim that man's duty is the 'will of God' if one means to stress the objectivity of duty as an enjoined—one might say 'intended'—possibility. If one asks 'intended by whom?' or if one asserts that, even supposing one knows that something is the will of God, one still has to ask, 'Ought one to do the will of God?', these questions must be rejected as inappropriate. For one is supposing that there is an objective moral purpose for men, and signifying this belief by simply *calling* it an 'intention'; and, again, one is simply *identifying* what one acknowledges to be right with this objective intention (the 'will of God').

Is it not, then, a matter of trivial definition, a matter of exchanging words, and nothing else?

In answer to this question I think it would be just to put another question in return; namely, why should anyone have thought that there was anything more to it? To suppose that one is giving some additional information in saying that the objective moral purpose is an objective intention, and that the unitary character of this purpose, which determines the specification of all the moral values involved in its implementation, is signified by the term 'God', is to suppose that the theist falls into the mistake of carrying over the connotation of these words in other areas of human discourse into the moral realm. So long as this is not done one is free to use the term 'Divine intention' as one wishes, and one needs no other justification for it than that it is convenient to have a phrase which neatly expresses the sorts of consideration mentioned in this chapter. Then, to conceive the moral life as one of realizing the Divine intention, or the will of God, is to see it as the realization of distinctive human possibilities in response to a unitary moral demand which calls us to become what we ought (and thus what we are, in the intention or content of the demand). It is to see human life as purposively constituted, its purpose being the fulfilment of the Divine intention and its constitution being such that fulfilment is possible, but not necessary.

# VII

# THE WILL OF GOD

1. In the previous chapter I tried to suggest some sort of justification for the Christian's interpretation of moral objectivism in terms of 'the will of God'. I did this by developing the notion of a unitary ground of values which demands an interrelated set of attitudes from men, a set which is specified, for the Christian, in the exemplary life of Christ who alone, it is believed, is in a position to apprehend this unitary ground adequately. And the personalistic language of 'Divine intention' was held to be an appropriate expression of the nature of the moral demand as claiming a distinctive human possibility from men and thus imposing an end or purpose on their acts and attitudes.

It may still be asked, however, whether all this is really sufficient to license one in speaking of a 'personal' God. As Professor Maclagan succinctly puts it, 'The God to which (the moral consciousness) testifies . . . is a God that not only need not but cannot be conceived under the form of a person.'[1] The reason for this 'cannot' is that 'if we are not to use anthropomorphic concepts the theory cannot be stated and if we are to use then it cannot be defended.[2] In other words to speak in personal terms of the moral demand is either empty talk signifying nothing or else plain wrong in trying, to construe moral facts as positive facts about the 'will' and 'understanding' of some person.

The first thing to be said in answer to Professor Maclagan's points is that it is not the traditional Christian view that God is 'a person'. If anything, there are said to be three persons in the Blessed Trinity; and though this doctrine certainly has difficulties of its own, it illustrates that the Christian view must be that the reality of God cannot fail to include all distinctively personal perfections in itself, not that it is the being of a person. Nevertheless, this does little to meet Maclagan's point; for his real objection to using personal language of the 'God' disclosed in moral experience is precisely that it is supposed to be used in such a stretched, analogical way as that just suggested. There would be

nothing wrong with this, he suggests, if it was in principle possible
to take concepts ordinarily used of 'persons', negate some of their
essential features, and still use them meaningfully. But this, he
holds, is impossible in principle—'we cannot mean anything by
the term "person" except what we mean by it in those human
contexts from which the concept is derived'.[3] There is no middle
way between meaninglessness and univocity; either words are
used in quite different senses of two different objects, or there
must be some real resemblance between the objects; in which case
the words used of both must be univocal, at least with regard to
those resembling features.

Without at this point wishing to defend the Scholastic doctrine
of analogy, which Maclagan chiefly has in mind here—and of
which I shall say more later—I think it is worth remarking that
Maclagan's dilemma—'either equivocal or univocal'—seems to be
an unduly restrictive principle even when applied to non-theo-
logical human discourse. For how does one proceed to draw the
strict dividing line, which is necessary on this view, between
univocal and equivocal word-uses? Take almost any word in
common use and apply the principle to it, and a host of border-
line cases at once becomes apparent which erodes the hard-and-fast
distinction the principle attempts to impose. To give just one
example, consider the word, 'sea', used both of a body of water
and of a large expanse of grass. One would hesitate to say that
the word was being used univocally, in just the same sense, in each
case; for what is the 'sense' in question? The expanse? The wave-
like appearance? The colour? It might be any of these things or
all of them.

Or it may be that there is no one common characteristic which
the word is intended to mark. One may, for instance, use the
word 'sea' because of its connotations of romance and mystery,
so that speaking of a 'sea of grass' may serve to set a mood without
specifying any particular property. Even in the case in which one
does wish to point up some similarity, there are very indeterminate
limits to what can count as a similarity. For example, the expanse
does not have to be *precisely* the same; but how different can it
be? No doubt there are limits beyond which few people would
attribute any similarity, and there are cases where similarities
are very obvious. But even there the similarity has to be in a
certain respect; and what one picks out as a similarity, and the
degree of similarity one requires before conceding that two things

have the *same* feature, will depend very much on one's own interests and concerns: it is a largely subjective matter, not capable of precise formulation. All one can say is that if one is attributing resemblance to two objects there must be some respect in which their properties are relevantly similar (the grass must cover a large area, but not necessarily 200 square miles exactly). What counts as 'relevant' is, to a great degree, a matter of taste or judgement.

Moreover, there does not have to be one specific resemblance in virtue of which the same word may be applied to two objects. Metaphor is built into the language, and we often talk of things in terms of images that seem appropriate but do not serve to identify real, exact resemblances. Consider, for instance, in the last sentence, the image of 'building a metaphor into language'. The word 'build' is quite comprehensible and may even seem appropriate. But it would seem silly to try to pinpoint some qualitatively identical activity of 'building' common to both speaking and house-construction. And it would seem wrong and restrictive to hold that one could not mean anything by the term 'build' except what one means by it in contexts of house-construction. Yet this appears to be the doctrine that Maclagan would advocate in posing the rigid alternatives 'either equivocal or univocal'.

I would, in fact, wish to reject Maclagan's dilemma to such an extent that I would propose, in opposition to it, the doctrine that almost all uses of language are analogical in some degree. That is to say, whenever a word is applied to two different objects it is not in virtue of one clearly definable common property; it may be in virtue of a whole range of characteristics which resemble one another in some, but not all, respects. And even in these resembling respects there will probably not be any precise qualitatively identical property; again it will be a matter of resemblance to a greater or less degree. As Wittgenstein put it in the *Philosophical Investigations*, 'we see a complicated network of similarities overlapping and criss-crossing: sometimes overall similarities, sometimes similarities of detail'.[4]

It is hopeless to ask the question, 'Is this word being used univocally?' when once it is conceded that there is no one clearly defined 'sense' but a whole range of uses, in various contexts, which continually adjust the range of meanings (both connotation and denotation) of words as our language is used to characterize constantly changing situations. One rarely speaks of identical words as being used 'equivocally', except where there seems to be no natural connection between the contexts of their use at all.

I would propose, then, that it is the terms 'univocal' and 'equivocal' which are peculiar, and to be defined by contrast with the normal case of the 'analogical'. The 'univocal' can only be properly used of objects which are qualitatively identical in some clearly definable respect—thus to call most words 'univocal' in use would be to subscribe to an Aristotelian notion of an 'essence' denoted by words. The vast majority of word-uses in ordinary language are analogical in that they stress partial resemblances; and what are taken as 'resemblances' largely depends on the associations and connections which are made by the agent between various contexts in which words are used. To press this argument home, it may be pointed out that the very title of Maclagan's chapter under consideration here is 'The Moral Demand'; and in what sense is the word 'demand' used if not an analogical one? One could say, I suppose, that the word was being given an equivocal use, so that no similarity between moral experience and the receipt of bills was being supposed at all. But then why, since 'demand' is being given a philosophical use, could not some more distinctive, less misleading term have been used? Like Maclagan, I too use the words 'demand', 'claim' and 'bind' of the moral experience; and is this not clearly because there is some sort of resemblance between being morally obliged and being commanded or constrained by a judge or superior? If there is such a resemblance, then, must the word 'demand' not be being used univocally of both phenomena? But what is the characteristic which is common to situations both of moral demand and of legal order? It may be suggested that the resemblance is that they are both situations of 'being ordered'; but, of course, this is simply not so; for moral obligations are not promulgated or enforced as legal rules are. Could it be, then, that both are felt as a constraint on the will? But, again, this is just to say that I usually admit legal orders to be morally obligatory; they need not always be so, and so 'obligatoriness' is not an identical characteristic of legal rules and moral obligations. It seems clear that, whatever is suggested, there is no characteristic of human and moral demands which is qualitatively identical.

Now it is precisely this doctrine—that there is nothing which is qualitatively identical between two things, and yet that there is something appropriate in speaking of them by using one term—which is the basis of the doctrine of analogical attribution. The moral demand, it may be said, is unique in its character; and yet it has an obvious affinity with contexts in which one is ordered to do something which it does not have with contexts of, for example, being seasick. Now in calling it a demand one is perhaps not explaining or illuminating its character to oneself, for it may be said that that character is best known in its uniqueness. But one certainly is locating it in a general linguistic framework, inviting one to explore its affinities with certain concepts and its differences from others; and it is not at all inconceivable that in doing this even the moral experient himself will increase his understanding of the moral experience. For it might be said that one only understands an experience as one brings it under concepts; and concepts are essentially discursive, uniting many diverse elements of experience under a unitary conception. Thus the moral experience itself may be better understood as one continues to explore the sorts of conceptual affinities and disaffinities it is amenable to.

In this process of continual exploration to which the making of analogies prompts one, one may attempt new and untried analogies, while always being careful to qualify them so that they do not detract from the uniqueness one is, after all, trying to understand. But I think that it may be truly said, in general, that unique types of human experience—such as is moral experience—cannot be understood at all without the use of discursive concepts; and these concepts will necessarily be analogical, if only because they are not capable of being intersubjectively verified and agreed upon by different experients of a common and public world. Thus it seems to me plainly false to say, as Maclagan does, that 'it is only in so far as the derivative object is capable of duplicating characters possessed by the original, not just of symbolizing and suggesting them, that it is even meaningful to assert a resemblance between the two.[5] And its falsity is well shown by Maclagan's own use of the concept of 'demand' to refer to an experience which is at best symbolized and suggested by, and never duplicated by, experiences of juridical command.

2. It thus appears that Maclagan's objections are not to the doctrine of analogy as such, but only to personal analogies in

particular, when used to characterize the moral experience. Even so, there is surely a meaningful sense in which the concept of 'demand' is personal rather than impersonal. That is to say, the contexts of human life from which it draws the analogy it exploits are contexts of interpersonal relations. I think that Maclagan would concede so much, but would reply that this does not make the moral demand a 'person' and so does not conduce to belief in a personalistic God. I would suggest that the doctrine which Maclagan here objects to is not one which Christians should be concerned to maintain. For I should have thought that anyone with a sense of the infinity and mystery of the being of God would be loath to claim, and indeed quick to disclaim, that the personalistic analogies which are appropriate to speak of God enable one to have any direct insight into the being of God itself, as would be the case if one could say that he was a 'person' in just the same, univocal sense that human beings are persons. So all that the Christian claims in saying that God is personal is that the most appropriate and illuminating ways to talk of God use concepts drawn from personalistic contexts.

But Maclagan would perhaps still wish to question whether personalistic analogies do in fact provide illumination in talking of the moral demand; and his objections to such talk may be elucidated by distinguishing two different theses which he supports. The first might be called his 'weak' thesis; and it is, as he puts it, opposition to 'the pretence that values themselves can be taken for something less than Deity and that they then both must and can be given a "ground" of such sort as would be properly described in terms of an independent, and personalistic, concept of God'.[6] I have certainly been able to assent to Maclagan's view that moral values do not gain in authority by being related to a concept of God, attained in a distinct way. I have agreed, that is, that the theist must affirm that, in some sense, the order of values is identical with the being of God, and that we know what God is by knowing them.

Nevertheless, even with regard to this weak thesis, I think that the theist should hold that there is a certain point to using the term 'God' of the realm of values which Maclagan does not explicitly allow. As I have held, one is thereby stressing the unitary character of the moral demand, and the nature of values as integrated attitudinal responses to it rather than as discrete and unrelated existents. In some sense, then, the theist does assert that values have a 'ground' which assures their unity and integration in the call to the moral life. But this is not in the sense which Maclagan opposes, namely, that one could not accept values as objectively binding unless they were enforced by the understanding and will of a personal Deity. The ground is simply the unity of values themselves; and the concept of God's understanding and will, if one goes on to form it, derives from the notion of such a unity and not vice versa. The introduction of the concept of 'God' in this sense, as unitary ground of values, does provide a distinctive view of the 'realm of values'; and if, as I believe, it is a more adequate view than one which fails to provide for such unity, that gives positive reason for interpreting moral experience theistically.

But this is where Maclagan's 'strong' thesis comes into play; the thesis, namely, that the 'God' which is defined in some such way as I have just attempted 'not only need not but cannot be conceived under the form of a person.'[7] So even if he allowed one to define 'God' as the unitary ground of values he would resist any move to give the concept of 'God' a personalistic interpretation, because the experience even of such a unitary ground does not gain either support or illumination from the use of personal language to characterize it. In particular, the concept of a Divine understanding which somehow creates or is identical with its own objects, and of a Divine will which is necessarily good, are more perplexing and obscure than the ethical data they are supposed to interpret.

I think that the theist must reject Maclagan's strong thesis, for he has a certain interest in characterizing 'God' as personal. This is in part because of the various other characteristics besides strictly moral values which the theist wishes to build into the concept (such as having knowledge of and causal efficacy in the world). But the case for a personalist interpretation can be defended even on moral grounds alone. The theist, however, should not want to claim that God is 'a person', but simply that the reality of God can be most adequately characterized by the use of analogies drawn from contexts of *personal*, rather than impersonal, discourse. It is the former claim which Maclagan attributes to the theist; and though he admits that most major theologians would renounce such a claim, he justifies forcing it on them by supposing that the concept of 'person' must be used either quite anthropomorphically or meaninglessly. I have already claimed that

Maclagan himself is driven to use analogical language to characterize moral experience—the language of 'claim' and 'demand'—
but the real point is that it is not the concept of 'person' with
which theologians are primarily concerned. Consequently, they
do not have to settle the question of what attributes are essential
to 'persons', how many of them 'God' possesses and how like
human persons he is. All they have to settle is what sort of concept
most adequately interprets moral experience and what sort of
context this concept is ordinarily used in.

The chief basis for the theists' claim that concepts drawn from
personal contexts are most appropriate is to be found in another
feature of moral experience which Maclagan does not explicitly
recognize. That is what I have called its 'ideal' or 'purposive'
character—that in speaking of universal exemplary concepts one is
speaking of an existent, demanded possibility which men ought
to realize; and thus one may appropriately speak of them as
expressing the objective purpose for men. It is because these
values are forms of a unitary ground that one may speak of 'one
purpose' for all men rather than simply of a plurality of binding
values which certainly, because of the diversity of values, would
be less naturally amenable to characterization as 'purposive'.
The concept of 'purpose' is in order here to just the same extent
as is the concept of 'demand'; as the experience of obligation has
affinities with contexts of being commanded, so the acknowledgement of a unitary demand to be realized has affinities with contexts
of concurring in someone's intentions and seeking to implement
them. In both cases, a stress on the analogical character of the
terms used will prevent one from illegitimately reading into
moral experience all the features of positive, human, demand
and intention situations, and will enable the distinctively moral
characteristic to be preserved.

In speaking of 'the will of God', then, one need not be interpreted as attempting to explain a moral experience, clearly
cognized in a logically prior way, by introducing an even more
puzzling concept of a 'personal will'. One is in fact saying that this
is precisely how the moral experience is cognized—rendered
comprehensible to oneself—by the use of a concept of 'purpose'
drawn from contexts of human purposes, used in a way which does
not simply 'take over' some precise features of human purposes
into the moral experience, but which seems appropriate because
of a certain unspecific and non-formalizable affinity between the

two sorts of context. It is like saying, 'The nearest thing I know of to moral experience is the recognition of and agreement with another person's intentions.' There is a likeness which in no way threatens to undermine the radical disaffinity between inter-personal human relationships and the absolutely demanding Divine purpose. One is, one may say, speaking of 'a purpose without a purposer', just as Maclagan speaks of a 'demand without a demander'. There is appropriateness without anthropomorphism; and this is the middle way between univocity and meaninglessness.

The final answer I would thus offer to Maclagan's strictures on the use of personal language to speak of 'God' (considered only in his character as moral demand) is, first, that no Christian should wish to conceive God 'under the form of a person': and the doctrine of the Trinity warns him against so doing; second, there is a middle way between anthropomorphism and meaninglessness, and it is one which Maclagan himself, in the concept of 'moral demand', uses; and third, it is in the characteristics of unity and exemplarity that one finds a basis for interpreting moral experience, conceived as experience of a realm of objective values, as ac-knowledgement of a Divine intention; and the existence of such a unitary moral purpose is what the phrase 'the will of God' means.

Acceptance of these three points would seem to me to be sufficient to license one to say that one characterizes God, the moral demand, as 'personal' in an analogical sense, though certainly not as 'a person'. It is only because Maclagan rejects any doctrine of analogy that he refuses to distinguish between 'being a person' (in the full human sense) and 'being personal' (being such that personalistic analogies are appropriate descriptions). I would agree with Maclagan in saying that the concept of a personal God, in the sense of an omniscient, omnipotent being, can neither add anything to nor be deduced from the mere experience of moral demand, as it has been here conceived; though, as I argued in Chapter IV, there are grounds in moral experience for attributing both omniscience and omnipotence to God. But I disagree with him in holding that that demand itself is most adequately characterized in the personalistic language of objective moral purpose, 'the will of God'.

3. I should emphasize that I am not claiming to have given an analysis of the complete meaning of the phrase 'the will of God'.

I have been concerned to say what the phrase means when it is licensed only by a general belief in moral objectivity. There are certainly other elements of its meaning which do not derive solely from one's conception of the moral demand itself; and probably the most important of these is the notion of what God purposes for the world, and what, as omnipotent, he will eventually bring into being. This is the sense in which people say of some event—usually one which brings pain or grief—that it is 'God's will', meaning, at least, that God will embrace it within his general purpose for the agents concerned to bring about some result he desires. In this latter sense God's will is to be inevitably consummated at some time. But to conceive this situation as one in which a specific being does something because he is bound to do it by some external cause is to take anthropological imagery— which has its uses in devotion—and pervert it out of all recognition. What is being thus crudely pictured is the Christian belief that certain states of the world will be brought about which are in accordance with the demands of the objective moral Ideal. That is, not only is the Ideal binding on men as their final end; it is also destined to be actually realized in men, however man, in his freedom, opposes its specific injunctions. To speak of this as a person's will being constrained by an external force is plainly distorted; but even to speak of it as that person's will as constrained by his own goodness (and so as naturally expressing his real character) is inadequate. For what is being said is that there exists an Ideal which exercises a real teleological causality on the world, as well as imposing binding claims to realize specific ends on free human beings. God is his own goodness (in that he is the moral fact which determines ultimate moral principles as true); and his 'purpose' is the teleological causality of his nature on the world.

A man might thus accept certain absolute moral obligations ('God's will' in the first sense) but yet not believe that any state of the world which could completely fulfil those demands, and indeed will do so ('God's will' in the second sense), ever would exist. For the contingent nature of the world might be such that the complete demand for perfection could not arise in it, or that if it did it might never be implemented. So a man may consistently believe that the world contains absolute moral claims and also that it cannot fulfil the conditions of a morally ideal world, or that, even if it could, it may not do so. But such a belief would

constitute a denial of what Christians call the creativity and omnipotence of God; namely, that God so constitutes the world that it
necessarily can, and thus ought to, conform to the moral Ideal,
and that his purpose will triumph in the end. In this sense a person
who believed in the objectivity of morals, even construed as 'the
will of God' in the first sense, might wish to deny that he was a
theist on the ground that he was not committed to a belief that
moral purposes will or even could triumph completely in the
world, as Christian theists are.

4. Moreover, though I have maintained that it is justifiable to
speak of God as 'personal' simply on the basis of the view of
morality elaborated thus far, it is certainly true that the Christian
view of the personal nature of God contains much—and, it may
be said, the most important elements—that mere reflection on the
foundations of morals cannot give. For the Christian, God is the
holy, loving and righteous Father who is active in history, who
calls men to fellowship with himself, who freely gives or withholds
his grace, creates and redeems his creatures. How can such a
view of the nature of God be compatible with the doctrine of an
objective moral teleology, changeless and necessary in its being?
If one treats these concepts as being descriptions of some entity,
they do seem to be directly contradictory—God cannot be both
free and necessary, active and changeless, an austere Ideal and a
loving Father. But a closer examination of the logic of theistic
concepts shows that such expressions are not contradictory but
complementary.

The principle of complementarity is essential to an understanding of Christian theism; it is, basically, the principle that
two sets of concepts which are *prima facie* incompatible can each
be shown to be essential to the understanding of certain features
of a phenomenon; the consequence of this is—if the logical law
of non-contradiction is to be preserved—that each set of concepts
must be denied literal applicability but may be taken as outlining a
conceptual 'model', the use of which remains essential for certain
purposes.

In physics the principle has been formulated in some detail
by Bohr and Heisenberg,[8] though it probably has its roots in
Kant's doctrine of the necessity of both mechanistic and teleological principles for an explanation of nature.[9] To explain the

results of one experiment (the two-slit experiment of Thomas Young) light must be regarded as propagated in waves, while another experiment (the photo-electric effect) requires that light be understood as the emission of particles, or quanta. Since these accounts of the nature of light cannot both be true, the concepts of 'wave' and 'particle' may be regarded as models or pictorial devices which are each essential for different experimental purposes and which thus truly characterize the phenomenon of light, though not in a straightforward, representative way. The exact interpretation of this situation is a matter of dispute, since some physicists hold that it only demonstrates a temporary incapacity to find one consistent adequate model. But the important point for theism is in the notions of complementarity and of non-picturing models which, in the case of physics, help one to understand various microcosmic phenomena which cannot be visualized in normal terms. For these notions have a use in theology, too.[10]

It is fairly evident that the reality of God cannot be visualized or known in any normal manner. Furthermore, since God is an absolutely unique being, and since all our referential concepts are discursive (that is, they identify common or reidentifiable features in our environment), it is impossible to refer to him in any normal way. Indeed, theistic language is never used to pick out God from other things or to describe him in an abstract way. It is used in worship, thanksgiving, petition and supplication; and seeing such language in its natural and original context of devotion it does not seem unrealistic to say that the concept of 'God' is used as a 'model' for the purpose of evoking and sustaining certain characteristic attitudes in ourselves and others. That is to say, in speaking of God as, for example, 'holy Father', we are not describing what some being is really like; what we are concerned with is our own life, with regulating and directing our attitudes by positing such a model. If description was the primary task, one would have to say what God was like by showing his similarity, in this example, to earthly fathers. But then one would presumably have to have inductive criteria which were publicly accessible for identifying and describing such a being; and such criteria seem peculiarly unconvincing to many impartial observers. It is clear that, in fact, in its religious usage, the concept of 'father' is deprived of empirical criteria for instantiation; the connotation of the concept is left intentionally open and incomplete, leaving a free play for the imagination in allowing the image to shape one's

H

attitudes and give a general affective tone to devotion. Thus while it is possible and essential for the Christian to interpret his experience in the light of such a concept—for example, to view events in his life-history *as* moments of grace, forgiveness or judgement—it is not possible to identify an event as a 'judgement of God' by generally agreed criteria of what is to count as such a judgement. Moreover, the believer must be very wary about locating particular instances of Divine judgement in his experience; while having a general belief in the providential ruling of life, he should be very diffident in claiming to discern its specific detail.

One can say of the religious use of concepts, then, that they are not constitutive concepts—deriving from specific cases of empirical instantiation—but regulative, directing one's interpretative attitudes to experience, one's 'way of seeing' the world, in general ways. This regulative function is exercised in two main ways: in devotion, worship and meditation; and in interpreting experience. In both cases the main use of a 'model' is will-directive; the mind is directed to a conceptual image of 'father', for example, which is a mere thought-entity shorn of all specific analogies with empirical criteria of application. What is left is an undefinable area of connotation and association; strictly conceptual thinking, which restricts the mind to the empirical conditions of knowledge of spatio-temporal objects, is here transcended, and the indeterminate idea becomes a symbol for what cannot be clearly conceptualized. Yet this non-conceptualizable 'object' which the model calls before the mind does give a distinctive affective tone and evoke a definite set of attitudes in one who uses it in devotion; this in turn directs his reactive attitudes throughout all his practical experience.

The concepts of 'God' as holy Father, caring, condescending and feeling for his children, may thus be seen as models which are regulative and will-directing for the believer. Their function is not to describe literally, but to specify characteristic attitudes. The models are received on authority: the Christian takes Scripture as authoritatively laying down the ways in which God must be spoken of. In Part Two more will be said about the nature of the predicates which are ascribed to God on the basis of revelation, and about the sort of authority which could authorize the ascription of such predicates. But in being based explicitly on revelation, these models for conceiving 'God' naturally differ from the model of God as necessary ground of values, which arises from rational reflection on the nature and presuppositions of moral experience. Both sets of models are equally essential to Christian theism; indeed, without some rational notion of what one meant by 'God', one could not accept anything on the ground that it was a revelation *from* 'God'. The rational metaphysical images help to locate the reference of the Biblical images; in referring them to a transcendent, necessary ground they help to avoid a naïve anthropomorphism or the idolatry of identifying God with any finite being or beings. The revealed, Biblical images give life and vivacity, a particular emotional tonality, to this rather abstract metaphysical framework, and thus help to avoid a sort of theistic agnosticism in which one asserts a necessary being but knows nothing more about it.

The former set of models assert that there are necessary moral Ideals, grounded in a Necessary Being; the latter set assert that this Being can, by revelation, be described as a 'loving Father' for the purposes of devotion and practical life. Thus they reveal that the ground of moral claims is itself the proper object of those morally demanded attitudes which define the Christian virtues, and, when modified by relation to particular circumstances, constitute the fulfilment of specific moral demands. The revelation of God as Incarnate, caring and condescending as well as absolute and demanding adds another dimension to God, *qua* moral ground, one that is not derivable from the concept by reflection, yet does not refer to a different being. It gives another set of images for conceiving the Divine reality, specifying a particular set of attitudes to what may have seemed an abstract moral demand. The two sets of models are therefore complementary in that each complements the other and is necessary to an adequate notion of 'God'; they do not contradict because their function is not to ascribe properties, which may be incompatible, but to show how 'God' must be conceived in different, complementary ways for different purposes.

So while God must be conceived as the unchanging ground of obligation, to support moral objectivity, he must also be conceived as freely active in creation and responsive to his creatures in loving concern, to support Christian devotion. The former concept alone leaves God remote and unconcerned, a moral ground which is not necessarily an object of moral attitudes. The latter concept alone leaves the being of God arbitrary and morality ungrounded (except in the power of the Divine *fiat*). Both concepts must thus be taken together to give an adequate Christian concept of God, for which God is both the ground and the proper object of all moral attitudes. Consequently, the justification I have given for speaking of the moral ground as a 'personal' reality, in terms of intention and demand, will certainly be insufficient for a Christian believer. Nevertheless it is, I think, a necessary part of his conception, and even a necessary condition of understanding what 'revelation' is and of assessing the claims of different putative revelations.

It is an important task for the Christian theist to examine more closely the relation of these complementary concepts of God, to show in which aspects God must be conceived as one, simple and changeless, and in which aspects he can be talked of as acting, loving and caring. Admirable work has been done by Professor Hartshorne in this area, and is well worth looking at.[11] But I will defer consideration of the concept given by Christian revelation until Part Two, and conclude my examination of the concept of 'God' which is licensed by an interpretation of moral objectivism alone.

5. It has already been seen that the objectivist must hold that there is an element of necessity about moral claims—namely, that only certain possibilities open to moral agents can be morally demanded. But one also seems compelled to say that there is something necessary about the very nature of the moral demand itself. It is not enough, for instance, for the Christian simply to say that God is totally free; for God cannot be free to be evil. His freedom to change, adapt and create must work within certain limits of necessity. For it does not seem conceivable that a quite different set of attitudes could have been morally obligatory, that anything could have been right, had God's will been other than it is. Thus one must say that God's will could not be other than it is, at least in its most general features.

It is for this reason that a Christian cannot adopt a purely voluntarist account of the being of God as, for example, Austin Farrer does in *Faith and Speculation*, where he talks of a 'God who is all He wills to be, and wills to be all He is'—an Unconditional Will.[12] By contrast with this voluntarist view, Farrer regards the Aristotelian account of God, which argues a *contingentia mundi* to a necessary, changeless, all-perfect Being, as an 'empty', 'merely formal' and 'inferential notion of diety', which is at best 'merely problematic' and at worse a 'logical monstrosity'. He claims—not without courage, in view of his own intricate defence of this argument in the past[13]—that such formalist accounts lack any practical religious concern; that they do not speak of the reality with which we have to do, in the Christian life. They are, he says, just supposed entailments of an outmoded physics, the 'ghosts of Aristotelian causal theory' which pretend to conclude to God from a disinterested contemplation of the physical world.

This may be true of some presentations of the cosmological arguments for the existence of God, which assume that it is self-evident that every event must have a cause, that the cause must be like its effects, and that the cause must be greater than its effects—and that these are principles which can be known to be true apart from any particular religious faith or experience. Yet it is surely of very great practical religious concern that Christian devotion should be to a will which is in some sense necessarily, changelessly and supremely good, rather than to a totally un-conditioned will, more reminiscent of the blind, purposeless striving of Schopenhauer's vision than of the 'Father of lights, from whom all good things come.' The Divine will to which the Christian seeks to conform must be a necessarily good will if it is to be the object of worship and devotion. It is even nonsensical to suppose a completely 'self-positing positer'; for if, as Farrer avers, 'God wills to be all He is', there must be a being of some antecedent nature to will its consequent nature. God cannot somehow create his nature out of nothing; even the first act of creation would have to be conditioned by the existent nature of the creator. So one must suppose the goodness of God to be a funda-mental, uncreated and unchanging datum which could not be otherwise than it is. In other words, one must suppose that God is necessarily good and that goodness is necessarily what it is—no other demands than these *could* be morally binding.

God's will could not be evil, for one *calls* 'God's will' whatever is the unitary ground of the moral demands made on one. But one must say, further than this, that only the demands which *are* moral *could, in principle, be* moral. That which the moral fact demands, it necessarily demands—it could not demand any other sorts of action and attitude. So one must say that if there is a moral demand at all it *must* be what it *is*. This is the basis, in moral experience, for the doctrine that the being of God is necessary, not contingent—that is, it is not just a matter of fact, which might have been otherwise, that God is as he is. Further, it does not seem sufficient to say that if there is a moral fact then it must have such a character; one must also say that there must (necessarily) be a moral fact. Otherwise, what could determine the necessity of its having such a character? If there is a moral fact its character is necessarily determined; but by what? If it was determined by something other than itself, it would be determined by a non-moral fact; and this, as has been argued at some length, is impossible. It must, therefore, be determined by itself. This, however, is not to say that it determines itself to be what it is, as if it could have determined itself to be otherwise. It is only to say that there must exist something which determines that only certain attitudes can be demanded; and this existent cannot be other than the moral demand itself which must, therefore, exist necessarily with the character it does have.

6. The supposition that there is a being the existence and general nature of which is necessarily what it is, but is not determined by anything outside itself, is a deeply mysterious one. Some philosophers, following David Hume, have thought that the very concept of a 'necessary being' is senseless, on the ground that a necessary being would have to be a being the non-existence of which was inconceivable, whereas one can conceive the non-existence of any being whatsoever.[14] This doctrine is a tangle of confusions. What human beings can or cannot intuitively conceive is a very unreliable guide as to what is really possible. Perhaps one can visualize very clearly the impossible (for instance, a thing existing in two places at once, or going back in time). And it may well be that 'logical possibility' must be distinguished from 'factual' or 'real possibility'. The non-existence of God may be logically possible (one can construct a linguistic formula denying it) but factually impossible (God could not not exist). Since we do not know what the grounds of factual necessity, possibility and impossibility may be, we cannot rule out such a possibility. Further, as Aquinas argued,[15] since men can in no way conceive the reality of God in itself, they are in no position to know whether they could conceive its non-existence or not. Finally, it is difficult to see what criterion is being used to show that the concept of 'necessary being' is senseless. It is certainly not self-contradictory;

and how else could one decide that a certain sort of being was impossible?

It may be suggested, as it was in a well-known paper by J. N. Findlay, that the concept of 'necessity', like that of 'contingency', can only apply to propositions and not to things.[16] He has since retracted this doctrine, and I see no reason for espousing it. It is true that we cannot see what could determine that a being not only will not change but could not change in certain respects; and thus we could never pick out a particular existent as being necessary or state the conditions for being such an entity. But, I have maintained, one can find, in moral experience, reason for saying that there is a necessary being; so since nothing precludes us from forming the concept, we may assert it, though it must remain incomprehensible, in that we cannot understand how such a thing can be. Nevertheless, it has been the fundamental supposition of metaphysical and religious thought for perhaps the major part of human history; and, I have argued, it seems to be required by the fact that what is good or right is not just a contingent matter which could have been otherwise.

It may seem that if the moral demand necessarily exists then there must also exist a universe on which its demands can be made; otherwise, it may be said, it would not make sense to speak of a demand which could never be realized. It is partly this thought which had led many philosophers to say that the existence of the world is itself necessary, and that the supposition of God without a world is as ultimately senseless as the supposition of a world without God.

This conclusion does not, however, seem to follow from the account given here of the moral demand. If, indeed, one spoke simply of a realm of values, it would seem plausible to suggest that, for example, a 'courage' which never had any instances in a physical universe was a highly peculiar, even an incoherent conception. For what could 'courage' mean as an unrealized quality of non-existent human acts? But if one speaks of 'God' as that existent which, when its nature is apprehended by men, demands the realization of various values from them, then one can distinguish between the nature of God in itself and the nature of God as known in the moral demands it makes upon us. And one can then say that, if there is a physical universe, then God's being will necessarily make moral demands of it; but the necessity of the being of God does not, so far as one can see, entail the existence of a world in which beings could apprehend his nature in the form of a moral demand.

We must conceive 'God', then, as a necessary being—a being which could not be non-existent—and which necessarily has the general nature it has. If there is a physical universe (as, of course, there is) the moral claims which exist in it will be necessarily determined to be what they are by the being of God. And it will be appropriate for moral agents in this universe to speak of the being of God, as apprehended by them, as an objective teleology of the world, morally binding on them; that is, in the language of 'Divine intention'. It is in this highly qualified sense that the being of God, even as expressed in moral experience alone, can be properly spoken of as personal and also as incomprehensibly far beyond personal categories; and it seems to me that sustained analysis of any moral objectivism will disclose such a theistic view as the most adequate basis of the moral life.[17]

# PART TWO

# ETHICS AND CHRISTIAN AUTHORITY

# VIII

## MORAL KNOWLEDGE

1. The will of God has been described as the necessarily existent ground of moral values, demanding a reactive attitude from men, which is uniquely exemplified in the life of Jesus. It is the purpose of human life to realise that attitude and so to imitate, in this respect, the life of Jesus. If this is so it is clearly of the very first importance that one should know what the demanded attitude, the 'telos' for man as such, is. And one needs to know, also, how the realization of such an attitude is relevant to the making of all those concrete decisions about particular principles and courses of action which go to make up the fabric of the moral life. However, before these questions about the nature and implications of the theistic attitude can be answered, there arises the logically prior question of how, in general, one can know moral facts. This question of the epistemology of morals only arises for moral objectivists, since only they claim to *know* moral facts in any real sense.

So far I have been developing what I take to be the Christian view of the meaning of moral terms—that they purport to refer to an objective reality—and I have sketched, in a general way, the sort of response that reality demands. The characteristics thereby elicited could almost be taken as a definition of religious morality— that it lies in the pursuit of personal perfection which is founded on some conception of an absolute value. But within this general description there still lie many possibilities of alternative inter- pretation, both of the value in question and of the sort of perfection to be pursued. Indeed, it is at this point that I would locate the central differences between various religions, which determine the development of many different creeds.

To take just one example, for purposes of comparison, the most influential world religion which is explicitly non-theistic is Buddhism. It finds its exemplar in the Lord Buddha, the one who achieved supreme enlightenment. To put it in a necessarily crude way—though not, I think, a false way—what the Buddha was enlightened about was the fact that all existence entails sorrow and suffering; that existence is founded on desire; and thus that the 'goal' of human life (in an extremely paradoxical sense of 'goal') is Nirvana, a state of the cessation of all desiring, sometimes call 'non-being'. There is, then, in Buddhism a personal perfection to be pursued; though that perfection is the attainment of complete non-attachment. And that pursuit is founded on a particular conception of the absolute value; namely that only non-being, or Nirvana, the passionless state, is to be valued in and for itself. Naturally enough, Buddhists do not talk of a 'Divine intention'; and yet they seem committed to the view that human life has a purpose or goal which it is right to pursue, and that this is grounded in the ultimate structure of reality; for they do not regard it as simply prudent to aim at Nirvana but as morally right.

From a Christian point of view the doctrine of Nirvana is perhaps characterizable as a doctrine of the nature of 'God'; but that doctrine will be very much more negative in its characterization than is the Christian one. Christians may find part of the reason for this negativity in the reticence of the Buddha himself in speaking of any supernatural reality. But it is also due to the Buddhist description of the human attitude which is thought to be the appropriate response to the ultimate facts of human existence; which is, in turn, founded upon the authoritative experience of the Buddha himself. It is therefore evident that there exist quite radically diverse accounts of the nature of the ground of moral values, and consequently of the appropriate human response to it, even when a generally religious attitude is adopted of pursuing what I have termed objective and attitudinal morality. In view of this fact it is necessary to enquire what the reasonable grounds for claims to knowledge in this sphere may be; only then can competing claims be assessed in the light of the sorts of reasons one accepts as relevant.

2. The basic epistemological question to be asked, when anyone makes a claim to knowledge of any sort, is, 'How does he know that?'; or, more exactly, 'What sort of thing, in general, would entitle him to claim that he does know that?' Of course, philosophical volumes have been and will no doubt continue to be written on what the proper answer to this question should be, even in the case of the most ordinary sensory experiences like those of seeing chairs and tables. But it seems to be generally agreed among

philosophers that in the case of any item of knowledge about empirical matters of fact there is always some set of sense-experiences which could, in principle, count for its truth or falsity. This could, indeed, be taken as a definition of what is meant by an 'empirical matter of fact'; and such facts are often taken as paradigms of knowledge by contemporary philosophers. Sense-experiences can be checked by getting other observers to agree with one's own observations. If there is disagreement one can proceed to carry out certain tests on one's sense-organs to see whether they are defective in some way. Moreover, one can usually check the information provided by one sense against the information of one's other senses—if one thinks one smells an orange one can look for it, feel it, and taste it. Thus in the case of sense-experiences there are a large number of tests which one can bring to bear on any alleged experience, which will enable one to decide whether it is to be classed as veridical or illusory.

None of these tests is available in ethics; one cannot check one's intuition against other senses, since there are no other moral senses; one cannot have one's moral sense-organ tested, since there is no such organ; and one cannot ask others to check one's intuition for, if they disagree, there is still no way of deciding who is right. On such grounds as these many philosophers have held that it does not even make good sense to talk of intuiting moral truths, if one has in mind any sort of analogy with sense-perceptions; for the analogy breaks down at all these vital points.

It does not seem to me, however, that these points should seriously trouble the objectivist. For he is himself committed to affirming the unique status of moral facts as facts which are *ipso facto* perceived as *claims* to action; if this were not so the moral 'ought' would be naturalistically reduced to a neutrally perceived 'is', which removes the whole point of introducing *moral* facts in the first instance. If a moral fact is intuited at all it is *ipso facto* intuited *as* a claim. It is a falsification of the moral situation to hold that one could intuit a moral fact and yet not believe that one was bound by it; and such a procedure would, of course, lead to an infinite regress, since one would then have to ask whether it was true that one ought to be bound by such a fact, and then one would have to posit a further fact which made it true; and the same question would arise with regard to that fact . . . . The moral objectivist, then, is committed to asserting that the basic moral facts, whatever they are, cannot be intuited at all, unless they are intuited as binding on one. To this one might say that one must first know *what* it is one is to acknowledge before one can acknowledge it; and therefore that apprehension and acknowledgement must be distinct acts. These elements are logically distinguishable; one can conceive a moral proposition without assenting to it. But if one does assent to it, that is because one believes it to be true—that some *moral* fact makes it true. To assent is thus precisely to admit that there *is* such a moral fact, a fact whose existence cannot be established in any other way. One can conceive without assent, but then one conceives only a proposition of undetermined truth-value; one cannot admit the moral fact without acknowledging its claim upon oneself: to say the proposition is true *is* to acknowledge such a claim. Thus in this case one cannot separate, even logically, the intuition of a fact from the acknowledgement that it is binding. It is in this sense that one must acknowledge the truth of Plato's dictum that virtue is knowledge;[1] that is, that to know the Good is *ipso facto* to acknowledge its absolute claim upon one's being.

But it may be objected, as Christians have traditionally said against Plato, that one can, after all, knowingly do evil. One can know that it is right to do a certain thing, and still refuse to do it: that is the essence of human freedom. It is even necessary to affirm this in order to preserve the moral intelligibility of Christian doctrine. For, if man is constrained to do good as soon as he clearly sees it, there appears to be no intelligible reason why God should not, from the first, have revealed himself to such an extent that man was constrained to obey him. What is important about human freedom if it must depend *essentially* upon ignorance of the good? It seems to me that human freedom can only be regarded as a value if it is a freedom which remains in the face of a clear knowledge of what it is rejecting. In other words, freedom is not particularly good in itself; it is good only as a means to a further end, good in itself, which could not exist without freedom. What is this further end? It is the fulfilment of man's nature, which, for the Christian, can be accomplished only in a certain relation to God. It is because this relation, good in itself, *presupposes* freedom as a condition that freedom is to be valued. But if one believes that, knowing God, one *cannot but* accept him—that is, that the final good for man does not presuppose freedom as its *condition*—why then should freedom be valued? The reply may be that, though when God is fully known it becomes senseless to speak of human freedom, nevertheless it is better that men should have *chosen* to know God than that they should know him willy-nilly. But how could they choose, rationally, that of which they were necessarily ignorant as to its true nature? Or how could they be blamed for rejecting what they were not able properly to conceive? In any case this view is still committed to asserting that there is *some* moral fact the claim of which men must acknowledge but which they can refuse to obey; it is only being said that God, when fully apprehended, not only *claims* but actually *necessitates* action. But if one concedes a sense of 'obligation' which does not entail 'necessitation' it is difficult to see what reason there can be for introducing a stronger sense which does entail 'necessitation'. And thus there seems no good reason to suppose that clear know-ledge of God would in some way constrain one to obey him.

What I have said is that to *intuit* a moral fact is *ipso facto* to *acknowledge* an objective claim, and this does not entail that I will *do* what it is thus incumbent upon me to do. So it might seem that there is no reason why all men should not be able to intuit the moral demand with equal clarity, even though they differ markedly in their moral practices. One might, then, expect to find universal agreement on what the moral demand is; so at least one could avoid the problem of incompatible clashes between diverse demands with no way of telling which was the true moral demand. Even this, however, is denied to the moral objectivist. He need not be unduly distressed by his inability to test his moral sense-organs or to check their deliverances against those of other sense-organs; and this is simply because there are no physical organs for per-ceiving moral facts. But it is distressing to find that there seems to be no conceivable way of finding out which of two conflicting moral assertions is true, especially when men do disagree so violently on moral matters. It is as if two men in the same room, under precisely the same conditions, looking at the same object, both described it quite differently—one as a brown chair and the other as a blue bed. If no further confirmation or disconfirmation of their opinions could be obtained it would be very tempting to conclude not merely that one of them must be mistaken, but that neither of them really had knowledge at all. So, in morality, be-cause of the seemingly irresolvable differences in moral opinions of men to all appearances equal in intellect and sincerity, it has been widely concluded by moral philosophers that it is not proper to speak of 'moral knowledge' at all. If the only thing that entitles a man to claim knowledge of a moral truth is that he just intuits it, then there is no possible way of distinguishing truth from error, the veridical intuition from the illusory. And it may well be said that in such a situation there is not even sense in talking of correct or incorrect, knowing or mistakenly believing; for no one knows what a mistaken intuition would be like or how it could be detected.[2]

3. In trying to answer this powerful objection to the whole notion of moral knowledge, it will be helpful to make a distinction between the test of the truth of a proposition and the conditions of its truth. For example, what makes the statement 'Jesus rose from the dead' true is the fact that he rose from the dead at a particular time and place—that is its truth-condition. But that cannot be the test of its truth for men now, since it is not something which can be tested. The tests used to determine its truth will have to be such things as assessments of the reliability of the historical evidence, the probability that certain subsequent events can only be adequately explained on the assumption of its truth, the practical consideration of whether one's religious experience requires such an assumption as part of the system of concepts used to interpret it, and so forth.

This distinction between the tests and conditions of truth may be blurred by the use of the notion of a 'criterion of truth', since the term 'criterion' may mean either 'what makes a thing true' or 'what ways there are of deciding that a thing is true'. The distinction is very relevant for an ethical objectivist; for whereas the truth of moral propositions is determined simply by the existence of moral facts, it is not a sufficient test of their truth to say simply that one sees them to be facts. What, then, are the available tests for the truth or falsity of moral propositions? I think that the best way to approach this question may be not to begin from a study of actual moral opinions and then attempt to account for their diversity but to work in the opposite direction, to ask what the actual state of moral opinion might be expected to be, what tests of truth might be expected to exist supposing that moral values are objective (or, as I have put it, that they characterize appropriate responses to a moral demand which is necessarily and objectively what it is). It might be thought that, on such a supposition, everyone would have a perfectly clear and precise understanding of what he ought to do; and further, that all men would agree in the list of principles accepted as morally binding. But these characteristics by no means follow from the objectivity of moral values. To suppose a perfect understanding of what ought to be done is to assume infallibility of moral knowledge; whereas one may wish to allow for the possibility that one could be mistaken. As in sense-perception one can be mistaken because of carelessness, inattention, defect of vision, memory, or reasoning; so in morals one may be inattentive, or fail to see all the implications of one's situation, or be blinded by vested interests and partiality, or lack the experience to judge how best to put one's ideals into action. In all these ways one can allow for mistakes in moral knowledge; it is just not true to say that there is no way of distinguishing veridical from mistaken knowledge in this realm. Moral knowledge is indeed incorrigible, in the sense that I must in the end stand by what I believe to be right whatever others think; though even here the qualification must be made that if any of the features listed above could be correctly attributed to me it would be absurd, and even immoral, for me to insist against all others that I know what is right. But when these features are not present I must regard my moral beliefs as incorrigible—not, in principle, correctable by others; though not as infallible, as if their truth was somehow guaranteed. Knowing what ought to be done is the concluding state of a long and difficult process of cogitation; one must know all the facts of the situation, assess probable consequences of one's acts, aim to rid oneself of all partiality and prejudice, judge the consistency and coherence of one's moral judgement with one's other general moral beliefs, weigh the different possible values involved against each other and find the most effective means of their implementation, balance the abstractly ideal course of action against the actual social conditions of the situation, and retain a respect for the accumulated experience of custom while remaining open to new possibilities and experiments. It seems that such a process could only be completed by a genius who was also a master of practical wisdom and had unlimited time and means at his disposal. And since a world can hardly be imagined which would consist only of such beings, it seems that even a moral objectivist would expect a great amount of moral diversity even among equally sincere people, according to their different intellects, temperaments, social environments and training.

One may object that moral knowledge should not require such

I

difficult preconditions; but this is rather like saying that human knowledge should be infallibly imparted, and not learnt through a difficult process of exploration and insight. In this respect moral truths are more like scientific truths than like those which are based on simple sense-observations. In each case there is un-doubtedly an objective state of affairs (one that is independent of the existence of any human minds), but it does not follow that one only has to 'intuit' it to know it fully and immediately. In trying to discover the fundamental laws of physics men do not simply begin with false statements and suddenly discover the true ones; rather there is a slow process of developing insight into the inter-connections of various phenomena, a development from the perception of fragmentary and superficial correlations to the apprehension of underlying principles, always liable to be revised in the light of new experiences.

So, in the discovery of moral truths, men and societies advance from acknowledgement of values which arise out of the particular conditions of a certain time and place, which are not fully general-ized or seen in all their implications, which are not clearly conceived either in their nature or in the means necessary to attain them, and which are not clearly distinguished from emotional and prudential considerations. And they develop their conceptions of these values, in their true character, by gradually divorcing them from particularities of time and place, extending the range of their application, exploring all their implications and the possibilities and priorities of combination with other values, and learning to modify their emotional reactions in accordance with a rational conception of the greatest compossible combination of acknow-ledged values.

I am not suggesting that such a development is a necessary historical process; societies may recede in moral development as well as advance. What I am suggesting is that, somewhat in the way that physics develops by the employment of criteria of unity, coherence, consistency and so forth, so moral insight may be said to develop by the employment of very similar rational criteria. One would accordingly expect the moralist, rather like the physicist, to be hesitant about claiming that he knows the truth and yet to be unconditionally committed to the use of the criteria he has to discover the truth, and to be certain that there is a truth to be found—though that does not imply that men will ever fully understand it.

The moral objectivist is not, therefore, committed to saying that he knows, for certain, the truth of any specific moral principles; indeed, on the account of moral experience I have given, it is rather artificially abstract to talk of 'knowing principles' at all. Principles are abstract formalizations derived from acknowledgements of particular values; and one's knowledge of these is, in the nature of the case, limited by the imperfection of the human faculties.


4. One might expect diversity of moral opinions not only because of the unclarity and imprecision of our cognitive faculties but also because objectivity in no way implies the universality of what is cognized. That is to say, it may be the case that the realization of all values at once is not possible, and so a choice has to be made between various sets of values. But one need not therefore say that one set of values must be better, in all circumstances and for everyone, than any of the others. It may even be true that different, incompatible sets of values are objectively right for different sets of people precisely because of their different circumstances. In this way moral values might be objective, and yet it might not be possible to list one set of values which it is incumbent upon all men everywhere to realize.

To take a familiar example, it sometimes shocks those who live in a highly civilized and law-abiding Western country to read the bloodthirsty exploits of the Israelites in the Old Testament. Time and again the Prophets of Israel (whom Christians also accept as being inspired) proclaimed as God's will that all the enemy were to be slaughtered and that no toleration was to be admitted to their state.[3] It is clear that one of the chief virtues of the ancient world was that of valour in battle; and with this there necessarily goes an element of insensitivity to the suffering of others and the cultivation of a stern, almost callous character. Such an ideal style of life does base itself on the realization of certain characteristic values; but they are, we might say, values which are quite foreign to us now; or at least they need to be balanced by other values such as sympathy and benevolence. This is an easy enough thing to say, however; the fact remains that, in order to keep the peace in which our sympathy can flourish, some men must kill our enemies; and they must kill efficiently. These men must therefore be given such a training that they will kill without hesitation and without question when ordered to do so; and one can clearly not expect them both to do this and to have a developed concern for the good of their victims. In our society the group of men who need to be trained to accept such values is relatively small; but in primitive societies it includes almost every man. It is not surprising, therefore, that the system of acknowledged values in such societies tends to be one that stresses valour and minimizes sympathy for others; that it tends to favour a restricted group-morality which is not extended to include one's enemies.

It is also obvious, upon reflection, that the existence of groups of manual workers, aesthetes and scholars, for example, is for the general good of society as a whole. But such diverse groups of men with very different temperaments and interests can hardly be expected to share precisely the same hierarchy of values. The aesthete will seem effeminate to the man who takes pride in using his physical strength to dig ditches, and the worker will seem coarse and stunted to the scholar. Since the existence of groups which will naturally tend to have such different values is for the good of society, is it not reasonable to say that it is really (objectively) right for different men to have diverse sets of values? This does not imply that, for any of them, it is simply a matter of choice which set they adopt. It implies that there are values of strength, artistic appreciation and scholarship, but that which of these oblige a man, and to what extent, must depend upon his temperament and social situation. Men have obligations to realize values; but their obligations are limited by the sorts of values which are available to them in their specific situations. One may well argue, in other words, that a plurality of values is both good and necessary, and in no way contradicts belief in moral objectivity.

5. One can thus allow for development and diversity in the knowledge of values. But there is another vitally important factor in the moral life which has not so far been mentioned. That is simply that men are free to reject any of the values they acknowledge; they can apprehend a value and intentionally fail to realize it. Now if a man acknowledges something as right and nevertheless constantly fails to live up to it, he is liable to collect a permanently guilty conscience, to become depressed or even neurotic and, in the end, to seek to avoid the moral demand whenever possible. Such a man will take every occasion to avoid a clear confrontation

with the moral demand and will attempt to lighten its claims by adjusting them to a more 'reasonable' level. There is, in fact, every sort of inducement to do this; for—as will be made clearer later—the moral demand is, in a real sense, impossible to fulfil; so one has good reason to reduce those demands to a manageable level. But that means that one is prepared to avoid the demand as it really is on the grounds that it is unrealistic—it is not accidental that men use 'idealistic' to mean 'not practicable'.

Thus many, or even most, men will have a vested interest in self-deception in the realm of morality, in distorting or avoiding the apprehension of moral values which they do not wish to implement. And if they are put in a position in which they have to train young people, whether or not they explicitly teach the higher values they do not follow, their pupils will see, in the conduct of their teachers, the perverse or minimized values they actually pursue and will adapt their own conduct accordingly. Children will therefore be trained to behave and react emotionally to a distorted set of values, and it will be extremely difficult for them to gain sufficient impartiality and objectivity to cognize values in their true nature. Education sets an almost indelible stamp on a human life; and the education of children by immoral persons (by which I mean anyone who fails to pursue the clear apprehension and implementation of values as well as he ought; which means almost everyone) will almost certainly prevent them from developing the temperament, ability and disposition necessary to attain a clear apprehension of moral values. It is thus quite consonant with moral objectivism to suppose that whole cultures may, far from developing in moral insight, become increasingly blind to even those values they used to acknowledge. Thus in a situation of economic crisis, as in Germany before the Second World War, the most perverse values, of racial pride and aggressive spirit, may take precedence over all other human values and captivate a whole people who have grown unused to the clear and constantly renewed apprehension of moral claims which is necessary to prevent moral decay and even collapse.

It is a fairly common phenomenon in the moral life that the apprehension of one value which is opposed to all one's inclinations and desires may be effectively blurred and even repressed entirely by attaching one's desires to a more amenable value. Thus it might be that one does in impartial and unemotional moments acknowledge that men should be equitably treated, without discrimination of race. Yet one's strong fear of racial threat, of conquest by aliens, may blur this knowledge; and experiences of objectionable aliens may lead one to generalize unfairly about all aliens. And finally, one's natural dispositions may be enlisted by an unscrupulous leader in the cause of patriotism or pride in one's cultural heritage. So one can devote oneself virtuously to the pursuit of this value which happens to be amenable to one's prejudices, and one will be inclined not to examine or cogitate enough upon the proper demands and interrelation of the values of, say, patriotism and equity. It is usually in this way, rather than by overt rejection of moral values, that immorality is propagated; one value is distorted by association with violent emotions and extended beyond the bounds of its reasonable claims so that it encroaches upon other values, obviates them, and so becomes an aggressive and destructive force. It was in a rather similar way that the value of religious devotion, by its ready association with fears of radical change and natural intolerance, led to a rejection of open-minded scientific investigation into the origins of man. One value was first distorted by association with certain temperamental aberrations and then extended into areas over which it had properly no claim so as to crush and destroy other values (for example, that of truth) which, for one reason or another, contradicted the natural inclinations of men. In this way various values may be entirely obscured in certain social contexts, so that it will require real moral heroism and independence of spirit to transcend the socially imposed norms. The conventions and norms governing social conduct may obscure claims, or else pervert them so that they become malign instead of beneficent influences. In this way, too, the objectivist might expect that development in the apprehension of one moral value may be counterbalanced by distortion or repression of other values; and thus he might not expect to see a uniform development so much as an oscillating balance of various ideals, all of them in some way distorted by social and temperamental forces which qualify their full implementation.

In view of these characteristics of relativity, development and distortion in the apprehension of values, it might be thought surprising not that men differ in the moral values they accept but that they ever agree! In fact, however, as Westermarck says, 'the moral rules laid down by the customs of savage peoples . . . in a very large measure resemble the rules of civilized nations'.[4] Some anthropologists even suggest that there has been no change in basic moral values but only in the changing pressures of economic and social life (Boas and Dewey, for example).[5] Certainly, I can see no need for total scepticism about the possibility of moral knowledge. One must, it is true, simply believe certain moral propositions to be true while not perhaps being able to demonstrate their truth to others. Thus there are no decisive and precise tests of truth in morals. But this is not to say that there are no tests; and I have tried to suggest some tests for assessing the partiality, development or distortion of the beliefs both of oneself and of others. What I am maintaining is that though one cannot provide a decisive test for the truth of any specific moral assertion, one can provide a set of criteria stating what sorts of pursuit are conducive to an increase in moral insight; one can say how to set about pursuing moral truth and thus, sometimes, which moral assertions are more likely to be true. And this situation is quite a common one in human experience, being closely paralleled by, for instance, the tests of a man's truthfulness in describing his dreams, which must include such considerations as his general reliability, ability to check imaginative supplementation, vividness of description and so forth. In such situations one cannot decisively test the truth of any specific assertion, but one can provide tests of truth-likelihood in general. The tests are imprecise and are inevitably matters of personal judgement; but in many areas of human life they are tests which we are constrained to apply and refine to the best of our ability.

6. This discussion may be clarified by reference to a particular example of an ethical dispute, of the kind which moral sceptics adduce to undermine belief in the objectivity of morals.

One of the most clear-cut cases of an ethical dispute is that between retributivists and utilitarians over the question of punishment.[6] A retributivist will hold that a person who does wrong should be punished for no other reason than that he has done wrong; he must have harm inflicted upon him in proportion to the harm he has inflicted upon others. The basis of the retributivist case must simply be that he intuits a moral principle of 'justice' or desert—that men should be treated as they treat others. On the other hand, a utilitarian will maintain that offenders should not be punished just because they have done wrong (though they may be punished as a deterrent or reformative measure). The utilitarian rejects the retributivists' alleged intuition of 'desert' and relies on a different intuition of his own, that two wrongs do not make a right, or that it is always wrong to harm anyone, offender or not, unless it may bring about some positive good or happiness. Nothing can alter the harm done in the past, he may say; and any harm inflicted now which is not at least aimed at making the world better in future must be itself an immoral act.

Here we have as direct a conflict over a vitally important area of morality as could be desired by any sceptic. The retributivist says, 'The criminal ought to be punished', on the basis simply of an intuition of that principle. And the utilitarian says, 'The criminal ought not to be punished (for no other reason than that he committed an offence)', on the basis of an intuition that it is wrong to harm others except to bring about a greater future good. Thus the moral propositions they assert are mutually contradictory; they exhaust the possibilities of the situation and so one of them must be true and the other must be false, if one allows a truth-value to moral propositions at all. But what way is there of telling which proposition is true? Each opponent in the dispute seems to confront the other with his own basic intuition; which is just to say that each is equally certain of the truth of his belief and that the reasons they adduce for their beliefs are identical (that they intuit them); so there seems to be no way of adjudicating between them, even though one is certainly false and though it is of the utmost practical importance to find out which.

This is, however, not a completely adequate account of the situation. For the fact is that this alleged impossibility of discriminating the true belief from the false does not lead all reasonable men to adopt an attitude of moral agnosticism to this issue. Some decision has to be made, and the decision is not felt by the agent to be arbitrary even if it appears so to the theoretician. If it was really just a matter of selecting one of two intuitions, equally plausible, then the agent would no doubt feel that it did not matter which he chose. But moral decisions are not in any case made by consulting one's intuitions; they arise as a development of a certain complex of attitudes and beliefs which the agent already has, in response to specific new experiences and contacts with the environment. The starting-point of moral experience lies in the pre-rational life of the human child, when he is partly conditioned and partly taught to adopt certain characteristic responses to human situations, to cultivate certain behaviour-patterns and accept certain evaluations of what is acceptable by his parents or teachers, and what is not. Children have various character-traits from the earliest age: some are aggressive, some shy, some extraverted and some introverted. The interaction-patterns which they establish with their parents help to determine these traits, either by cultivating them (as when aggressiveness in a boy is commended by his parents) or by repressing them. Thus at a very early and certainly pre-rational age children possess characteristic and often highly individual behaviour-patterns and complexes of feeling associated with them. And far from the rise of moral perception in humans being a matter of the filling in of a *tabula rasa* with lots of clear intuitions, it is essential to see it as beginning from an already well-formed character with its own predispositions to act and evaluate.

In the face of this account, obvious enough as soon as it is stated, the language of intuitionists about the clear apprehension of abstract moral principles by equally intelligent and impartial agents appears almost naïve in its neglect of the plain facts of human development. On the other hand, consideration of these plain facts had led some modern theorists to give an account of morality solely in terms of infantile conditioning or the striving for role-satisfaction in a social group. Whereas moralists of old tried to pretend that men were never children, social theorists of today occasionally suppose that they are never anything else. What is needed to correct the balance in each case is the intro-duction of the notion of 'development' of inborn human drives and capacities towards a fully rational, emotionally mature and controlled life. The sceptic will, however, object to such a notion, for its presupposes some assumption that the more developed is the better, and thus the same sort of dispute will arise over what is to be called more developed as did over what was to be called good. It is simply begging the question, he may say, to think that one's own is the more developed of two competing moralities; and it might be more honest to confine oneself to the statement that the moralities conflict and that is all there is to be said.

This seems to me, however, to be a counsel of despair. To take a case which is analogous in some respects: suppose that a child is brought up to a ready acceptance of popular light music and a rejection of symphonic music as 'highbrow'; he will naturally tend to value tunefulness and simple harmonies more highly than complex thematic development and advanced chord progressions. Now is this just a straightforward conflict with those who do value classical music more highly, or does it make sense to speak of 'stages of development' in appreciation of musical values? One reason why it seems more natural to speak of 'development' than of mere 'incompatibility' is that the classicist does not just disavow the values espoused by his opponent. He too values tunes and common chords but finds them monotonous and lacking in variety and complexity, in the qualities which demand ever-renewed efforts of appreciation, and which always seem to offer new and unsuspected rewards to those who strive hard to understand them. Variety, complexity, difficulty of apprehension and economy of form combined with depth of expressiveness emerge as some of the values which the classicist believes to fulfil and supplement the basic qualities of tunefulness and harmony. The popularist himself will probably concede that classical music is a 'development' of popular in one sense, namely in a technical sense; but he need not concede that it is more valuable to have a more complex technique. But at this point I think the classicist would be quite justified in making the assertion that there is an intelligible sense of 'development' in which various elements become more, rather than less organized, coherent, rich and integrated—and perhaps the ideal limit of such a process would conform to something like the Leibnizian criterion of the richest possible diversity of elements organized according to the most economical set of principles.[7] Armed with such a notion of development one may construe moral differences between men as expressions of different general emphases and partialities in the development (or possibly the failure of development) of a coherent set of attitudinal responses to manifold human situations. Thus, in order to see the sort of moral commitment that underlies the advocacy of such a principle as 'criminals ought to be punished', one would need to explicate almost all the beliefs of the person concerned about the nature of society and of human personality, the importance of emotion as opposed to reason, and so forth. These will almost inevitably be at least partially undeveloped and even inconsistent, embodying lack of knowledge or limitation in experience of the criminal mentality, for example. And the same will go, of course, for one who maintains that criminals ought

not to be punished. When the general background attitudes have
been elaborated and systematized it may be found, for example,
that the retributivist places great stress on the notion of 'desert'
or 'fairness' whereas the utilitarian rather tends to emphasize
values such as 'sympathy' and 'benevolence'. In other words,
although, when phrased in an abstract way, it seems as though
the retributivist and the utilitarian are just having contradictory
moral intuitions, this way of putting the matter is grossly inadequate to the situation. The propositions they utter about the
subject of punishment are expressions of much more general
commitments to certain ranges of values; and the real difference
between them lies in the stress they put on different values and
the unavoidably partial and experience-conditioned interpretation
they give to various values (for example, does one 'respect a
person' by interfering with his life or by letting him go his own
way?) Views will differ on this matter, and the line will be drawn
at different places by different people. The objectivist must say
that there is a right place to draw the line; but because of human
limitations and frailties he will not expect all men to agree on
where that is.[8] He can only seek sincerity for himself, never
knowing with certainty what incorrectness in his views is due
simply to incorrigible error and what to culpable imperfection.

But he can certainly seek to systematize, extend and develop the
attitudes he inevitably begins with; and at every stage of this
ongoing development the objectivist may suppose that he becomes
more able to discern accurately what is objectively demanded of
man. It is somewhat as if one must begin from a necessarily
obscure and distorted apprehension, able to know only the direction
in which one may proceed to clarify and correct it, and aware
that this process is not completable but is necessarily imposed on
one by one's nature as a rational moral agent.

It may now conceivably be said that what I have really done is
to construe moral principles as expressions of particular value-
orientations; and this is just another way of saying that morality
is founded upon the human sentiments, that we are not to seek
for universalizable rules but to seek the most common and
compossible realization of man's emotional nature. In a sense I
would not deny this. I do think that it is an unrealistic and
unprofitable pursuit to try to formulate completely universalizable
moral rules; and I do think that the moral life is much more a
matter of controlling and developing one's attitudinal responses

to the environment. But I also think that it is most important to assert that certain attitudes or value-commitments really are demanded of men—that fundamentally it is not just a psychological fact that we commit ourselves to the pursuit of certain values; but it is true that we *ought* to acknowledge these values. And it seems to me that one cannot give due emphasis to the words 'true', 'ought' and 'acknowledge' unless one is prepared to speak of existent values which claim one's response to them, and of one's value-commitments as a form of moral knowledge (or moral belief—in the sense that what one believes, one believes to be true).

# IX

# VOCATION

1. A difficulty which is raised by the account I have given of the diversity of moral values is that it seems to be incompatible with the Christian conception of the moral life as one of the adoption of a specific set of attitudes to a unitary moral demand, attitudes which are exemplified in the life of Jesus. Thus, though I have spoken of the ideal human life as one of total self-abandonment to others, as that of Jesus was, it would seem vastly unrealistic to suppose that this ideal was binding on a professional soldier on active service in a guerilla war. In this, as in so many cases, the nature of a man's vocation is conditioned by the evident facts of moral ignorance and corruption creating obligations which are, in an ideal and abstract sense, not even desirable. It is clear, therefore, that it is a quite inadequate account of moral experience to maintain, as was suggested, perhaps, in Chapter VII, that the will of God for men could be a perfectly general will, demanding exactly the same attitudinal response from men whatever the facts of their particular situations. One must also speak of a particular will of God for individuals in unique and humanly unforeseeable circumstances. And since these circumstances will be inextricably tempered by the whole network of evil acts which engender and circumscribe them, very few of them will make it possible for the agent to adopt that attitude towards God, as ground of moral values, which is abstractly ideal for man as such. This does seem to imply that the fully ideal human life is available to the few, while the majority of men in any society must devote themselves to the pursuit of values which are less than the ideal.

This is a position against which many Protestant Christians have reacted violently. It is admittedly an Aristotelian view that the ideally good life should be possible only to the few who could devote themselves entirely to contemplation, and as such it was incorporated into the ethical system of the Catholic Church in the form of a 'doctrine of orders'.[1] The best life is still conceived to be the contemplative life, and its realization is the supreme good for man. But the pursuit of such a life is a vocation only for the few; most men are necessarily concerned with practical aims in a world in which they must continually come to terms with violence, passion and vice, and to this extent they are precluded from the highest human vocation. Against this view the Reformers stressed that the Christian life was for all men; that contemplatives, far from realizing the best life, in fact betray their duty to help others by retreating from the world; and that there are no 'levels of attainment' in the moral life since all men equally are in sin and are redeemed not by moral striving but by grace.[2]

This dispute introduces the important and difficult concepts of sin and grace, and thus cannot really be analysed fully until these concepts have been clarified. For the moment I think that the dispute can, however, be avoided if one asks the question, 'Is it true that different men, by virtue of their different roles in society, different temperaments, and the different cultures in which they live, ought to realize different values, or at least values in different orders of predominance?' Asked simply as a question in ethics, rather than in theology, it seems to me that the answer must be 'yes'. The worker must realize different values than the scholar, and the soldier than the statesmen, the emotional person than the intellectual, the Indian savage than the American managing director. If this is so, one must introduce the concept of 'vocation', of the calling of each man to his appropriate virtue and to the station in life in which this virtue can be realized. For the Christian it is the man with a vocation to poverty, chastity and obedience who aims at the highest ideal of life, in the sense that he most nearly imitates the exemplary life of Christ. But not all men are called to imitate Christ so exactly; and it is in fact a peculiar emphasis of the Christian conception of the moral life that each man has his own individual and uniquely important calling. The Christian emphasis on particularity and on the ultimate value of the individual is in fact radically antagonistic to any conception of the moral life as the mere following of universal moral rules. Part of the importance of the doctrine of the Incarnation is that it shows God as concerned with an individual human being rather than with men in general; and this doctrine can be readily extended to all men, so that each man is seen as having his own particular vocation for which he has responsibility.

Recent moral philosophy has tended to be very much concerned with rules or general principles. Sometimes these have been elevated to the status of criteria of morality itself, so that what *makes* a decision a moral decision has been said to be the fact that it can be formulated as a universal rule.[3] And sometimes the foundation of morality has been said to lie in the construction of general rules—constructed, perhaps, by an impartially sympathetic observer of the human scene—which co-ordinate diverse human interests equitably.[4] At any rate it has been widely suggested that it is one, or even the, fundamental characteristic of morality that it is rule-like, and thus that to be moral consists in following general rules of conduct.

One could, of course, make this a stipulative definition of what 'being moral' is; but if one takes the fundamental business of morality to be the formation of a personal decision as to how one is to live, then this 'rule-following' notion of morality seems to evade just those issues which are of the deepest human concern. Naturally one does not wish to say that rules have *no* place in the moral life, or that one cannot formulate general principles of conduct to which one adheres, or that it does not matter which general principles one espouses. But there is another area of decision-making altogether; the area in which one decides what course of life one will adopt—what, for example, one's job will be, what one's ends in that job will be, what sort of character-traits and attitudes one will adopt, what interests one will cultivate or ignore. It is in this area that the concept of 'vocation' finds its place.

The man who has a vocation is one who feels that what he does is not just a matter of choice; that he is under an obligation, he is 'called' to perform a certain job; or that, being placed in a certain situation, he is 'bound' to remain in it and implement, so far as is possible, an ideally conceived manner of performing his role in it. Thus a man might feel 'called' to the priesthood; or an incurable invalid may believe that it is his life's vocation to endure suffering with patience and fortitude. But if such vocations are perceived as absolute obligations it would be false, if not absurd, to say that they were binding on all men, even on all men similar to oneself in relevant respects. For the only respect one can be sure to be relevant is that one is called to that vocation. And to say that, is only to say that one is under obligation if one is under obligation, which is tautological. Perhaps someone else, in an apparently identical situation, would not feel such a vocation. So it is with many of the things, and those the most important, upon which the direction of our lives depends. They apply uniquely to oneself; and even to raise the question of whether they would be binding on anyone in that situation is to miss the whole point that it is just the particularity of one's own situation that is in question.

Since one's vocation is what one *ought* to be, in a particular situation, it must appear as one among other possibilities of one's own situation, as a person with such a character, born into such a set of social relationships, in a nation with such an historical tradition. All these things condition and set the framework of one's decision; what is required is the decision to realize one possible line of development, implicit in one's situation, to the exclusion of others. And what the man who seeks his vocation seeks is that destiny which is uniquely and peculiarly his own, which will conform him to what he ought to be; he seeks himself.

That which occurs to many, at least in their most profoundly questioning moments; the adolescent and yet Socratic question, 'Who am I'? is, for those who ask it, the decisively ethical question. It is not answered by describing all one's character-traits and social functions, though the investigation of these may suggest an answer. For what is to be decided is which of the possibilities of action that one's situation limits is to be chosen at the expense of others? The wrong choice will be the loss of oneself; and though, in that choice, one may follow all the moral rules, the decisive thing will have been betrayed; one will be without direction, without fundamental ethical purpose; because, whatever one *does*, one is not what one ought to *be*.

It is certain that there are many for whom the concept of 'vocation' has no force. But to those for whom it has force it has a sort of ultimacy and importance which even moral rules do not have; for, of course, one must keep moral rules; and at times that may call for the sort of serious decision in which one's very life must be put at risk. Nevertheless, most of the time and for most people the moral rules can be kept with minimal inconvenience; but one cannot avoid the decision on how one's life is to be lived. Or, rather, one can avoid it; but even the avoidance, the passive acceptance of whatever time and place and set of conventions one happens to find oneself in is, unavoidably, a decision against oneself. One may say that it does not matter what one's situation is as long as, in it, one does what is right. But that, it must be seen, is just to state an alternative view of what morality is; it is, in effect, to deny that there is anything uniquely important about *oneself*, about the being which one allows to come to fruition in the situation of one's own choice; about the being which *ought* to be, here and now, but which is delivered into the freedom of my decision.

To stress 'vocation' is thus to stress the ultimate moral importance of human individuality. And it is perhaps only a religion of incarnation which can give such a notion an intelligible and central place in the concept of the moral life.[5]


2. But how is this conception of individual vocation compatible with the view that there is only one true ideal for man, and that the life of Jesus is the exemplary life for all men? What is required is a deeper understanding of what is meant by a human ideal. To say that something is an ideal for man is not to say that it is something which all men are actually under an obligation to realize. Indeed it is quite possible to speak of the life of Jesus as the ideal life without ever supposing that one can come near realizing it oneself. As in geometry one may speak of an 'ideal' circle without believing that there ever will exist such a thing, so, in the moral life' one may talk of an 'ideal' life without supposing it realized. The ideal life will be that which embodies an appropriate response to the moral demand as it really is. And, as I said in Chapter VI, each human value is given its true character only when it is seen as an element of one total attitude to the moral demand; for the Christian, when it is controlled by the sort of charity that Jesus exemplified. The Christian is bound to believe that the life of Jesus is both ideal and exemplary in that it represents a perfect human response to the reality of God and that it presents, in a living image, the pattern of values in one integrated total response. But though some men are called to follow Christ in the detail of his life—in its poverty, self-sacrifice and martyrdom—most men will find their vocation in very different spheres of life—in the affluence and competitiveness of an industrial society, for example. One can hardly seriously suggest that the Christian faith has nothing to say to such men, or that it precludes them from following their particular occupations (though it will, in some cases, condemn human occupations as such—perhaps mercenary warfare and prostitution are examples of this).

K

It does seem, however, that such men will have to say that even if they fulfil their vocation completely their lives will still not be ideal lives. And I do not see why this should not be said. As, in human society, there are only a few men who have power, or great ability, or fame, and other men, if they are not envious, will take pleasure in the eminence of their fellows; so in the spiritual life it may well be that few men attain close proximity to the perfect adoration of God which was Christ's, and that others take pleasure in their greater capacity and achievement. The Bible seems to sponsor such a view in speaking of the different rewards of the souls in heaven.[6] In this sense, then, an 'ideal', though it stands at the head of a scale of perfections, is not something to be realized by all men regardless of their capacity or inclination. But it is something which all men ought to recognize as ideal, as the supreme fulfilment of human life which they can neither attain nor desire for themselves if they have true self-knowledge. It is as if one said, 'I can see that the ideal of human excellence is to love God wholly and completely, to the exclusion of all else; but I am not capable of such love, nor do I truly desire it. I will accordingly revere those who do attain it, but remain true to that vocation which, though lower in the scale of absolute perfection, satisfies me fully.'

In somewhat the same way the man who feels that it is his vocation to pursue intellectual studies may allow the pursuit of truth to be the predominating value in his life; and in so doing he will not, of course, be 'imitating Christ' in any direct sense, since Christ was not a scientist. But, at the same time, an acknowledgement of the Christian ideal of life will temper the scientist's attitude to his own vocation. It will prevent him from erecting an ideal of intellectual superiority (something of which Aristotle may not unfairly be accused), from despising the ignorant, and from supposing that the pursuit of truth is the only value which should be acknowledged by all men. Rather as the spiritedness of Plato's Auxiliaries in *The Republic* was modified by their acceptance that the Republic was to be guided by the wisdom of the Rulers,[7] so the intellectual endeavours of the scientist should be modified by his acknowledgement that the value he pursues must always be controlled by that ideal of charity which Jesus exemplified. Even though it cannot be predominant in his life, as it was in that of Christ, he can accept it as modifying and developing his pursuit of his own vocation. Thus the exemplary life of Christ is for most men an ideal 'focus' which helps to give form and direction to their own vocations; it is the regulative ideal which gives a distinctive, Christian 'form' to all the moral virtues; and for some men it is itself the vocation which they must pursue.

3. One can, however, say rather more than this about the moral demand upon all men to adopt the theistic attitude. For the different values which predominantly claim men can be seen as stresses on different aspects of one demanded attitude, which are due to the varying conditions of temperament, culture and social role, in which the moral demand is apprehended. Thus, a man who has been educated to be a professional soldier may see that, given the world is as it is, he must cultivate a specific set of values in which preparedness to kill takes a major part. But he may also see that the character he must adopt in virtue of his social role is not one that is essential to being a soldier, in other conditions, perhaps. Thus he may try to bring about those other conditions. And he may further see that, in a perfectly moral world, there would be no place for soldiering at all. The man who sees all this will not be disposed to say that an ideal human life is open to him—he will see the necessity of repressing some values he might otherwise have wished to realize (such as a secure home life, for example) and of allowing other values to exercise an unduly prominent influence (one can hardly imagine Jesus allowing his sense of honour to be as predominant as that of a regimental commander). He may even allow that those values he does realize will be necessarily perverted by their contact with evil, both in others and in himself (so that it is hard to prevent 'honour' from becoming aggressive pride), and he will have to accept that even the best course open to him, abstractly judged, is far from ideal.

Now I suggest that the proper course for such a man will not normally be to renounce his commission and preach the gospel to the poor (though it may be, in an exceptional and unpredictable case). It will be wholeheartedly to embrace the values demanded by his role and culture—honour, discipline, courage and determination—but to incorporate these values within a wider set of attitudes derived from the exemplary model of Christ. It may be that God demands courage as my predominant virtue in my particular situation; but I know that, in the ideal response to the moral demand, courage will be controlled and modified by charity: it will be steadfastness in the love of God. Nevertheless, it is not my vocation to pursue the love of God above all things. What, then, should I do? I suggest that every man should pursue those values that are demanded of him in his particular role and situation (except in the limiting cases where even pursuance of the role seems incompatible with the Christian attitude), while always cultivating the general Christian attitude of worship, obedience, thankfulness and humility.

It is possible to do this because it does make sense to speak of a general will of God for all men as such, as well as of a particular will for individuals. The particular will of God is modified by particular circumstances of historical time and place; and yet it cannot be thought of as varying indeterminately, according to no general principles, so that his will for one man might be the opposite of his will for another with no explanation of the difference being necessary. It was maintained in Chapter VII that the being of God must be necessarily what it is; and part of the reason for saying this is precisely to exclude such arbitrariness in the Divine will as is here being envisaged. On the other hand, if one is to speak of a particular will of God at all then one cannot mean that the being of God is completely unchangeable in every respect. What is required, therefore, is a doctrine which will preserve the necessity of the being of God in its general nature, while allowing for the modification of his will in the light of particular historical circumstances.

Such a doctrine in turn requires the development of a more precise view of the relation of the moral demand to the empirical world. It has already been suggested that any doctrine of an objective moral demand requires the assertion of some conceptual relation between the demand and the world, however general and unspecific in its nature, in order to ensure the moral necessity of human obligations. But that relation must be conceived as being much more specific, if one speaks also of a modification of the moral demand by contingent and historical facts. What one wishes to say is not only that the demand specifies conceptually the most general characteristics of human being which will give rise to specific moral claims but also that the developing response of human creatures is able to bring about new and more specific demands as the possibilities of human action are limited or extended by constantly changing human responses. At each moment of historical time, therefore, the moral demand is modified to accommodate different ranges of possible action; but this always happens within the sphere of the more general, and necessary, Divine intention which has been construed as the objective teleology of the world.

It is this doctrine that is expressed by Christian language about the 'knowledge' of God. As in the case of 'intention', a concept derived from contexts of human existence is used analogically to express something, without asserting that 'God' is a knowing mind in anything like the same sense that persons are. One says that God 'knows' the hearts of men, not claiming any understanding at all of how this knowledge functions or what it is like, and without really wishing to assimilate the concept of 'God' itself to that of a human person. But the word seems appropriate to express the fact that there are particular moral demands as well as a general moral purpose for the world, and that these clearly differ according to the difference in contingent historical situations, even though one is precluded, by one's commitment to the objectivity of morals, from supposing that empirical situations can be themselves the sole ground of moral obligations. One must consequently speak in terms of a modification of the Divine intention by empirical circumstances; and it thus seems appropriate to say that God's will for particular men is modified by his knowledge of their situations in all their complexities and ambiguities.

4. The moral life of the Christian may therefore be considered at different levels of generality. In the first place, there will be many moral rules to which the Christian will conform because he accepts them as conditions of participating in a relatively stable society. These rules may be specific to his role in society or they may be general principles of social cohesiveness; and, in general, the Christian will obey them, in common with all men of good will, doubting or disobeying them only when they seem to have lost their socially integrative function. But the 'good will' of the Christian—that which disposes him to adopt the duties of social utility—will be reinforced by what I have termed his attitudinal approach to the moral life. That is, he will see himself as obliged to develop in himself certain virtues or attitudes, apart from all consideration of their social consequences; and these will include

the attitude of benevolence, which naturally leads to a concern for social utility. It is here that the notion of 'vocation' finds its place; and though perhaps all men do not have a strong sense of vocation, many believe that certain virtues are demanded particularly of them. I have suggested that the sense of vocation is a central feature of the Christian life and that it finds its paradigm in the unique calling of Jesus to be the Messiah. Different vocations require the realization of various values in varying degrees; and thus, while admitting the desirability of a diversity of vocations, the Christian will not regard them as all equally high in the scale of abstract moral perfection. The imitation of Christ, in a life of teaching, healing and martyrdom, is the highest calling; but it comes to very few. Nevertheless, that ideal remains a sort of 'imaginary focus' towards which the particular vocation of each Christian must be continually referred. It is true that the Reformers tended to protest against this notion of a hierarchy of vocations, mainly on the ground that it seems to assure a few men of a certainty of salvation not universally available. But such protests are quite needless if it is clearly seen that the hierarchy is intended to be solely of moral perfection, not of the more or less saved, or worthy of salvation. It would seem to me totally unrealistic to suggest that different men are not really at different levels of moral perfection, or that some lives are not really capable of greater moral perfection than others. But to admit that rather obvious fact is by no means to suppose that the less perfect are in some way deprived, any more than to admit that some men are better footballers than others implies that the worse ones are deprived. A man is only deprived if he lacks something that, given what he is, it is possible for him to have. Thus the man who is not able to be more perfect without becoming a different man is not deprived by comparison with the heroic Christian saints. Indeed, it is right for him to glory in their achievement. Moreover, being higher in moral perfection by no means assures one of 'salvation' to a greater degree than others; the Biblical view rather suggests that, of those to whom much is given, much will be required;[8] and it is not humanly possible to know by how much more a highly virtuous man might have failed in accomplishing what was possible for him, than a poor mentally inadequate child of a criminal family who may have done all he could. Furthermore, it may be recalled that the most perfect of men is 'in sin' just as much as the greatest sinner, and therefore both stand under an equal need of redemption. Now in saying this I have introduced the terms 'salvation' and 'sin' without providing any explanation of them; but I hope that this may be allowed for the moment in view of the fact that I am merely attempting to rebut the objections of those who might oppose the doctrine of hierarchical vocation by relying on these terms.

5. There is, however, I have said, another aspect of the Christian conception of the moral life. As well as particular attitudinal demands there is one general attitude which is demanded of all Christians. Whereas the diverse particular attitudes demanded of men have, as their objects, various personal and social situations, and consist of policies of action and apprehension in relation to other men, the more general theistic attitude has, as its object, no particular set of social contexts, and is neutral with regard to all possible social situations. In Chapter VI, I spoke of God as the unitary ground demanding a set of related attitudes which were fully exemplified in the life of Christ; and in this chapter, by an elaboration of the notion of vocation, it has been seen that only very few men are called to realize precisely those virtues which Jesus, in his unique situation, fully realized. To that extent the life of Jesus remains an ideal of human life for the Christian rather than a pattern to be slavishly duplicated, regardless of circumstances. Nevertheless, there are respects in which the attitudes of Jesus can, in principle, be duplicated in the life of every Christian; and this is because of the generality of the object to which these attitudes are directed. That object is simply the ground of moral claims itself. I have tried to show, particularly in Chapter IV, that as well as saying *what it is* that the moral demand requires of us one can also properly enquire into the nature of the moral demand itself. One can say, for instance, that it may naturally be conceived as a creative power; and one can say also that, by whatever means, men continually reject and refuse the demands made upon them and so are unable any longer to perceive those demands clearly and unambiguously. The whole notion of vocation testifies to the defection of men from the moral demand, for it is largely designed to establish what ought to be done, not absolutely and ideally, but in the face of circumstances which are ineradicably bound up with evil acts and intentions.

Here, then, are two elements of the human situation which are quite universal in scope—they apply to all men everywhere—the vision of a total demand which may be further understood as creative ground and demanded goal of human existence; and the radical inability of men to perceive or meet adequately the demands made upon them. The Christian believes, as will be more fully shown, that a third universal element of the human condition is expressed in the Divine promise that, in the end, the moral demand will be fully met in the world and human rejection of it will be overcome. The belief in this promise is grounded chiefly on the Christian experience of regeneration through the objective power of Christ. The Christian 'good news' is that man's rejection shall be transcended, but by the coming of the Spirit, not by his own efforts—that is, by grace.[9] Faith is founded firmly on the work of grace in men, not just on an ethical commitment: it is the hope for completion of a work already begun, and based on the promise of Christ.

But in saying this it should be noted that one is not here making an abrupt transition from evaluative statements to factual statements. The very readiness to assent to these factual statements is conditional upon the sort of evaluation of human experience which sets them in a context of intelligibility. That is to say, the preparedness to say 'yes' to the work of the Spirit in oneself, and the willingness to interpret this work *as* the work of the Spirit, logically presupposes an evaluative interpretation of experience as mediating absolute and objective moral demands and of one's own endeavours as radically ineffective in meeting those demands. These are evaluative decisions; or, more properly, they are reflective explorations of the metaphysical foundations of the morality we accept. Christian faith arises out of moral experience (if it does) as a certain way of understanding that experience gradually becomes clearer, and as these tentative interpretations tend to be corroborated (if they do) by experiences which seem to be adequately describable by the use of the interpretative concepts one has already elaborated. Thus fact and evaluation proceed indivisibly; and if, by harsh analyses, the purely factual elements (for example, 'there is a Holy Spirit') are strained out from the purely evaluative elements (for example, 'I ought to rely on the Spirit'), the inner truth of the situation is at once destroyed. For the situation is that how one interprets certain experiences *as* facts, and thus what one *counts* as facts in this realm, depends essentially upon the set of concepts which express one's evaluative stance in the world. Thus one might ask if belief in the existence of the moral ideal is a matter of fact or of evaluation; since it speaks of 'existence' it must be a matter of fact; and yet this is not a fact which can be established by any experimental methods of verification. Why does one say that it is a fact at all unless one feels that the demands of morality are to be taken with ultimate seriousness? And is this not an evaluation of human experience? Thus it is one's evaluation of experience which leads to the postulation of non-empirical facts; and then, as if in the next progression of the dialectic, this fact may in turn lead to new evaluations; so that one's commitment to an objective Ideal (for example) may lead one to an attitudinal ethic; and this, too, will generate questions about the attainability or unattainability of human fulfilment; and so doctrines of the Fall and of Redemption will be generated. If one says these are questions of fact, the answer is 'Yes; but not ordinary, empirical matters of fact; they are questions of adequate backing for our evaluations, corroborated by the occurrence of specific experiences which they seem able to illuminate'. And if one says they are questions of evaluation, the answer is 'Yes; but not simple approval or aversion; they are ways of seeing one's experience, of allocating importances and decisive insights; and they often arise out of specific factual contexts towards which they come as appropriate responses'.

It is the acceptance of such a general structure of human existence, as it stands in relation to the moral demand, which is in an indissoluble way both factual and evaluative, which provides the object of the theistic attitude. It can be universally binding on all men because these structural elements of the human situation are universal. Thus it is reasonable to say that all men ought to adopt the same attitude, in so far as there are structural elements common to human life as such, over and above the particularities of individual human situations. So whatever values the individual Christian feels called to pursue, he will be able to devote himself to the development of the basic theistic attitude—seeing himself as a creature alienated from and in need of reconciliation to the ground and goal of his existence—at the same time.

We may suppose that it was his acute perception of the structure of the human situation that led Jesus to pursue, and thus exemplify in himself, the ideal pattern which gives to the Christian virtues their characteristic form. And though very few are called to realize this ideal in its fullness, all men are called to adopt the general attitude of creaturely reverence and gratitude, contrition and repentance, trust and moral commitment, which is the appropriate response to the structure of human existence. Thus the Christian refers his interpretation of the moral life back to the historical Jesus in two distinct though related ways. He understands the specific virtues he feels called to pursue by reference to their place in the ideal pattern exemplified in the life of Jesus; and he adopts a specific attitude to the ground of these values, as it conditions the structure of human existence, which is ultimately founded on the authoritative declaration of Jesus. Christian morality is consequently seen to be a morality based on authority rather than on autonomous apprehension of moral values. But the notion of authority in morals is an extremely complex and even potentially dangerous one, and will need to be explored in some detail in succeeding chapters.

# AUTHORITY IN ETHICS

1. In exploring the nature of Christian ethics, certain major characteristics have emerged which, if not all unique to Christianity or necessary to it, do seem to be basic features of a Christian view of the moral life. The first such characteristic is that of *objectivity*—the assertions of Christian ethics claim to be true, and to be made true by an extra-human fact (or facts). The second is its *attitudinal* character—the fact that it demands the development of specific attitudes and policies of life, the pursuit of personal perfection in the moral agent himself and not just obedience to moral rules or the bringing about of good ends in the world. Associated with this are four other characteristics which I tried to elucidate in the foregoing chapters; first, the *unitary* nature of the moral demand, a unity which develops into the notion of a creator or necessary being as the ground of all actual beings; second, the *purposive* conception of human life, as being called to achieve a specific end or purpose; and third, the *exemplary* character of Christian moral doctrine, which locates the demanded attitudes in one paradigmatic life. Connected with the purposive element is the Christian concept of *vocation*, which stresses the great importance of the individual life precisely in its unique individuality. The stress on individuality is integrated with the element of exemplarity by the introduction of a hierarchy of vocations which come more or less close to the exemplary ideal for human life as such without reference to particular exigencies; and also by distinguishing between the content of the moral demand for a particular person at a particular time and the relation of human existence in general to the moral demand, the recognition of which requires an attitude from all men which is compatible with a great range of particular demanded virtues, varying with persons and times.

In this scheme, both the exemplary moral ideal and the general attitude to the moral demand itself are, as was said at the end of the previous chapter, accepted by the Christian on the authority of Jesus. And it is probably true to say that the most striking, and often repugnant, feature of Christian morality for a non-believer is the way in which it falls back on authority for its ultimate moral judgements rather than relying on the agent's immediate insight. Religious ethics is essentially *authoritative* in nature. And for some people this is sufficient to condemn it; for, it may be said, a man should only accept as right what he himself sees to be right; to do otherwise is a betrayal of conscience. But I think that the Christian will consider the situation to be rather more complex than this. He should certainly deplore the suggestion that a man should accept as right what he sees to be wrong; and he will be wise to point out that the decision to accept a certain moral authority itself involves a prior moral decision. The assumption of the secular moralist which he will wish to dispute is that every man is an equally good judge of what is right, and that therefore each man should trust his own moral insight, on every matter, as his final guide. This assumption relies on what I regard as one of the most fundamentally mistaken views of the nature of moral experience—namely, that knowing what it is right to do is a simple matter of intuiting, or calculating in accordance with a simple rule (for example, of universal prescriptivity), or discerning one's immediate emotional reaction. While these theories differ widely from each other, they agree in what they deny, that moral knowledge requires the arduous development of certain skills and capacities and is not freely available to anyone who cares to seek for it. An ethical objectivist is, however, by no means committed to such a denial; indeed, since he is claiming that there are moral facts in the Universe, it is almost a natural corollary to suppose that the apprehension of these facts, in their true perspective, may be open only to a few men, and then after long and difficult training. Such is, approximately, the view developed by Plato in *The Republic* where he declares that an apprehension of 'the Good' itself is a feat almost impossible of human achievement.[1] One can know that there is, and must be, such a demand as the ground of morality, but one also knows from experience of the ambiguity and relativity of the moral situation that the demand is, in its true character, hidden from one.

2. It may be objected that moral insight cannot be as rare and difficult as this, for nearly all men do sincerely hold moral beliefs

of some sort; and does this not assume that, whenever their beliefs are true—as they often must be—they have moral knowledge? This, however, is not so; for one of the things which distinguishes knowledge from true belief is that one can be said to know something only if one has adequate grounds for one's claim, whereas true belief might be based on very inadequate grounds.[2] So the question is, what sort of things constitute adequate grounds for claims to moral knowledge?

At this point some sort of parallel might be made with human knowledge of physical laws. Probably every educated man accepts that there is a universal law of gravitation, even though most men are perhaps unsure of what its exact formulation is. And, of course, the fact that many primitive societies would not acknowledge such a law in no way weakens its claim to be objectively true. But very few men could work out the gravitational law if left to themselves, however obviously true it seems when pointed out. Those who can be said to possess adequate grounds for claiming knowledge of the law are only those who know what tests to apply and measurements to confirm in order to establish the law as true.

The parallel with moral experience which I wish to draw is that most men accept moral beliefs in somewhat the same way as they accept scientific beliefs—they do not themselves 'intuit' moral truths as objectively binding facts. On the whole they accept what they are taught as morally commendable behaviour, only modifying it in the light of new experiences which go beyond the rules. And this is not to say that they are immoral or non-moral; it is only to say that, lacking any direct insight, they accept in its place the tested experience of mankind as to what ought to be done.

The parallel breaks down when it is a question of giving a positive account of moral knowledge, however. For moral truths are not laws discoverable by hypothesis, deduction and the application of confirmation-tests. In morals the final appeal must be to a definite experience of a moral demand; the adequate basis for a knowledge-claim in ethics is such a particular experience, as experienced by one who is able to interpret it adequately. There are two main requirements here—the occurrence of an experience and the capacity of the experient to apprehend it. As has been suggested, many men have no specific 'moral experiences' at all; and most of those who do, have them either infrequently or in an extremely obscure and rather tentative fashion. Thus when men say that they just 'feel' or 'intuit' something to be right, they usually mean these terms in a purely negative sense. That is, they are not claiming to have had some definite experience of demand; they mean only that they cannot justify their belief in terms of anything else, and so it has a sort of ultimacy and irreducibility which is signified by the word 'intuition'. It is rather like assenting to the truth of a proposition without a clear apprehension of what it is, in the facts, which makes it true—like accepting the law of gravity because, when stated, it seems the best available thing to believe even though one can neither demonstrate it nor, perhaps, show it to be true. So possibly the vast majority of Christians believe that it is right to love; and they do not believe it solely because Jesus commanded it and for no other reason; yet they do not believe it, either, because they clearly apprehend the nature of the moral ideal which demands love from them.

3. It may be objected that to drive a wedge in this way between the acknowledgement of ethical ideals and the real objective demand is not faithful to the facts of moral experience, which must see one's ideals *as* objective demands: and that it introduces a radical scepticism with regard to the possibility of knowledge in morals which, once introduced, can in no way be overcome. But my contention would be that the account I have suggested does precisely fit the facts of our moral experience. In particular, it provides some account of the rather paradoxical situation, in ethics, that one *cannot but* believe that one's deepest ethical convictions are right; and yet one is reluctant to speak of 'knowing' moral facts. Thus, on the one hand, one cannot claim to have an unshakably clear knowledge of what is demanded of man: this is perhaps why the language of 'choosing' principles comes more naturally to the lips of many philosophers than that of 'apprehending' them. While, on the other hand, most men do not really believe that it is *just* a matter of choice and so would rather speak of 'acknowledging' principles than of deciding on them. The principle of 'universal love', when clearly placed before reasonably impartial and sympathetic men, will have a clear moral appeal, a strong claim for acknowledgement, in that it seems to fulfil their other moral commitments. But the limits and implications of the principle will be unclear—what does it demand in war, for example, or in the competitive world of business, or in

international politics? So whereas one may incline to assent to the principle of 'concern for others', one can be very unclear indeed about what it is in the facts which makes such a principle true, and thus about what exactly, and in particular, is demanded from one at any time.

The acceptance of such a principle may or may not derive from some vision or experience of an objective demand; it is certainly conceivable that, for a Christian, it will be generated by the experience of a claim centred on the preaching of the life, death and resurrection of Jesus. But for many people born and brought up in the Church the principle itself will be learned both by precept and example, and so enter into the very fabric of their moral conduct, without being associated with any particular experience of its factual ground. Moreover, even if there does occur some particular experience of ethical demand it will almost inevitably be an obscure and fleeting experience which is as tantalizing as it is compulsive and which promises a completion beyond that which it offers.

4. It may be objected that some men do claim to have continual experiences of moral demand, and their experiences still differ enormously from each other. This must be conceded; and one must then rely on the second of the two main requirements, the moral capacity of the experient, to distinguish probably true from probably false claims. The moral demand claims certain responsive attitudes from men; and what these attitudes are thought to be will depend very much upon the context in which claims are felt, the general pattern of claims which is built up throughout the development of one's own formed character and outlook. Though it is difficult for the moral agent himself to be sufficiently dispassionate to recognize the influence of social and personal prejudgements, other people can usually recognize them quickly enough. They will be able to tell if the agent's intellect is advanced enough to be able to distinguish and relate all the various aspects of a problem; if his experience seems broad enough to make his judgement impartial; if his feelings are sufficiently strong yet controlled to enable full appreciation of the situation to take place; and if his life is morally virtuous—on the theory that moral practice sharpens moral perception. There are not, and there cannot be, precisely definable tests in this area of human life;

but the vague tests that do exist are sufficient to exclude almost everyone from any certainty of attaining knowledge in morality.

The two major features of the account of morality I have here developed are, first, that morality is ultimately founded upon claim-situations; second, that such situations are not common among men and are not therefore necessary features of the moral life of every individual; and furthermore, that even when they do occur they are likely to be apprehended in a distorted form, according to the total situation of the apprehender. As an example of what I have in mind, consider the apprehension of a moral claim to pursue truth for its own sake.

5. When does man feel the claim to pursue truth? In specific situations; but it cannot be stated in advance what these situations will be: to state them would be to state the biography of a particular individual. So, perhaps, a man will become a scientist simply because he is good at physics, because it pays well, and so forth. But then one day he is asked to conceal the results of an experiment because it might prejudice sales of a product marketed by the firm he works for. At that point the man may (or may not) feel a conflict of conscience produced by the aroused perception of the claim to pursue truth for its own sake, which opposes the vested interests represented by his firm. In other words, he perceives the claim, in however distorted or obscure a fashion, in a certain context and at a certain time in his individual biography, at which decisions involving such a claim are forced upon him. It follows that some men, having an exaggerated, one-sided vision, will feel impelled to devote their whole lives to pursuing truth; any hint of lie or deception will to them be unthinkable, a denial of humanity itself; for their humanity, their fulfilment, is found in total devotion to that ideal. Others will acknowledge the same ideal, but complement it with other ideals, and so be prepared to compromise this one ideal by lying or deception if it is overruled by other ideal-claims they admit. Still others will not have been confronted with the claim in any direct way; they might assent to the general rule 'lying is wrong' out of conformity to convention, far-sighted self-interest (that people must be able to trust one another) or a strong, conditioned distaste for deceit.

What is an unrealistic account of the situation is that there is

some general ethical *principle* which is intuited; or that every act
of deceit carries with it a non-natural property of 'wrongness'
(whatever that could be). The problem which faced the British
intuitionists was that it seems obvious that, if lying is wrong,
then all acts of lying are wrong, at least *prima facie*. It is because
all identical acts must be equally right or wrong that Ross had to
assert an *a priori* connection between ethical properties and
certain naturalistic properties;[3] if the connection was only contingent, two otherwise identical acts could easily differ in their
ethical properties. On the interpretation I am suggesting, however, there is no question of there being ethical properties attached
to things of a specific type. If a man feels impelled to pursue
truth as a goal and fulfilment of his own life, he does not have
to intuit any distinct ethical properties; indeed that would be a
very unrealistic suggestion and would not account for the diversity
of the goals which men acknowledge, the varying intensity with
which they are said to obligate men, or the differing particular
judgements of value which equally committed men derive from
the same basic claim. To account for these things one must see
the perception and acknowledgement of ethical claims as intrinsically bound up with the life and experience of particular individuals.
A man does not, then, intuit particular properties in principle
equally perceptible to all by a sort of 'common moral sense',
equally present and developed in all. In his particular life-
situation some moment of decision gives rise to his acknowledgement of a claim; and one must say that there is something existent
which binds him (or is acknowledged by him to bind him) to
pursue a certain value.

General moral principles are abstract principles which are
generated out of such claim-situations. To say that one feels
committed to devote oneself to the pursuit of truth is not the
same as to assent to the principle 'lying is wrong'; but that
principle seems to follow naturally from commital; if one says,
'One must always seek to promulgate truth', this entails, 'One
must never lie.' Particular judgements on moral situations can
also be derived from the assessment of the ways in which various
claims can be fulfilled in those situations. But such assessment
is always a matter of judgement and decision rather than of simple
direct 'intuition'. Thus although there are occasions upon which
a man will feel impelled to take a stand on what his own conscience
dictates, very often—and even in the development of that conscience

L

itself—men will align themselves behind the insights of those whose judgement they respect. This, I would think, is actually the case in human morality; and it is perfectly natural. For since what men acknowledge largely depends on the sort of men they are, the environmental factors which influence them, and their inherent moral insight, if one accepts that there are specific truth-making features of reality in morality, one must also accept that some men will be more liable to acknowledge the moral truth than others. Thus it might actually be a moral virtue in a man to accept someone else as a moral authority rather than to insist that his own moral standards must be final and incorrigible for him.

This statement must, however, be treated with great care. One cannot simply say that one should renounce all one's moral standards, or that one should put oneself unquestioningly into the hands of some external moral authority. Just as one will admit a man to be of exceptional intellectual ability only if one already has some ability oneself and if others tend to agree in admiring him; so, in morals, one can accept a man as a moral authority only if he somehow seems to transcend one's own moral achievement while being recognizably better in the *same moral direction*. A case which some Christians have put to unfortunate use is that of Abraham and Isaac.[4] It has been said (for instance, by Kierkegaard) that Abraham here overruled his moral belief that it was wrong to kill his son simply because of his belief that God commanded him to kill Isaac.[5] Thus particular commands of God are said to be able to overrule even a man's most firmly held ethical convictions. The truly iniquitous consequences of such a doctrine can surely be seen by the most Kierkegaardian Christian if he applies the same doctrine to alien faiths. Thus the 'thugs' of India could justify any enormities by appeal to the commands of God—and so could Hitler. But, the Christian may say, God did not really command Hitler to massacre the Jews. Perhaps not; but if one can apply no moral criteria to God—if he really can command what opposes our most deeply felt ethical convictions—how do they know that God did not command this? Plainly there is no test at all here for truth or deception. Did God really command Samuel to command the slaughter of the Amalekites?[6] One may well react by exclaiming 'God forbid!'; by which one means that such a course would contradict all that we know of the existent ground of our ethical norms. If God can do that then no moral man will want any part of such a God;

and if one says morality is of no importance, being a sign of man's fallenness, then it is useless and hypocritical of Christians to appeal to the moral goodness of Jesus or to the sublime morality of the Christian concept of love or to the ability of the Holy Spirit to help men achieve a new level of morality; for Christian faith is compatible with the most radical evil imaginable if God really can overrule the 'fallen' moral law of men at his pleasure.

A study of comparative religions and ancient history surely suggests that Abraham was not torn between duty and obedience to God's command; at that stage in Jewish history it was common belief that human sacrifice *was* a duty; the point of the Genesis story is not to demonstrate a 'teleological suspension of the ethical', but to show Abraham's total devotion to the ethical as he believed it to be. We would now say that Abraham was misguided in this belief—a warning that Christian devotion is no guarantee against deception. Yet one could hardly use this example to point the lesson that one should *never* be devoted to the ethical because of the danger of making a mistake. For there are occasions—fortunately rare—when total devotion, even as far as death, is required of any man who has any moral beliefs at all, unless, indeed, he is a complete egoist.

One cannot, then, rationally be required to accept any authority which *contradicts* one's moral beliefs. Perhaps an analogy can be made from music: if one regards tuneful popular music as the best sort of music, one certainly has some sort of musical appreciation. But, in listening to a master discussing his craft, one may become aware of subtleties which one is oneself unable to appreciate but which clearly represent a development of one's own appreciation to a very great degree. In somewhat the same way one may reasonably suppose that some men are 'masters' at apprehending the factual ground of all ethical claims and at seeing more clearly than others what it requires of men, the true ethical demand.

6. The notion of 'revelation' is closely allied to the notions of 'authority' and 'experience'. The moral authority is one who has a greater and deeper experience of that which his followers experience in some degree; and what he tells them of his own experience becomes 'revelation' for them. It has been rather fashionable, in recent years, to disclaim any propositional view of

revelation—any view which regards it as the acceptance of propositions as true, on authority. Instead it has been proposed that 'revelation' should be regarded as 'self-disclosure' of God's nature directly to men, on some historical occasion, so that it becomes something like a disclosure of personal depths in the world of one's experience.[7] I would not wish to suggest that there are no such disclosures; indeed, on the view of morality I have outlined I am committed to admitting disclosures of moral claims to specific persons in specific situations. But what must be firmly stressed is that such disclosures, because of the relativity and ambiguity of our situation, vary very much in their quality and the interpretations put upon them; and it is probable that very few persons ever come near to apprehension of the truth of God's nature (the nature of the Good, *qua* ground of ethical claims) in this way. My objection to this view would therefore be that it assimilates the notion of 'revelation' too closely to that of common human experience, thereby subjecting it to the uncertainty and variability of human experience of this sort, and leaving unexplained the fact that God has disclosed himself to so few people on such rare occasions.

On the other hand, the notion of 'revelation' cannot be entirely dissociated from that of 'experience', for otherwise it would be difficult to see on what grounds anything could be accepted as revealed. It seems that what is required is the notion of an 'authoritative experient', whose word other men take on trust as expressing a level of insight to which they cannot attain, but whom they have reason to believe is trustworthy in these respects because his insights transcend insights of their own in the same direction.

Thus the Christian belief in an *authoritative source* of morality also finds a clear foundation in the notion of objectivity. It is not that the Christian subordinates his own judgement to that of the Church in an arbitrary way, but, basically, that he accepts the notion that in morals as in most other spheres of life there are expert authorities who are worth listening to. One must first, of course, assure oneself as far as possible that they are experts; and even then one must not leave their teachings untested. On the contrary, one must put them to the test in one's own experience to see whether they are consonant with the insights one has oneself achieved, or if they find any corroboration in subsequent experience. Such testing is necessarily a matter for sensitive practical wisdom; for one would not be dealing with 'revelation' if one could wholly demonstrate for oneself the truth of what is revealed. Rather it is a matter of using very inadequate tools to test whether the revealed doctrine does illumine one's own experience, or seem to fulfil or complement it in a new but perhaps not entirely unforeseen way; whether it marshals one's own ethical insights in one unitary vision; or whether, perhaps, it proposes only one more visionary dream which crumbles as it comes into contact with the hard facts. What one has always to bear in mind is that it is 'revelation' with which one is dealing, a claim to knowledge of truths one cannot oneself attain. How else, then, can one test it except by probing the reliability of the one who reveals, and the ability of the revealed truths to fulfil and transcend without contradicting one's own partial and obscure glimpses of the ethical claim on man? One can and should examine the fruits of the doctrines in men's lives in the way of fulfilment and moral excellence; and one can measure their fruits in one's own life as a power for renewal and regeneration. In fact, I would go so far as to say that, without such a personal experience of an immanent presence of the objective ideal in one, the claim of a transcendent objectivity remains a barren and austere one. When faced with its denial by naturalism of all types, one must perhaps ultimately fall back on some real experience of the Good, some immanence of the ideal which can stand in face of the assertion that it is a delusion.

I am certainly not saying that commitment to the Ideal is to be *founded on* personal experience—as though one could establish the existence of something by the simple claim to have experienced it—what I am saying is that without any such experience the argument to the objectivity of morals must remain at an abstract level, where it can have little force to counteract the strong claims of a naturalistic view which proposes a reasonable blend of benevolence and self-interest as its creed.

It should also be clear that I am not suggesting that the truth of a religious doctrine is to be judged solely by its efficacy in bringing about an integrated state of the human self. G. E. Moore has forever quashed the doctrine of pure pragmatism, that any assertion is true if it 'works'.[8] For I am not saying that a certain doctrine is true *if* it brings moral renewal; but that it would be rather more difficult to *establish* the truth of a certain doctrine if it did not have some effects on one's own experience.

7. This analysis helps to provide an answer to the question of whether, and how, Jesus can be a revealer of moral truths to men. For it might be said that if any moral principle is true it must be true everywhere and for all men, and knowable equally by all. But moral principles are grounded upon and derivable from specific truth-making features of reality (in the way suggested above); and the experience of these features is not equally available to all men. For the Christian, *what* is demanded is a specific responsive attitude, an attitude which is 'appropriate' to its object in that it is—uniquely—*demanded by* that object. The inculcation and constant maintenance of that attitude is the chief aim of the Christian life and the fulfilment of man's ethical goal. But for the average Christian there can be no question of a direct experience of 'the Good', demanding always and clearly the appropriate attitude to it. (It is to be noted again that this reactive attitude is *demanded*; it does not just happen to occur as a natural response; and so one must allow that, even in clear view of the demand, it could be refused. In this fact lies the resolution of the hoary problem of how Jesus, if he was other than we are, could genuinely be tempted. He was other than us in having a clear and constant knowledge of the Good; but like us in being susceptible to disobedience.) Thus, for the Christian, the response which is demanded—a response which must be specified by the description of the object which demands it—can only be received *on authority* from one who is believed to have the knowledge of the Good which we lack.[9]

Thus *what* Jesus reveals is the nature of the factual ground of ethical claims, not just a set of moral principles; he thereby specifies decisively the attitude which it is incumbent upon all men to aim at and adopt. He is able to reveal it because he alone of all men, Christians believe, had clear and constant knowledge of the Good. If men say that they do not stand in need of any moral revelation this is basically because—whether or not they reject objectivism as such—they reject the idea that there are degrees of vision of the objective ground of all moral rules. This, in turn, probably implies that they are content to accept a morality of rules or principles as opposed to one of attitudes. There is no logical reason, indeed, why men should not accept just the same principles, or attempt to cultivate just the same attitudes, as Christians, even though they do not do so *because* such attitudes are revealed. What the Christian would not allow them to claim is that they themselves attain such a clear vision of the ethical demand that they *see* what it requires without need of revelation—that is, that they base their attitudes on direct experience rather than on revelation by a unique experient.

Why should such a claim be ruled out of court? From what has been said so far it cannot be ruled out of court. All that can be said is that, as a matter of human experience, it is extremely rare for anyone to claim such direct and constant experience of the Good. This is sufficient to establish the notion of authoritative revelation in religion, and to show how it has a moral basis; but, of course, it is not sufficient to establish the truth or uniqueness of the Christian revelation. That cannot be accomplished without an examination of the concepts of 'the Fall', 'Atonement' and 'Redemption', which assure the uniqueness of Jesus, and which will be undertaken at a later stage.

# EXPERIENCE AND ANALOGY

1. The question which must now be examined is the thorny problem of the validity of religious experience; for it is, after all, in the religious experience of some particular person or group that revelation must find its source. The first feature of religious experience, which has already been stressed, is its essentially moral character. It is experience of that which, by its very nature, claims a specific responsive attitude from men. This fact already delineates some of the characteristics of the object of religious experience—it cannot be a natural, or empirical, object, which is perceived by means of some sense-organ. It cannot even be a supernatural object, which is perceived by means of a supernatural sense-organ or faculty of perception; for it is not just apprehended by a particular sense; it claims the whole person in an active and total experience. Thus it is that when men speak of knowledge of God they very often speak of such knowledge as being due solely to the initiative of God, to an overwhelming power of his grace, taking them out of themselves completely. It is because God's nature is to be the total claim on man's existence that this is so; but that should not blind one to the fact that it can very often be a long and arduous process, involving great discipline of the will, to tear away the veils which prevent this claim being encountered in its full reality.

Some recent theologians have tended to speak of 'knowledge of God' in terms of interpersonal relationship, or encounter, so that to have knowledge of God is to encounter the Divine Person.[1] There is a qualified sense in which this account is not misleading for one who is already a Christian (see Chapter VII). But as it stands it seems a very inadequate account of what experience of God must be. In the first place, it makes such knowledge too easy; as though it was a thing of no great difficulty to apprehend the Good itself; but this would make nonsense of 'revelation'. Then, it reduces the concept of God to the anthropomorphic level of 'personality', and so obscures the distinctive and central characteristic of total moral demand, which has no adequate analogy in the discourse of persons with each other. Finally, it is an inadequate account of the character of the experiences of those throughout the Christian tradition, and indeed in all the religious traditions of the world, who have spent their lives in the pursuit of God. To speak of the 'Divine Person' is, indeed, usually permissible for them; but only as part of a much wider concept which includes the *mysterium tremendum* as well as the 'Divine friendship', the *horrendum* as well as the *fascinans*.[2] In fact, apart from the specific Christian revelation, there is no reason at all to suppose that experience of God would be pleasant and fulfilling for the average man. If one can envisage a total moral demand, and contrast that with the rejection by man of that demand—a rejection which is obscured by the ambiguity and relativity of his moral situation but which is revealed by his apparently irremediable immorality—there is every reason to think that a clear vision of the Good would tear man asunder in revealing his rejection of that from which he cannot escape. This is part of the meaning of the doctrine of Hell, and no doubt part of the reason for the hiddenness of God in the world; that if men could see God as he is then, being what they are, they would suffer almost unbearable agony. God veils himself for our sake, that our freedom should not destroy us completely. (It is not, as Hick suggests, that complete knowledge of God would deprive us of freedom,[3] but that it would make our freedom unbearable.)

This account helps to answer the philosophical question, 'How do you know that it is *God* you experience, that you are not mistaken?' It does not provide a positive criterion but a negative one, in that it rules out a number of possible candidates for the divine object. Thus it cannot be any natural object; it cannot be any object which is not apprehended as total claim; and it cannot be any object which does not demand of us both dread and reverence—dread before the total claim which we deny, and reverence for the claim which we cannot fail to acknowledge. It can be seen that these criteria are established not just on the basis of some supposedly 'self-authenticating' experience, nor yet on the ground of a supernaturally infused revelation which contradicts our natural, 'fallen' reasonings; but by reflection on the foundations of our moral beliefs, the facts of the human situation in the light of those beliefs, a sympathetic consideration of the claims of those whom we believe to be more ethically perceptive than ourselves and an honest appraisal of our own state of moral development and insight. In other words, it is not just the intrinsic character of an experience which certifies its genuineness as an experience of God; it is also its consonance with a whole system of concepts by means of which we interpret our moral experience, and which do or do not support and corroborate each other as we find them leading us to expectations (about the character of future experience) which are subsequently fulfilled.

There can be no question, then, of having a bare, uninterpreted experience of 'God' which guarantees its own genuineness; any such experience will have to be interpreted by the use of concepts already available to us. Yet this fact should not lead one to the opposite extreme of saying that there is no specific characteristic, or inner quality, of the experience itself, over and above that 'read into' it by the interpretative concepts one brings to bear on it. That would be like saying that no matter *what* one experienced it could always be regarded as God, if one so interpreted it. Whereas the clear fact is that one can positively exclude all natural and most supernatural (or non-empirical) objects of experience from any possibility of being identified with God.

The great difficulty of characterizing the religious object is that it is, by its essential nature, unique; whereas all the concepts we ordinarily use in our language are universals which can be instantiated in many particular instances. Thus the concept 'table' is a class-concept which is properly applicable to many members of the class, each differing in specific detail but being recognizably similar to other members of the same class. And when we apply a concept to anything we pick that thing out from its environment and bring it under a general concept which relates it to many previously cognized, similar, discriminated entities. This, however, is just what cannot be done when one seeks to characterize the religious object by applying concepts to it. For it is not a member of a class of similar objects.

One might say that one should, nevertheless, be able to define ostensively the object of religious experience; but again the usual mechanism for ostensive definitions is lacking. One cannot, for example, use a finger to point to it; and one cannot even rely on the same phenomenon appearing to several observers in similar situations; for moral insight and reflective judgement are here at issue, and these cannot be determined in advance, or indeed at all, with any precision.

Perhaps one will say that at least one could ostensively define 'God' *to oneself*. But then, how could one convey to others its meaning? Or how could one convey its implications even to oneself? Indeed, how could a mere ostensively defined experience have any practical implications for one's conduct at all? Yet the essential characteristic of God is that he demands something—and something specific—from those who experience him. Thus it is not enough simply to invent a name for a special religious experience, as though all that was being done was to affix a label to it. Since what is in question is a specific attitude which is demanded, one needs to characterize that demand in terms which allow the attitude to be specified correctly. For this purpose, certain analogies drawn from the world of our dealings with objects and other people will have to be exploited and yet continually qualified, so that the nature of the demand can be recognized by its similarity to a range of other attitudes and yet the uniqueness of the demand may be preserved.

2. After the *via negativa* has done its work, then, and all particular and non-unique objects of experience have been decisively rejected as being possibly identical with God; then the way of 'qualified analogy' must come into its own. There is a vast literature on the theological doctrine of analogy; and the way in which I am using the term must be carefully defined. In the first place, I am postulating such a thing as a clear experience of a total moral claim, something which occurs to very few, and then very rarely on the whole. There is then no possibility of describing this claim by a specially coined ostensively defining name—for it has not only to be labelled in any way that occurs to one; it has to demand a specific responsive attitude from one—nor of describing it by univocal attribution—using a class-term in just the same way as when applied to similar members of the same class; for this claim is unique. Nor would there be much point in describing it by the use of an equivocal term—using the same word in two quite different senses, as in 'boot' as applied to a car and an item of footwear—for one would then be back in the position of attempted ostensive definition of one of those senses. The only remaining possibility is that terms drawn from other contexts of language must be applied to God analogically; but, apart from saying that this means 'neither univocally

nor equivocally', what exactly *is* meant by analogical attribution?

The classical discussion of the doctrine of analogy is to be found in St Thomas Aquinas' *Summa Contra Gentiles*.[4] The discussion presupposes acceptance of an Aristotelian metaphysics of essence and existence, act and potency, form and matter and of the arguments of the *Five Ways* which establish that ,God is pure act without potency, pure form without matter, and a being whose essence is simply to exist in a full and unlimited way. It is in the light of these doctrines that Aquinas constructs his doctrine of analogical attribution. He is certainly not speaking of a unique experience which has to be characterized in a unique way; in fact he denies the possibility of a natural vision of God. Nevertheless it is useful to recall what he said, if only because it is a *locus classicus* for this subject.

Aquinas begins from the doctrine that for every thing there is a genus, or essence, and that all such 'perfections' are to be found in God as the perfect source of all beings. According to *Summa Contra Gentiles*, Book One, Chapter 28–34: 'In every genus . . . there is . . . a measure for all other things in the genus. . . . Now the measure of all beings cannot be other than God. . . . No perfection, consequently, that is appropriate to this or that thing is lacking to him.' It follows from this doctrine that every perfection can be properly attributed to God; yet perfections cannot exist in God in the same way that they exist in creatures, which are finite and limited in their being and therefore always to some extent imperfect.

Some names, of perfections without defects, can be directly predicated of God—names like 'goodness', 'wisdom' and 'being', for example. Yet even here it must be noted that 'as to the mode of signification, every name is defective';[5] that is, they express things in the way in which the intellect conceives them, namely always as embodied in sensible things, not as simple and self-subsistent, pure forms. So these names, though they apply properly to God, cannot apply in the ways in which we must conceive them by means of 'our intellect, taking the origin of its knowledge from the senses'.[6] Other names can be applied to God only metaphorically; and they should always be qualified by a prefix of supereminence—'highest', 'first' and so on. These prefixes either negate sensible qualities—as in 'infinite' and 'eternal'; or they show how other things are related to God—as when we call him 'the first cause'. 'For we cannot grasp what God is, but only what he is not and how other things are related to him.'[7]

'It is thereby evident', Aquinas concludes, 'that nothing can be predicated univocally of God and other things.'[8] 'The things that God has made receive in a divided and particular way that which in him is found in a simple and universal way.'[9] On the other hand, the attribution of names to God is not completely equivocal. For created things are like God in the respect that their complete perfections are to be found in a simple, substantial and undivided way in him. The attribution of such names, then, must be analogical.

We come to know the meaning of the names applicable to God by means of his effects in the world; but in reality that which is properly denoted by the name belongs to God alone, and to created things only derivatively and partially. 'The reality in the names said of God . . . belongs by priority in God according to his mode of being, but the meaning of the name belongs to God by posteriority.'[10] So the word 'goodness', for example, is learned from certain empirical contexts; but in reality it applies to God by priority; and as human goodness stands to human nature so divine goodness stands to the perfections of the divine nature. The word applies to each thing in a way appropriate to the nature of that thing, and so is applied to each by the analogy of proportionality.

So, for Aquinas, every word which denotes a perfection can be applied to God; and as God is perfection itself such words apply most properly and completely to him; yet, our intellects being limited, we can only conceive the applications of the words to various sensible things; and we must say that they apply to God in a different way, which is proper to his perfect nature; and the relation between God's nature and this attribute is proportional to the relation between some finite nature and the attribute as conceivable by us. In this way we can never conceive what God is in himself; but we can conceive the relation in which created things stand to God, or the proportional difference which must exist between various attributes as we conceive them in created things and as they must exist primordially in the perfection of God's nature.

For Aquinas there are three kinds of analogy. First, there is the Analogy of Attribution; when a term which is properly attributable to one thing is applied to another. For instance, one may speak of a 'healthy man' and of a 'healthy complexion'. Here the term 'healthy' is only attributed extrinsically to his complexion; that is, it does not properly apply to the complexion itself but signifies only that the complexion is the symptom of health in men.

Second, there is the Analogy of Proportion; when a term is predicated of two things in a slightly different sense. For example, if one speaks of 'the light of the sun' and 'the light of reason', the term 'light' is used neither univocally, so that it means just the same; nor yet equivocally, so that it has quite a different meaning; it is applied analogically. There is some similarity of structure, at least in some important respects, between the two things.

And third, there is the Analogy of Proportionality; when a term is predicated of two things, the nature of one of which is unknown. This is the sense in which all perfections are predicated of God. We say, for example, that Divine goodness stands to God's nature as human goodness stands to human nature. There is a resemblance of relations here—the respective relations of 'goodness' to beings of a certain nature—but no claim to know what the nature of God is. So what is being said is that all perfections are ascribable to God since he is the First Cause of the world; but we cannot know how they apply to him since his nature is inconceivable to us.

The distinctive claim of the Analogy of Proportionality, then, is that certain concepts are appropriate to attribute to God; but their applicability must not be taken to imply that there is any structural isomorphism between God and those other things in the world to which the concepts apply; the concepts apply to God in a way proper to his nature which, in itself, is unknown to us. Moreover, the appropriateness of such attribution is to be found in the relation of things in the world to God (a relation, for Aquinas, of 'likeness of nature' between effects and their cause). For Aquinas this doctrine is a consequence of the basic postulates of Aristotelian metaphysics, that everything that comes to be has a cause, that the cause must be greater (or possess 'more reality') than its effect, and that it must be similar in nature to its effects.[11] I am not presupposing these postulates, nor attempting to construct a metaphysical concept of 'God'; my task is to enquire how one can talk of the Good, the ground of total ethical demand, in a way which may illuminate its character while preserving its uniqueness. Nevertheless, even in this very different task,

Aquinas' notion of the Analogy of Proportionality is not unhelpful. For he posits a way of talking which does not affirm any identity of structure between God and natural objects, but which nevertheless signifies a particular relation of the world to God which compels us to ascribe a certain term to him. Thus, for instance, we must say that God is good; the term 'good' *must* be affirmed of God in virtue of the fact that all good things are caused by him; but we cannot say that he is good in the way that other things are good, or in any particular way conceivable by us; he is good in a way proper to his own nature.

If we transfer this doctrine to the characterization of experience of the Good, one might say, first, that it is *ipso facto* experienced as demanding a specific responsive attitude. Suppose, now, that the attitude demanded—though naturally unique—is one that is very closely allied to the attitude of interpersonal love, in the sense of total devotion to the well-being of another person. In seeking to clarify the nature of the demand, to oneself as well as to others, one will be forced to attribute to the object of the demand those characteristics which would make the attitude appropriate and understandable. One may in this case, perhaps, have to characterize it as 'personal', 'worthy of esteem' and 'loving'. These are all terms which are taken from ordinary everyday experience; but in applying them to the Good one does not wish to suggest that it falls into the same class as such objects—one wishes to deny structural similarity. They must therefore be qualified by adding some term such as 'infinite' or 'holy', which makes clear this lack of similarity. Yet without applying some such terms it will be impossible to characterize the attitude which is demanded.

So, as in the Analogy of Proportionality, one *must* say (for instance) that the Good is personal in virtue of the fact that it demands a response as to a person; but one must deny that it is personal in the way that men are. One can only say that such characterizations are not seriously misleading: the attitudes they specify are the appropriate attitudes to the Good; but neither are they literally descriptive, even of any conceivable formal similarity between the Good and ourselves. It is because we are related to the Good in a way that demands a specific attitude or set of related attitudes from us, that we must characterize it by certain object descriptions which are then qualified to avoid any literal signification.

The doctrine of analogy is here being used in a different context from that of Thomism. It does not proceed on the basis of the causal postulate that 'the greater cannot come from the less', and thereby conclude to a simple unitary ground of all possible perfections by way of reflection on the general nature of the world. It proceeds from the ethical postulate that an objective Good lays a total claim on men and that exceptional individuals may be in a position to discern this claim without distortion, to ask how this discernment may be characterized in a way that may become authoritative for the conduct of others who do not or cannot achieve it.

3. A recent account of theistic language that also exploits the parallel with moral discourse rather than with scientific, is to be found in I. T. Ramsey's *Religious Language*.[12] Ramsey tries to take account of the cognitive claims and of the call to commitment which religious language involves; and he does so by means of the notion of a 'disclosure-situation'. Such situations are distinctive in two ways—first, in that they contain a unique discernment 'of the spatio-temporal and more'; and second, in that they involve total commitment following from the discernment. He provides a number of entertaining examples of discernment–situations, situations in which suddenly and unpredictably the 'ice breaks' or the 'penny drops' and we see something characteristically personal in a situation which may have been quite objective and impersonal before. 'To understand religious language or theology', he says, 'we must first evoke the odd kind of situation' for which it is the appropriate currency.[13] And, on the other hand, such distinctively religious situations can be evoked by suitably odd uses of language, when words are used, not to refer to or denote anything but to evoke an objective depth apprehended by a special sort of insight or disclosure. The commitment that such disclosure evokes is both total, in that it involves our whole personality, and universal—a commitment to the whole universe, or the whole of life.[14] Language gains such a use as this by taking certain object-words and qualifying them in a certain direction until, perhaps, they evoke a disclosure-situation. The object-words are models, and Ramsey suggests that absolutely anything can serve as a potentially religious model, though in fact some models are better than others in that they provide a richer source of fruitful metaphor and analogy. These models are qualified by the use of an operator-word which directs us to extend

the model-word in a certain way; thus 'change' or 'mutability' may be taken as a model and qualified by the prefix-operator 'im' to give the concept of 'immutability'. This prefix directs us to develop our concept of change until at some point we perhaps see 'the more' beyond all change; we have a disclosure which could only have come along this route, but yet lies on an entirely different logical level from any of the concepts along that route. Ramsey uses a helpful analogy from mathematics to explain this concept of disclosure as a sudden displacement to a new logical level. Take the number-sequence $1 + \frac{1}{2} + \frac{1}{4} + \frac{1}{8} \ldots 2$. The series converges towards the number 2, but never equals two except 'at infinity'. Now, writes Ramsey, 'If we said that "2" was the "infinite sum" . . . we can only mean that "2" is a number outside the series and of a different logical status altogether from the terms of the series, but a number which might be said to preside over and label the whole sequence of ever-expanding sums.'[15] Such a displacement as is involved in seeing that 2 is the infinite sum of the numbers in the series is what Ramsey would call a disclosure-situation, evoked by continuing the series until it discloses something beyond it and yet somehow completing it and making it intelligible. In this way disclosures might be evoked by talking in certain ways around certain themes until a displacement to a 'new logical level' occurs. That such a displacement takes place can never be guaranteed; no one can predict a disclosure, either as to where along the route it will occur, or whether it will occur at all, or which route might be most helpful for any particular person. But if one does occur, it will always disclose a transcendent 'X' seen through and by means of the qualified model, and it will call for total and universal commitment to what is disclosed.

But, it may be asked, exactly what *is* disclosed in these ways? The brief answer to this question is that what lies beyond the limits of referential speech cannot be referred to; and thus it is impossible to describe the object disclosed. All one can do is to say that it is whatever objectively declares itself to us as more than just the empirical facts along a certain route of qualification of a model. This being so, the qualified model as a whole is now taken to describe or stand for 'God'—the object of disclosure. But this description is nothing more than the allotment of a specific logical placing to the word 'God', giving its place in our language. The concept of 'God' becomes a 'keyword . . . expressive of the

M

kind of commitment one professes'.[16] We may thus call God 'love'; and what we are doing in this case is 'to claim that the word "God" can be given in relation to a total commitment which can be approached by considering those partial commitments which we normally describe in terms of the word "love".'[17] We take 'love' as our model and qualify it, perhaps by the operator 'infinite', so that we consider various situations in which the word ordinarily has currency, always seeking a greater and greater love; until, at some point, we do not come to the last term of this series of loves; rather we are suddenly enabled to pass outside the series altogether and find its completion on another logical level. This disclosure, and the commitment that inevitably comes with it, we designate by saying that 'God (the transcendent) is love'. And so we could designate God under many other descriptions so long as it was clearly realized that, in every case, the words were not meant literally, nor yet even analogically, but only to evoke or express a peculiar situation of discernment-commitment that has occurred in the process of qualifying some linguistic model in a particular way. In this way the meaningfulness of religious language is always traced back to a firm anchorage in experience; and it is in these 'odd' religious situations that the language of religion gains currency. And once this type of discourse is established it is developed in a way 'which, avoiding clashes with other well-established discourse about the Universe, leads to articulations which are subsequently verified, and is thus a context which in its totality is offered as the simplest, most consistent, most comprehensive, and most coherent map of the universe'.[18]

4. There are many points in this account which are substantially similar to the ones I have been attempting to make, but there are also one or two rather marked differences. Dr Ramsey is concerned with a non-empirical 'something' which demands total commitment and which has cognitive significance; which is objective, in my usage. And he develops the illuminating notion of a 'model', non-picturing in nature and qualified in various ways, which can be used to describe the object of commitment in a non-literal way. This is very close, though not identical, to the account I am suggesting; I have suggested that various models, or analogies, are chosen because of the attitudes which are felt to be

demanded of us; Dr Ramsey suggests that models are accepted
because they call to mind the sorts of context in which disclosures
(of a total non-empirical claim) have occurred. The similarity
between these accounts can be seen from Ramsey's example of
'love'. We call God 'love', he says, because the commitment
evoked by a specific disclosure is similar to and yet dimensionally
greater than the partial commitments normally described in terms
of the word 'love'. In the terminology of this chapter, the demanded
attitude is like and yet dimensionally greater than certain other
familiar attitudes characterized by the term 'love'. The fact which
makes this translation of terminology so easy is that the typical
situations which men tend to place themselves in, their habitual
responses to them, and the general way in which they develop
their moral insights, will naturally tend to affect the way in which
they characterize any apprehension of the Good, however partial,
which may fall to them.

But despite this similarity there are some aspects of Dr Ramsey's
analysis which seem to me to be potentially misleading. In the
first place, he undervalues apprehension of the Good—a rare
and momentous experience—by putting 'disclosures' on the
same footing as 'penny-dropping' situations, or even discernments
of 'personal depth' in some situation. These latter experiences
might well be called 'disclosures', sudden insight-situations, and
so forth; perhaps they occur quite frequently, and to most people.
But to place apprehension of the Good on this level is rather like
placing the scientific discovery of an Einstein on the same level
as the sudden feeling that I am in love. They are both 'disclosures',
doubtless; but there is a wealth of logical difference between
them; and it seems to me that apprehension of the Good must be
much more carefully guarded from confusion with other and lesser
insights than the use of the umbrella-term 'disclosure' will allow.

Again, it seems to me false to suggest that 'to understand
theology we must first evoke the odd kind of situation'. One can
*understand* theology without having oneself had direct experience
of its object—God—and if it were otherwise there would be no
room in the Christian faith for revelation, the acceptance *on
authority* that God is of such a nature. This point is bound up with
Dr Ramsey's claim that the use of religious language *springs
from* some 'discernment-commitment' situation which the user
himself has had, and that it has the *function of* evoking a similar
situation either in himself or in others.

One might say that one would not accept the Christian characterization of God unless one had a certain sort of 'disclosure', perhaps around the person of Jesus. But this would be a weaker sense of disclosure. It would in fact, I have suggested, be a decision to accept Jesus as an authoritative experient of the moral demand. Of course, this must be both a discernment of his moral authoritativeness and a commitment to what he declares to be true. Now it so happens that what Jesus declares to be true—and this is one of the things which differentiates him from almost all mystics—is that he is himself in a unique way the manifestation or representation of the moral demand; thus it is that the Christian has a commitment to Jesus as the *object* of his faith as well as a commitment to him as the *revealer* of that faith. Nevertheless, these are logically different types of commitment, and it seems to me that the Christians' acceptance of Jesus as the object of faith (as himself, in his human person, characterizing the ethical demand, the Good) depends upon the fact that this is a claim he made for himself.

There are undoubtedly those for whom the person and acts of Jesus formed the occasion of a specific discernment of the moral demand, which was then characterized in terms of analogies —of love, humility, service, and so on—drawn from experience of Jesus. But even for those who knew the historical Jesus this was evidently a slow, developing and unsteady experience. Peter's confession of Christ, not immediately attained, was succeeded by his denial. After the death of Jesus, succeeding generations of Christians have only the record of his life; for them it is the preaching of his death and resurrection which may sponsor a moral discernment; it certainly cannot be acquaintance with the historical person of Jesus. In any case, it is not just the loving conduct of Jesus which differentiates him from other men; nor his miracles of healing; it is his teaching about the coming of God's Kingdom, and his own central part in that coming. Without that teaching the crucifixion does not even make sense; it becomes just the death of an obstinate man unless it is seen in the context of a claim to Messianic status and destiny. I cannot see how anyone could have felt able to characterize the Good by the 'living analogy' of Jesus if he had not been able to assent to the teachings of Jesus. But how could men know that those teachings were accurate? Clearly they had to accept them simply on the authority of Jesus, though there were ways in which they might subsequently seek to verify them in experience (for example, will the Holy Spirit come with power?). It is thus Jesus' characterization of the Good which is authoritative, even, or above all, for the Apostles.


5. There are thus various strands of authority for the Christian. First, and supreme, are the authoritative declarations of Jesus concerning the Good and its relation to the world, and his own place in that relation. Even though it may not be possible to know what Jesus actually and exactly said, it is clear that his teachings formed the dominical basis of the utterances which are ascribed to him in the New Testament. Next come these writings of the New Testament, which can testify to an immediate disclosure around the person of Jesus. Third comes the tradition of Christian experience, shaped by the preaching of the Gospel and the shared experience of Christian community. It is only this third strand which is open to the individual Christian now; and it is quite incorrect to speak as though we, like the Apostles, could attain a disclosure centred on the actual historical person of Jesus. He has been dead for two thousand years; the context of our disclosures can only be the Church, the Bible and the activities of preaching and prayer. It is these which may sponsor an intuition of the moral demand and which constitute a testimony to its presence in the lives of the saints.

This admission of authority entails that there are various levels of intuition of the Good; that even if one believes oneself to have such an intuition one will carefully weigh it against the accumulated experience of the Church, against the Biblical writings, and subordinate it completely to the teachings of Jesus himself. Thus one will not say that all disclosures are of equal worth; and one will not suppose that one's own disclosures are of the same order as those of Jesus. If, indeed, some disclosure is required to become a Christian, it need only be the low-level sort of disclosure which brings one to see that Jesus is a unique moral authority. Thus religious language does not exist to characterize one's own disclosures; one must merely assent to certain spiritual experients as authoritative; and that may be an assent of will and reason rather than a matter of direct insight. Nor does it exist to evoke specific disclosure-situations. For though the Christian will hope for a clearer insight into the Good after death, he may not expect it on earth. One may even say that there are dangers in expecting it; for such expectation may lead one on a quest simply for 'religious experiences', which will deter one from attaining the true end of the Christian life—the love of God—and it is probable that the quest of the 'vision of God' is the vocation only of a few men, while most have other responsibilities and vocations. In other words, all Christians are not called to renounce the world; and all Christians must beware of seeking religious experiences just for their own sake—that is, for some emotional elation rather than for the pursuit of the Good in its total demand on the will for obedience. The Christian must, then, rely on authority, since few are able to achieve the vision of the Good; in the teaching of the Church, experiences of God are a matter of unpredictable and unmerited grace, not a matter of determination or resolute striving. Religious language is not primarily used, as Dr Ramsey seems to suggest, to *evoke* disclosures: it exists to characterize the discernment of an authoritative experient and thus to mould the responsive attitudes of Christians *whether or not* the cultivation of these attitudes tends to lead to a personal experience of 'disclosure'. Moreover, it is not sufficient to say that one can characterize the object of a disclosure by tracing the 'logical route' along which one proceeded to find it. For it is just here that one must defer to authority in selecting which vocabulary it might be appropriate to use.

Therefore, although it is true to say that the Christian characterizations of God (such as 'God is love') are based on experiences of a certain sort of moral demand, it must also be remembered that the experiences in question are those of Jesus, the uniquely authoritative experient. It is his clear and constant apprehension of the basic moral demand which is expressed by the predicates analogically attributed to God by Christians, and which remain authoritative for them whether or not these predicates spring from or evoke similar apprehensions in them. The function of such theistic predicates, in the Christian life, is thus not to express or arouse specific types of experience, however 'odd', but to specify a general attitude and policy of action towards one's experience. The achievement of some direct awareness of God, as the factual ground whose apprehension makes the Christian analogies appropriate, is a matter of grace, not of right, and the most that Christians can hope is that they will now see dimly what they desire to see more fully beyond this life.

# XII

# THE THEISTIC ATTITUDE

1. I have said that the function of the predicates ascribed to God by the Christian is to specify a general attitude to experience; and that such predicates are ultimately founded upon the authoritative experience of Jesus. In subsequent chapters the grounds for accepting such an authoritative experience will be examined; but first, more needs to be said about this notion of the specification of a general attitude. For it may be felt that human attitudes are purely subjective, psychological phenomena; and therefore that if Christian assertions are to be construed as fundamentally concerned with specifying such attitudes, they will lose all contact with putative objective realities. The facts, it might be said, are one thing; and our feelings about or attitudes to the facts are another.[1] So statements about God really must be about God; and what my attitude to God is, is a quite irrelevant matter.

This position is, however, vastly over-simple. To say one is ascribing a predicate to God cannot be like saying that one is ascribing a predicate to some physical object, say a table. For whereas a table is identifiable independently of any specific predicate, God is not. To speak of God is to speak of the moral demand; and naturally one cannot say anything about the demand without saying what is demanded—which is, I have held, a specific attitude. Thus to say, for example, 'God is love', is not to say that some independently identifiable being is loving. It is to say, in part, that the moral demand is such that it claims an attitude appropriate to a loving being (or at least analogous to it). The statement is thus about a demanded attitude of mine, rather than a description of some object. On the other hand, this ought not to lead one to the opposite extreme of supposing that religious statements can be solely about subjective feelings or attitudes and not at all about objective states of affairs. This is the extreme which Paul van Buren seems to espouse in *The Secular Meaning of the Gospel*; and it is aptly expressed by his statement that 'Religious language can be understood as outlining a way of life, *not* as a set of cosmological assertions' (my italics).[2] This position is not so much false as logically impossible, at least if a 'way of life' is interpreted as a characteristic attitude to all one encounters in life. For it is a logical truth that the expression of an attitude entails the existence of some factual as well as evaluative beliefs in the mind of the person who expresses it. One could not say of anyone that they expressed an attitude if they did not have certain factual beliefs about its object; and one could not describe their attitude correctly without mentioning the object to which it is directed.

The reason for this lies in what may be called the 'intentionality' of the human passions; the fact that they are essentially directed to certain objects outside themselves. Human attitudes are not just private mental occurrences which are recognized and named by introspection, just as colour-patches or physical objects may be picked out and described by observation. We learn from others how to use words for specific feelings; and though this does not entail that there is no private mental state which they may denote, it does follow that the use of such words must be learned in contexts of public action and behaviour, that it cannot be only to denote private mental states.

But if attitudes are not just private mental states, neither are they completely reducible to dispositions to behave in certain ways, as Professor Ryle suggests in the following characteristic analysis of the attitude of 'vanity': 'He boasted on meeting the stranger and his doing so satisfies the law-like proposition that whenever he finds a chance of securing the admiration and envy of others, he does whatever he thinks will produce this admiration and envy.'[3]

This account may have some plausibility in the case of a few human feelings and attitudes; but there are others, and among them some of the most important, which resist analysis into 'law-like propositions' about overt behaviour. Consider, for example, the case of 'worship'. Is it just the tendency to attend church, recite prayers and so forth? One may do these things without worshipping; yet one might not be feigning; one might want to worship but not feel one was succeeding, so it would not be deception or pretence, as Ryle might want to hold. Well, could it be the tendency to perform these acts by inclination? One may enjoy church-going without worshipping, however—one may enjoy the ritual. So one must enjoy performing these acts for the right reason, it seems. But the right reason is simply to honour God; and now it becomes plain that the very performance of the acts in question could not be accurately described without incorporating the intention with which they are performed—to worship—into the description. It would be wrong to describe such an act as 'inclining the head', for instance; but right to describe it as 'bowing'—that is, showing reverence—that is, performing the physical act with the intention of showing reverence.

'Worship' has been adduced as just one of a large class of intentional acts which, to be the sort of acts that they are, must be done with the intention of expressing certain beliefs; and in every case the verb characterizing the act is non-exponible—it cannot be eliminated in favour of any translation in terms of overt behaviour alone. 'Worshipping' is not a further act in addition to the physical acts of bowing, kneeling, and so on; it is one's intention in acting, and only if one has the intention does one worship. So at least in the case of intentional attitudes it is not possible to analyse them out as tendencies to perform acts of various kinds, since those acts can only be properly described as intentions to express certain beliefs about objects.

Just as intentional acts like 'worshipping' are expressions of non-exponible beliefs, so the attitudes which underlie them—in this case, 'reverence'—are not necessarily accompanied either by recognizable feeling-states or behavioural expressions. One may have the attitude of 'reverence' without expressing it behaviourally at all; and one may ascribe it to oneself not on the grounds that a specific feeling-state has occurred but solely on the grounds that one has those beliefs and evaluations which are characteristic of it.

In saying this I do not wish to deny that, if there were no overt expressions of any emotions, we could not in fact have learned to describe them as we do. Nor do I wish to deny that there are usually, in fact, overt verbal expressions of reverence by reference to which we learn the use of that word. On the contrary, I regard both these statements as true. All I want to do is to suggest that attitudes form a specific class of intentional acts—those which may be called mental acts, since these are not necessarily tied to any behavioural concomitances—and that consequently it is not possible to describe them correctly merely by describing either a sequence of behavioural dispositions or by describing a privately introspected mental state. An essential element in the correct description of an attitude is the mention of beliefs about and evaluations of the sort of object to which it is directed.[4]

For example, the attitude of claustrophobia is not described by saying what a specific inner state feels like; nor just by citing one's overt behaviour in confined spaces. It is properly describable only by citing the reason for such behaviour, which is a fear of being in a confined space; that is, by citing the subject's belief that confined spaces represent a threat to his safety or well-being. This is a belief about a sort of object—namely, confined spaces— as representing a threat. In this case the attitude is pathological, since the object of one's attitude, though it exists, does not have the characteristic (of threatening) which one attributes to it. But whether pathological (that is, mistaken in its description of its object) or not, my attitude could not be correctly and fully described without this mention of its object and the adumbration of my beliefs about and evaluation of that object; and it could not be expressed without my belief, whether consciously formulated or not, that confined spaces are dangerous or threatening.

It is consonant with this account that we often ascribe attitudes to others not on the basis of their bodily behaviour or introspective reports but on the basis of assertions they make which express their beliefs and evaluations. And we often ascribe attitudes to ourselves not because we detect a *sui generis* mental occurrence but because we interpret some elements of our experience in such a way as to specify particular attitudes towards them.

Thus the attitude of hope and confidence is specified by a particular description of the imagined future course of events in the world. The object which specifies that attitude is a future state, which I desire. So it is incorrect to suggest that an attitude can be held without regard to the facts, since the specification of the attitude depends on a particular description or interpretation of the facts—even though such interpretations may not be assigned on purely empirical grounds. This is true of all those philosophers and theologians who have tried to give an account of religious belief in terms of the expression of feelings or attitudes and their evocation in others.

One of the best known is Schleiermacher who writes, in a famous phrase, 'The self-identical essence of piety is this: the consciousness of being absolutely dependent'.[5] He cannot here be saying that religion depends only on the occurrence of a certain characteristic mental state; if this were so it is strange that no one seems to have remarked upon its existence before; and if it really is essentially a religious feeling it is equally strange that all arguments for religion should not have been replaced long ago by attempts to induce this feeling in those who have not yet had it.

But Schleiermacher is not pointing out a feeling which had previously escaped our notice. What he is pointing out is that we ordinarily feel dependent in many ways—on fathers, employers, governments; and that since there is a Creator of the world we ought to feel dependent upon him in every way—absolutely dependent. He is evaluating 'dependence' as a right attitude, and so hopes to inculcate the characteristic feeling associated with it over the whole range of human experience. There is nothing *sui generis* or uniquely important about 'dependence'; its importance lies in the fact, if it is a fact, that there is a Creator upon whom we are all dependent. So Schleiermacher offers us a new concept which we must learn to apply in our experience; or rather we have to interpret our experience in such a way that the concept may find an application. In recommending the attitude he is advancing certain beliefs about and evaluations of the world; and in deciding to adopt the suggested attitude we are also necessarily adopting the description of the world which specifies it.

To take one final illustrative example: Cook Wilson has maintained that 'reverence' is a *sui generis* feeling which in some way guarantees the existence of its object, God.[6] But again, this is not a case of the occurrence of a mental state being used as a premise in an existential proof. One could only characterize a mental state as 'reverence' by reference to a description of its object, not by mere introspection. Naturally, the occurrence of an attitude of 'reverence' guarantees the existence of a belief in its appropriate object, since only such a belief about an object enables the attitude to be specified as 'reverence'. But to know whether 'reverence' is a pathological or an appropriate attitude one must know, in a logically prior way, whether its object exists or whether its description is correct.

So far from religious beliefs being adequately expressible in terms of feelings or attitudes, the question of the appropriateness and even the correct description of those attitudes immediately drives one back to the consideration of the allegedly factual descriptions of the objects of belief which are required to specify the attitudes.

In this way, it can be seen that if the Christian commitment is primarily to a distinctively agapeistic attitude, then, since attitudes are only characterizable in terms of their objects, such commitment presupposes belief in the truth of the factual descriptions which are necessary to define the religious object.

2. Two problems which immediately arise are, first, what is the 'religious object'?; and second, what makes it specifically religious? My suggestions here must be very brief and rather impression-istic—an outline of a possible answer rather than an answer. First, I think that the main characteristic of the objects of religious attitudes is what I would call their 'totality', their unrestricted applicability over the whole range of human experience. To make this a little clearer I will introduce a technical definition of the term 'experience'. At any one point of time in the history of an individual person there exists for him a field of perceptual presentations of various sorts—visual, aural, olfactory, tactual, and so forth—which is of finite extent. Whether the objects so presented by the senses are directly perceived physical objects, or sense-data, or something else, I wish to leave an open question; but that there often exist such finite sets of sensory presentations to persons at particular times seems as certain as anything else known to me. I wish to call any such finite field, in its totality at a given time, an 'experience'. Then the history of any person will consist of a succession of such experiences, of such finite sensory totalities. It is experiences, in this technical and restricted sense, which are characterized by some set of descriptions of the religious object. It would be incorrect to restrict these descriptions to some particular features within any experience (as, for instance, we restrict descriptions of material objects, like 'tables', to some particular features within some experience); and it would be incorrect to restrict them to some experiences and not to others. The descriptions must be used to characterize *each* total experience and *every* experience in the history of the believer. Thus the religious attitude may be called 'total' in two senses; it applies to the totality of any experience, and it applies to the totality of all the experiences of the believer. Thus language about God is not intended to describe some remote being in a supernatural realm; it deals with man's relation to some present reality, the characterization of which enables us to specify a particular and

characteristic attitude towards the whole of our present experience.

To say that this reality—'God'—is the object of many human acts such as praying, worshipping, trusting, and so forth, is to say that it is an object towards which we direct one attitude or a set of related attitudes. To say that he is the subject of many acts—God loves, creates, sustains—is to characterize the nature of this object and thus to specify or articulate the appropriate attitudes more closely. There is no question of learning to identify God as the subject of many independently identifiable acts; we do not first identify an act of loving or creating and then identify God as the agent who performs these acts. On the contrary, to attribute such acts to God is simply to characterize him as the object which specifies our present attitude to the whole of our experience. Thus if one says 'God loves men', one means to recommend the 'appropriate' attitude of responsive love, an attitude of trust, thankfulness and obedience. And if one asks to which object in particular this attitude is to be directed, the answer must be, to no particular object within experience; and to no particular empirical pattern within experience. It must be directed to 'Being-itself', to the whole of reality, to God who is unlimited and pure actuality. And it seems to me that these expressions are all ways of saying that the object of the religious attitude provides a characterizing description of, without being identifiable with, every experience we undergo. The description which specifies our attitude is to be applied to every new situation we encounter, so that we meet and respond to each experience as (in the Christian scheme) a claim, or a gift, or a judgement—in short, an encounter with the object which is characterized by the set of theistic descriptions we accept. It is because the function of religious concepts is to specify an attitude, a reactive response to the whole of one's future experience in this way without exception, that one cannot identify God with any particular empirical occurrences within the world (though this does not exclude the possibility that such occurrences may be taken as manifesting the correct characterization of God, as Jesus is by Christians); and one cannot equate belief in God with the discernment of any distinctive occurrences or patterns in experience.

This, I suggest, is a way in which some objections to speaking of God as both immanent and transcendent may be overcome. One may, on the account I have suggested, say that God is immanent in the sense that the concept of 'God' provides a description which must be applied to every experience. And God is transcendent in that the concept cannot be said to be instantiated in any particular experience. Consequently, it is said to define a relation or set of relations which holds between every particular empirical experience and a reality which is transcendent with regard to every experience, and yet determines the description which must be given of the most general features of human existence, thus defining man's attitude to that existence in which he participates.

The point of a specific characterization of God, on this account, is that it should be able to provide a set of descriptions under some of which every experience whatsoever can be subsumed. Thus it might be said to provide a characterization of Being as a whole. But when I say this, I do not mean to imply that it can be used, for instance, to explain the occurrence of physical phenomena or to justify the axioms of scientific enquiry; in fact, I think that the areas of conflict between the empirical sciences and religious dogma have been largely produced because believers have thought, wrongly, that religious concepts could be so used. I have maintained, however, that the real use of concepts of God is not to explain empirical phenomena at all, but to specify a particular attitude to experience. To say that a concept of God characterizes the whole of reality, or Being-itself, is not to say that it denotes an impossible intuition of the whole of reality at once; it is to say that it specifies the attitude which it is proper to adopt to the whole of human experience, past, present and future—the concept is to be used to interpret all future experience without qualification. And a concept cannot perform this function unless it has existential force and asserts the appropriateness of some descriptions to speak of the relation between a transcendent reality and human experience. It is in this sense that the question of the existence of God must be a question of fact; and thus the existence of the theistic attitude is logically inseparable from the affirmation of that fact.

3. Applying this analysis to the Christian faith, the believer's attitude to each and every experience will be one which is specified by the concept of 'God' as Creator, Sustainer and Redeemer. His reactive attitude to each experience will be an attitude *as* to a sustaining, providential, personal being; but that being will not

be locatable anywhere within experience; it will be experience itself which is conceived in this way, and thus as mediating or manifesting a being of such a nature. This, I think, is how one can construe such statements as, 'We always live in the presence of God'. The aim of the Christian's life is to achieve and maintain the attitudes to experience which are specified by theistic descriptions of the religious object. Here, perhaps, one can understand what some moral theologians mean when they say, 'God loves you; therefore you ought to love God'. As an argument this is clearly a non-starter; it has not even enough logical form to be fallacious. But it can make sense if the statement 'God loves you' is taken as a description of the religious object—that is, 'There exists a loving being'—which then specifies an appropriate total attitude. And this interpretation has the merit of avoiding the reduction of Christian ethics to concern for others which, laudable though it is, is a purely human ethic.

The Christian description of the religious object is not a result of philosophical speculation as to the nature of reality; it is given on the authority of Jesus who claimed a unique knowledge of that object. He is authoritative for the Christian life not because he expounded a moral code or principle of agapeism—which anyone could have done—but because he revealed the nature of God as loving, redeeming Father to whom the appropriate attitude is worship, thanksgiving, humility, love and commitment. There is a place for authority and revelation in Christian ethics, then, when the distinctiveness of the Christian life is seen as the commitment to a total attitude which is specified by an authoritative description of its object, 'God'.

4. But what sort of factual description can be given of God which will serve to specify a particular total attitude to experience? It may seem that, since God is not an independently identifiable object, there is nothing that can be said about him except that he demands certain attitudes of men. And this could hardly be said to be the provision of factual data for specifying an attitude—it answers the question, 'Why should one love God?' with the statement, 'Because God demands love'. Such a reply, however, goes no way towards showing that love is the appropriate attitude to take to God. As I have tried to show in this chapter, if the attitude is to be called appropriate, God must be known to have

a nature that would make it appropriate. How can this be done? I think that the way lies neither in the purely moral observation that one feels obliged to take up a specific attitude, in a specific situation, to the things in that situation; nor in the purely descriptive observation that there is a being—God—which, as can be established by some factual technique, has such-and-such properties. The way lies in an examination of the moral demand itself, its relation to all the situations in which men find themselves and the consideration of what attitude it is proper to adopt to it. Thus one's attitude to God is not to be considered as just one extra item in a catalogue of duties—one which depends on whether or not one believes God to exist—but as an attitude to that which is the ground of all one's duties; and thus as an attitude which is of greater generality than and an all-pervasive influence upon the ways in which one conceives those duties.

In the Christian religion—and possibly in all religions deserving the name—there is a three-fold division within the general religious attitude; and the first element has already been examined in preceding chapters. This is the element of reverence, awe or dread which may, in a restricted sense, be called 'worship'. Kant was one of the first moral philosophers to examine this attitude in any detail; and he designated the Moral Law as the object of reverence, a law which categorically commanded men and at the same time lowered their self-esteem by exposing their inadequacies.[7] At any rate, the object of this attitude cannot be any human life, however exalted, since men do no more than *exhibit* goodness—and then deficiently. The object of worship, however, is the ground of goodness itself, 'the Good', that which commands the allegiance of all men without exception. Furthermore, as was suggested in Chapter IV, the notion of 'the Good' develops into the concept of a necessary Creator and goal of the contingent Universe; and thus 'worship', as one element of theistic belief, is an attitude specified by the concept of a necessary ground of all moral value, a Creator and foundation of moral obligation, a being beyond beings from whom we come and to whom we go, on whom we are absolutely dependent and by whom we are totally claimed.

This notion is not specifically Christian; nor does it depend upon any special revelation since it can be derived from an examination of the foundations of moral experience. It is rather a presupposition of accepting even the possibility of the Christian revelation as a revelation about the being of God. The second element of the theistic attitude is one which has also been mentioned in preceding chapters though it has not been developed at any length. That is the element of contrition, confession or repentance, which is sometimes and misleadingly, to my mind, called 'guilt'. It is produced by the acknowledgement that one always fails to do what one ought; and, moreover, that the human situation appears to be one of alienation or estrangement from the moral demand which is its ground. For the characteristics of relativity, ambiguity and perversion which appertain to human ideals all suggest that, in some way, the world of human existence is opaque to the moral demand as it really is. Again, this belief seems to be common to all world religions. But Judeo-Christianity is distinctive in its insistence that this 'alienated' condition of the world is due to man's free rejection of the moral demand, to what the Genesis story describes as a primal disobedience. It is this notion of a free rejection which cannot now be negated or overcome, a past act which cannot be annulled, which produces the peculiarly Judeo-Christian poignancy of contrition and the need for expiation.

The third element of the theistic attitude is that of thanksgiving, hope and commitment to practical action; and it is this element which enables the Christian attitude to be called 'agapeistic', which gives the predominating Christian mood of the 'love of God'. The object of thankfulness is primarily the redemptive act of God in Christ; the object of hope is the promise of the fulfilment of this redemption after death; and the incentive to commitment is the belief that the world is the sphere of Divine redemption—that it is not to be left to itself but to be changed, renewed and redeemed by men as the living body of Christ. When the theistic attitude is seen in its complete three-fold articulation it becomes more apparent how the one phrase 'God is love' can epitomize the whole complex attitude. The love of God is seen in creation; in the positing and calling of man into fullness of being; in the patience which endures rejection by the creation; and in the final triumph of redemption through suffering. These are the facts which specify the human responsive attitude to the Divine reality; they are facts about the human situation in relation to the moral demand; and the Christian believes that Jesus is in an uniquely authoritative position to apprehend these facts of the human situation, for reasons which will be explored

N

more fully in Chapter XIII. So it is that the Christian ethic consists in adopting a total attitude to experience, and depends essentially upon the acceptance of factual beliefs about the being and nature of God. It is in these beliefs (themselves, however, matters of assessment and evaluation rather than simple detached observation), in their function of specifying a particular way of life, and in these alone, that the distinctiveness of Christian ethics consists.

# XIII

# THE AUTHORITY OF CHRIST

1. The ethics of Christianity must be founded upon authority; and ultimately this authority must be traced back to the experience of the man Jesus. For it is he who, on the basis of his own experience, promulgated those factual characterizations of the nature of the moral demand in its relation to human existence which specify the total, specifically Christian attitude which is sometimes called 'agapeism' or 'the love of God'.

It is clear that, on this view, all forms of so-called 'secular' Christianity must be ruled out, as they are unable to offer any adequate account of the revelatory character of Christian ethics. Accordingly, they are not able to retain any essential connection of their faith with the historic person of Jesus; and therefore they fail to be distinctively—that is, uniquely and solely—Christian. Views like those of Professor R. B. Braithwaite,[1] which see the story of Jesus simply as an inspiration for following an 'agapeistic' way of life, cannot provide any plausible ground for distinguishing between the real and an imagined life of Jesus. That is, it would not matter whether Jesus existed or not for the story to have its inspirational effect; and, of course, one may doubt whether what Braithwaite calls 'agapeism' is the same as the attitude which I have called by the name. The attitude he recommends seems indistinguishable from respect for persons, which is the fundamental principle of humanism. There is, of course, nothing wrong with that; indeed it is wholly admirable. But I think that it would be a mistake to suppose that it is equivalent to that love of God which includes the elements of worship, penitence and thankfulness, and which is directed to the whole of one's experience. Concern for one's fellow men is just a part of this complex attitude; and there is a case for saying that it is only within the larger context of the total attitude that Christian concern for others can take on its own characteristic mode. It may well be that humanists will wish to reject the Christian interpretation of concern for others; but that again points up the objectionable vagueness of a word like 'agapeism', when it is not more precisely defined.

Just as it is quite inadequate to try to base Christian faith on a prior and independently selected moral commitment to 'agapeism' —since to know what agapeism is, for a Christian, one has to be able to specify his total attitude—so also it is useless to attempt to dispense with metaphysical assertions about the being of God and replace them with statements about the effect the historic Jesus has on those who hear about him. According to such views, one is said to see in Jesus an 'ultimate depth'; as Bishop Robinson puts it, 'It is in his [Jesus'] utter self-surrender to others in love, that he discloses and lays bare the Ground of man's being as Love'.[2] *What* is disclosed is the *ground* of man's being; but what is a 'ground'? Is it a cause? Or a goal? Or if not, what? One may say that here in this life we see a pattern of living—of total openness to others—which we feel compelled to accept for ourselves. The trouble with this talk is that it is absolutely ambiguous as between a prescriptivist and a teleological account of moral commitment. Is it just that this vision of a pattern of life fires one's imagination so that one prescribes it to oneself as a pattern? Or is it that in that pattern there lies the *truth* of human life; that is, the 'true nature' or 'final end' of human being, that which is an objective claim on all men? If the former, one does not escape the conclusion which prescriptivists must accept, that truth or falsity is of no concern to morality. If the latter, how can one discern man's final end simply by seeing Jesus? His example may, indeed, psychologically help us to see how we ought to live. But that insight is surely not wholly dependent on the life of that one man. And, in any case, religion is concerned not only with how we ought to live but with the nature of the facts which obligate us to live in a certain way. What is the fact about Jesus which obligates us? It cannot be just the fact *that* he loved; though it may serve as an inspiring example it is not a morally obliging fact. It must be a fact somehow disclosed to us *through* him.

Now we move on to the objectivist interpretation, that *something* declares itself in Jesus; not just that his life becomes a moral inspiration, an example of a fine human possibility to us. This fact is usually conceived as a 'Thou' or at least a quasi-personal 'depth'; one may perhaps say that in and through the love of the man Jesus one discerns a love which transcends human being and which is the 'ground' of it (in an unexplained sense)—a transcendent or non-empirical love.

Such a view, however, neglects the consideration that the Christian records of Jesus do not simply speak of a loving man; they record the teachings of one who spoke with, and claimed, authority. Since the New Testament records are the only records we have of Jesus, it seems very implausible to say that Jesus' life reveals an objective demand to others while doubting the truth of his own claim to a morally authoritative experience. If Jesus is to be regarded as a decisive figure for one's own life, one must stress his teachings about himself at least as much as the moral worth of his life. And thus one is compelled to assess not only Jesus' life but his claims to authority before there can be much point in declaring allegiance to him by taking the name 'Christian'.

2. But how can one assess claims to authoritative experience of this sort? Fortunately, perhaps, men who claim to experience the Good directly are exceptionally rare; and most of them do already accept the basic truth of a particular religious tradition (that is, the adequacy of the concepts current in that tradition to interpret the nature of the demand which is made upon them). It is the founders of religious traditions who, starting from a current set of concepts, feel the need to develop them in certain ways to correspond to their own deeper insights. There are two elements involved here: the question of the interpretative adequacy of concepts, which is largely a matter of rational reflection, together with an essential element of 'insight'—an ability to realize new connections, relate hitherto disparate points, and see all human experiences fitting into a new pattern—which is the metaphysical element; and the question of the character of the experience involved, which is what chiefly distinguishes the religious man from the philosopher. The philosopher may talk about 'salvation' or 'union with God' (though rarely in twentieth-century Britain); the religious authority claims to have achieved it. Only the former element is susceptible of rational assessment; for the latter one can only depend on the testimony of those who knew the authority at first hand. And even in the former case there is no direct method of assessment one can use, since what one has to assess are the doctrines of a few claimants to authoritative experience. But it is clear that general metaphysical considerations must inevitably enter into such assessment; even in outlining

what an 'experience of God' cannot be, I have drawn on considerations connected with a certain basic attitude to the moral life, and to a certain predisposition to see certain sorts of moral belief as fulfilling or transcending one's own, and other sorts of moral belief as falling short of or contradicting it. It is hopeless to pretend that one can start from nowhere, as it were, without any criteria of judgement or evaluation. At the most basic level, therefore, all one can suggest is that one should be sincere to what one is, and always be on guard against self-deception. What philosophical reflection can do is to make explicit the beliefs one tends to hold, to try to render them internally consistent and adequate to cover all the data of one's experience, to unify them so far as is possible into a coherent system, and to clarify the meaning and grounds of our beliefs. In extreme cases this reflective process may lead one to reject certain beliefs one has previously held; but the general effect will be in the refining and systematizing and therefore in the general strengthening and confirming of the system of beliefs one already has. What I am saying is that in most cases philosophy does not and cannot help to decide the ultimate grounds of one's beliefs, the criteria which one finally adopts: reflection works *within* the area of what is given. But what it can do in that area is of immense importance; it is only the activity of reflection which can modify general schemes of belief to cope with new human experiences, which can make them clear and consistent and which can place them within a coherent and intelligible pattern of experience. As examples of what I mean I would say that any Christian who now maintains the falsity of the theory of evolution on the basis of the Genesis creation-story, just cannot be concerned to establish a really coherent and adequate conceptualization of the whole range of human experience which is available to him, and which includes the sciences of zoology, geology and astronomy. Again, a Christian who says 'I believe, because it is absurd' is simply erecting a wall of invincible stupidity which will bar any attempt to render his beliefs consistent. And those who deny the existence of God but hope to find in the story of the death of Jesus some significant message for their own lives are flying in the face of all the demands of human reason—which does not demand strict proofs of everything, as is sometimes supposed, but which does demand some intelligible reason *why* the death of a Galilean peasant should be significant two thousand years later. It is only if some sort of real connection between Jesus and contemporary men can be made out that Christianity can be more than absurd; and it is the business of rational reflection to try and make clear what real connections there are (here a complex scheme of concepts will be needed, relating the historic Jesus to an eternal Christ, and these to an indwelling Spirit in men, and so on). Thus one must seek economy and consistency within the conceptual scheme of a religion, coherence of the scheme with conclusions in other areas of human investigation, and adequacy to interpret and illuminate the data of practical experience.[3] If these are not sought, one's religious beliefs will remain at a primitive and superstitious level; if they are not found, a religious scheme will, to that extent, become irrational.

3. As well as these general rational criteria for reflection on given data, there is also the element of 'insight', which is usually adopted as one's own from another person but which is a talent of specific individuals. This element helps to determine what the data of reflection are, and I can think of no better characterization of it than the one provided by Professor Wisdom in his paper 'Gods', which I shall summarize briefly here.[4]

He takes the ways in which two people can have quite different attitudes to someone they both know, even though they both know all that there is to be known about this person. One may say, 'He is mean and self-centred'; but the other may expostulate, 'No! on the contrary, he is prudent and sagacious'. Now what is the difference here? Wisdom says, 'The first may have noticed what the other has not although he knows no incident . . . about which the other doesn't know too'.[5] Even when what they actually observe is the same they may notice different facts, discern a different pattern, emphasize particular features, disagree about motives and the assessment of actions. In such cases as this, Wisdom claims, we see different facts, but cannot entirely dissociate 'what there is' from 'how we feel about it'; nor is there any question of finding out what the facts 'really are'.

In trying to evoke a discernment in others of the pattern we see, we use what Wisdom calls 'the Connecting technique', a sort of reasoning that 'is not vertically extensive but horizontally extensive—it is a matter of the cumulative effect of several independent premises, not of the repeated transformation of one or two (as in deductive or inductive inference)'.[6] He suggests that this technique is used by lawyers in deciding, for example, whether a certain body is or is not a public authority. To decide this we present and represent various features of the case which 'severally co-operate in favour of the conclusion'. To decide the issue we must weigh the cumulative effect of severally inconclusive premises; so also, he suggests, in aesthetic disputes where talk leads us to see paintings in a different light, to see the beauty we had missed; here reasoning, redescription and reobservation go together. Now this is in some sense, he suggests, a discovery of new facts, and may be rational or irrational; for we want 'appropriate attitudes' and reactions. So we sometimes try to dissuade someone from his attitude by pointing out various analogies and likenesses, patterns and connections we feel he must have missed; but then if he admits these and persists in his attitude 'we then feel that perhaps it is we who are blind and cannot see what he can see'.[7] To have the right attitude is to react appropriately to a situation; and it is the technique of 'connecting and disconnecting' which may help us to see what is and what is not appropriate.

There can be no formalizable set of rules governing this process of reassessing and redescribing in various ways and under different aspects. But it remains an essential part of any reasonable attempt to assess religious claims. It is by marshalling certain aspects, making certain stresses within experience, and so posing a series of hints and prompts, inklings and persuasions, that one will come to a view of the nature of human existence in its relation to the transcendent demands of morality (and to admit such a relation is already to have adopted a specific view, based on an acceptance of the ultimacy of moral claims). One must ask, for instance, whether suffering seems to be an integral part of existence as such which can only be relieved by non-existence; whether it seems rather to be a reflection of an alienated but fundamentally good world; whether it seems to express the birth pangs of a 'nobler world in travail'; or whether it signifies the demonic character of a world in opposition to goodness. These are the sorts of question which require an attempt to assess the character of human existence as it actually is, in the light of the final end which is demanded by the Good. And such assessment requires the sort of insight Wisdom speaks of, an increased sensitivity and awareness, breadth of vision and clarity of perception. There are no finally compelling answers; one can only stand by one's own fundamental convictions while being always prepared to adopt and extend them if others can help us to come to see what they see, but we do not.

Thus a Christian will claim that the most adequate interpretation of human existence is provided by the central concepts of his faith: the concepts of Creation-Fall-Atonement-Redemption. But great sensitivity is needed here; for the interpretation can be put in a crude and brutal form and without real regard to the facts of human existence at all. Some theologians even make a virtue of this failure by claiming that the 'Word of God' cannot be compromised with the world in any way, that human insight is always opposed to God's revelation, and that to try to argue from the nature of human existence to the Christian revelation is a monstrous assumption of intellectual arrogance.[8] These protests, however, miss the whole point of the enterprise. One is not trying to argue that the *truth* of Christianity depends on an analysis of human existence; what one is doing is trying to find out which of various religious doctrines it is *reasonable* to accept. The truth of a belief must be clearly distinguished from the reasons which we may have for accepting it; we may hold a true belief without any reason, and we may have very good reasons for accepting a belief which is in fact false. But it is a strange doctrine which asserts that one should believe something without any reason; and all I am claiming is that one of the sorts of reason which may be given in support of Christianity is that it 'fits the facts' of human experience. And, of course, to decide whether or not that is so one must analyse those facts.

4. These, then, are two ways in which one may assess the validity of religious claims (claims as to the nature of the Good and its relation to the world): by applying rational criteria of consistency, coherence and adequacy, and by assessing whether the insights such claims provide into the nature of human existence (seen as constituted by its relation to a transcendent reality) tend to fulfil one's own existence and to illuminate it in a helpful way.[9]

A related sort of consideration is the analysis of the historical context in which a specific authority taught. For to some extent one can decide that certain elements are appropriate only to a particular time and place, while others are capable of being extended to all men; that some schemes can (or cannot) be seen as developments from, and improvements upon others, in the direction of greater adequacy or breadth of vision; and that the contexts of some teachings are so unusual or different from our own that they cannot reasonably be adopted by us, at least as they stand. Again this is largely a matter of being true to one's own experience while trying to ensure that that experience is as broad and deep as it might be.

Another way of assessing religious claims is to examine the perceived effects of belief on the lives of those who accept and seek to practise the Christian attitude. Associated with this must be the assessment of the effect of belief in one's own life. For one of the claims of Jesus was that he, through the gift of the Holy Spirit, would transform human lives with power and overcome their alienated condition. There is thus a two-fold experiential test of this claim—whether it seems to be corroborated in one's own life, and whether it can be testified to by the confessions of those who have led lives of heroic virtue. This also, of course, is not so much a procedure for confirming the truth of the religious claim; its status might be more accurately gauged by saying that a negative result would disconfirm the claim. That is, the absence of perceivable effects of the requisite sort would undermine the claim, though their presence would not be sufficient to establish it.

Finally, and indispensably, for the acceptance of an authoritative religious claim, trust is necessary. When Jesus proclaimed the Kingdom of his Father, called for repentance and faith in him, and promised his power to become adopted sons of God, then he himself became the challenge to those who heard him and the judgement upon their lives. The sorts of consideration enumerated in this chapter would not in any way establish the truth of Jesus' claims about himself. But they might set those claims within a framework of facts which would make them intelligible. In such a context, his call for our trust can be heard as something not inherently alien and absurd, as it might otherwise be, but as a challenge which calls for total commitment and which must be taken seriously. Rational criteria of assessment are essential for thinking people; but in the last resort Christian faith must remain not a demonstrable truth but a challenge—'What think ye of Christ?'[10]

At this point, of course, the non-Christian may well say that the argument has been given up. So it has: but it would be an unrealistic analysis of the Christian faith which attempted to suggest that belief could be established by argument alone. From the Christian point of view the proclamation of Christ is itself the challenge to accept the truth, and it is the hearer who is put in question by this challenge. But for one who does not believe, Christian preaching must appear as just one more resort to emotional appeals when argument has failed.

5. Even if one takes the Christian view of this challenge, however, one needs to develop an adequate account of what sort of authority Christ was claiming, and what might have justified him in claiming it.

I have suggested that the final apprehension of the nature of the Good is achieved only when it is seen in the whole context of the human situation, in its total relation to human existence as claimed, alienated and reconciled. Men are called to trust in Jesus as the unique experient of the Good; for only Jesus fully understood the nature of the claim, the alienation and the reconciliation which constitute man's relation to the Good. And he understood himself as the reconciler in this scheme, and his life of total commitment to the Good as the surety that trust in the final realization of the Good will be justified, in the event. But, even for him, trust in the reconciling power of the Good was necessary; for the final triumph of Good in the world cannot be an object of knowledge until it has happened. For us, too, it is not possible to convert Christian trust into knowledge and thus turn a ground of trust into evidence. But one must set that trust within a context which makes it seem intelligible; in which the moral failure of man is made acceptable, a power of new life is made available, and a promise of ultimate fulfilment is found in the exemplary pattern of the cross and resurrection.

How could Jesus come to understand himself as the reconciler between alienated humanity and the moral demand? In asking this question I am not trying to explore the self-consciousness of Jesus as a psychologist might. What I am interested in is the epistemological question of how anyone could be *justified* in so regarding himself; and the most I can hope to do is to provide suggestions as to the sorts of thing that might count as justification; I am certainly not presuming any special insight into the mind of Jesus.

First, one may suggest that Jesus apprehended the ground of the moral demand for reverence and love in a particularly clear and constant fashion. In this apprehension his thoughts would undoubtedly be shaped by the Judaic thought-forms which spoke of a God Holy and mysterious to human thought, terrible in majesty and unpredictable in wrath, who was yet pleased to enter into a covenant relationship with men through the medium of one Chosen People. In this scheme, too, was a strong statement of the alienation of man from God in sin and of reconciliation through the law and ritual observances of Judaism. Jesus, we must suppose, saw with particular clarity the condition of alienation in which man stands; and one may establish his uniqueness in this respect by the consideration that though he naturally participated in the human condition yet he stood above it in being wholly without sin: that is, his will was not naturally inclined to 'the world', nor was he guilty of actual moral evil. His vision was thus not blinded or distorted by alienation and he perfectly conformed to the moral demand he perceived. It is in this respect, of total freedom from sin, that Jesus could be justified in perceiving a dimensional difference between others and himself. We are to suppose that he knew temptation but did not succumb; that he was keenly aware of the power of 'original sin' while being free from that power.[11] He could thus be aware that he stood above the Judaic cults of reconciliation, that he was not in need of reconciliation. Of course, there is the possibility of self-delusion here; I am not attempting to prove anything about Jesus by this account, but only to suggest conditions which might justify his apprehension of a unique status as between men and the Good. One cannot prove that the historic Jesus was not deluded; one can, however, attempt to substantiate the view that he might not have been deluded, that a situation is conceivable (though *we* could not be in that situation) in which one could be reasonably certain that one was not deluded. It is not that the experience of Jesus was in some mysterious way 'self-authenticating', but that his clarity in apprehending the moral demand and his ability completely to fulfil it renders his interpretation of the human situation in relation to the Good uniquely authoritative: it is the best a human being could have, and one that no ordinary (alienated) human being could achieve.

If we moreover suppose, as tradition teaches, that Jesus was able as a man to work miracles and heal sickness, these abilities, too, would confirm him in the apprehension of his unique role among men. We may think, also, that the experience of the indwelling Spirit, which is familiar in some degree to Christians, was with Jesus a constant and powerful presence throughout his life so that he felt no distinction between the rational, choosing Self and the (to us) mysterious action of Grace as it expresses itself in our acts and attitudes. With him, one might say, lower and higher Self were one. Supposing these sorts of conditions were fulfilled, it would seem that Jesus could be justified in claiming a unique and authoritative role for himself. And it would thus be entirely natural for him to come to see himself as the one destined to fulfil the Messianic hopes of Israel. In his own person the 'Kingdom of God' had come with power; he could see that he was above Judaic law and that the law itself was not the adequate reconciler of man and God; and no doubt, as he reflected on these facts, it became clear to him that the reconciliation of men to God was destined to be accomplished through him.

6. These are the sorts of thing which could justify Jesus in belief in his reconciling destiny and in the characterization of the Good which would naturally follow from his adoption of such a role; and it seems to me clear that the non-fulfilment of such conditions as these would considerably weaken the sort of justification Jesus could have for his beliefs. It would consequently also weaken the justifiability of the Apostles' beliefs about Jesus, since they accepted his Messianic status not by a direct and unjustifiable intuition but because of what they believed to be his justifiable authority.

One can see here the role which empirical matters of fact play in religious faith: what is in question is how one's beliefs, or trust, can be justified. The truth of certain empirical facts—as that Jesus was uniquely sinless, worked miracles, and rose from death—helps to justify claims to uniquely authoritative experience, even to the experient himself (for it is not that Jesus knew, but had to convince others; even his own beliefs stand in need of some sort of justification, or safeguard against delusion). Miracles do not in themselves provide a basis for belief (as if one might argue, 'This is a miracle, therefore God did it') but they are safeguards against delusion about the basis of one's belief (apprehensions of the Good, or trust in the authority of such an apprehender).

Now one might protest, like David Hume, that miracles are themselves almost certainly delusions, and so can hardly be safeguards against delusion![12] This is not quite fair to the religious claim, however. Certainly, the religious man must defend the possibility of miracles (events not falling under known general scientific laws), and of course he believes that they have occurred; but he is not committed to saying that he can provide good evidence for their occurrence, or even that such evidence, convincing to any impartial observer, could be found. It is true of almost all Christians that they accept the occurrence of miracles on authority; therefore the miracles cannot be evidence for them. They accept them because, had the miracles not occurred, it is hard to see how Jesus could be said to have known, in any sense, that he was called to be the Messiah. They are accepted, in other words, as epistemological conditions of supreme spiritual authority; they are accepted together with the authority and because of it. Thus they cannot function as demonstrations to us that an authority is reliable; they function rather as an integral part of the authoritative claim, as an epistemological backing (not an evidential guarantee) for the claim. If there were no miracles, this backing would disappear; but that there are miracles is, for most of us, itself part of the authoritative claim.

7. No Christian at the present time can be in the position of Jesus or his immediate disciples and can see for himself the moral pre-eminence and miraculous powers which he believes Jesus to have had. I think that it must therefore be the three-fold interpretation of moral experience as creation, alienation and reconciliation which is the primary object of the Christian's assent. And in giving or withholding such assent each man must consider how his own way of life is challenged and put in question by the Christian claims, and whether the testimony of the saints to the power of new life through the Holy Spirit holds out a hope and promise for his own life. The Church claims to reconcile men to God through Christ, and thus it offers what Austin Farrer has called an experimental realization of a life lived in conformity to the Divine Will.[13] The Christian interpretation of existence can become real in the life of each individual who undertakes to follow it; and so Christian assent is not abstract or theoretical; it is existential, in calling for personal involvement and commit-

ment. Nor is it assent simply to a particular metaphysical doctrine arrived at by natural reflection; the Christian must assert the authority of Christ for his faith. That is, his central claim will be that Jesus did authoritatively apprehend the Good, and the nature of human existence in the face of it; and that he does provide a power of new life, perpetuated in the preaching and sacraments of the Church. We cannot now say with exactness what Jesus said and what the New Testament writers may have read back into his teachings; but there can be little doubt as to the general character of his teachings, and of the new experience of Pentecost. The Christian therefore accepts the concepts in terms of which the New Testament speaks of Jesus as determinative for all his interpretations of the spiritual life. These central concepts or images—of God's Fatherhood, Heaven, Hell, the Coming of the Kingdom, Messiahship, and so on—are what the Christian is bound to accept; and he accepts them because he believes that Jesus gave them an authoritative status for the characterization of the Good. These are what might be called the *conceptual structure* of the Christian life—a general structure of concepts for interpreting experience in the light of the fact of the Good as revealed by Christ.

The core of Christian truth is this authoritative conceptual structure as presented in general terms, though not in detail, in the New Testament. The Christian will say that the structure is (1) *authoritative* for him; he accepts it for the sorts of reasons sketched out above, but then he accepts it as a whole, as going beyond what he might think out for himself. Those sorts of consideration only determine whether or not he should accept the authority of the structure, not which parts of the structure he might be able to incorporate into his own metaphysical system. He will accept it as (2) *revelatory* of the nature of the Good, in a particular teleological relation to man. He will accept it as (3) *exemplary* in its presentation of a human life whose pattern is determinative for his own life (the death and resurrection of Jesus must become his own dying to sin and rising to new life). And he will accept it as (4) *charismatic*, actually offering him the new life of which it speaks.

Now one can say that a certain conceptual structure is determinative for the correct interpretation of human experience as it actually stands in relation to its transcendent goal; but one is not thereby committed to any particular exposition of the nature of this structure. If one cares, one can say that the images themselves are infallible; but that is not very illuminating; for it is not at all clear what images mean. Thus it is quite possible to say that there is an unchangeable core of truth in Christianity—that is, a body of authoritative images;[14] and yet that all Christian affirmations are fallible—for they always seek to define conceptually what the images mean, and thus are always revisable in terms of the general conceptual methods and techniques available in any particular society and culture.

To take a concrete example, the image of 'the Fall' is part of the authoritative conceptual structure of Christianity; without it the doctrines of God's goodness, *qua* creator, and of sin cannot be coherently combined. But one may interpret this image as a defect in man's original nature, a deprivation of supernatural grace; or one may regard it as a total depravity; or one may even regard it as in some way a necessary condition of human freedom before God (as does John Hick).[15] None of these interpretations is ruled out, but none of them is entailed by the development of the concept of the 'Fall' which is found in the Bible from Genesis to the Book of Revelation. One must therefore, it seems, take the conceptual structure as expressing the general structural elements of the human situation in the light of the transcendent Good; but the exact interpretation of these images is a matter for constantly renewed clarification and reassessment.

There is a danger that the conceptual structure may be divorced from its historical association with Jesus; and thus the 'Christ-myth' could be separated from the historical Jesus, who would become logically, if not historically, irrelevant to the central Christian faith. This can be avoided, however, by a firm stress on the notion of authority. The Christian accepts as authoritative the experience of those who promulgated the images he accepts; and in particular the experience of Jesus as the one who established the scheme in its present form. Without the belief that Jesus was in a uniquely privileged position to be sure of the true nature of the Good and to have overcome alienation in himself, the whole Christ-myth could be no more than a tentative metaphysical theory. Jesus, the historical man, is the authoritative exemplar of the Christian scheme; his experience authenticates it, and his freedom from alienation (or sin) is what enables him to become the reconciler of alienated men.

It is thus impossible to separate the present fundamental

experience of rebirth in the Christian life from its historical roots; for the whole conceptual structure in which the notion of 'rebirth' finds its intelligible place is grounded in the authority of Jesus as unique experient, and it is his perfect life which assures us, the Christian would say, that we can in fact be freed from our past for a totally new future before God. The pattern of perfection is shown not to be illusory in his life; further, it is not just an example, bringing despair, but a pattern to be worked out over and again in each individual life as that life is, in the Sacraments, offered continually to men.

o

# PART THREE
# JUSTICE AND REDEMPTION

# FREEDOM AND SIN

1. Concepts which are undoubtedly central to the Christian faith but which are apt to seem alien to twentieth-century minds are those of sin, guilt, judgement, atonement, sacrifice, forgiveness, justification and sanctification. Rudolf Bultmann, himself a theologian of stature, writes, 'What a primitive religion it is, that a divine Being should become incarnate, and atone for the sins of men through his own blood!'[1]

It is certainly strange that a religion which claims to be the fulfilment of all men's moral insights should seem, in fact, to fall well below the moral standards of secularists and even to be abhorrent to them. Yet it seems even stranger that a Christian theologian should accept the criticisms of secularists at their face value and try to rid his faith of its most distinctive concepts in order to meet their demands. Christianity must have something distinctive to say to the secular view of life: it cannot simply accommodate itself to secular views and thus become merged in a general idealistic humanism. The task of the moral theologian is to present the distinctively Christian interpretation of the moral life in as sensitive and sympathetic a way as possible, so as to try to suggest its character as a fulfilment and enrichment of the secular understanding.

Something has already been said of the 'fallen' character of human existence, but so far it has merely been described as an actual feature of the human situation; nothing has been said about the difficult doctrines of responsibility, guilt and punishment. In many interpretations of Christianity, however, and especially in those which attempt to expound the Biblical images as literally as possible, these concepts assume a central position. It is said that men are responsible for their acts and therefore that they are to be held guilty of any sins they commit. Further, since 'the Scripture hath concluded all under sin',[2] all men without exception are guilty; accordingly they deserve and will receive the condemnation and wrath of a righteous God; in fact, for their sins all men are justly punished by an eternity of torment in Hell—excepting only those who believe in Jesus as their Saviour.

There are many ethical difficulties in this presentation of Christian doctrine. In the first place it may perhaps be accepted that 'fallenness' is a characteristic of human existence; that men are born into an alienated world as already alienated beings, defective in moral knowledge and willing. But even if this is so, and indeed, precisely because this is so, it is difficult to see how men can properly be regarded as responsible for and guilty of their moral errors. If men were born into a completely neutral state where the ways of good and evil were equally open to them then they might fairly be held responsible for their subsequent moral acts and choices. But then one would expect that at least some men, if not the statistical fifty per cent, would choose the moral course and thus that they would be perfectly good. There is certainly no reason why some or even all men could not be morally perfect in such a world. But then it is equally possible, even if highly improbable, that all men could make immoral choices as a matter of fact. In either case it would be a purely contingent matter that men do make the choices, for good or evil, that they do make; and it seems to follow from this that it could not be known in advance with certainty what their choice would be. Yet the Biblical statement is plain: 'If we say that we have no sin, we deceive ourselves.'[3]

It is possible that a Christian might believe that this statement about the sinfulness of men is just a highly probable induction; but if so he must concede that there may well be people who are not in sin; and presumably these people would not be in a condition of alienation or stand in need of redemption. This in turn would seem to undermine the uniqueness of Jesus as the sole revealer of the true nature of the moral demand to men. Moreover, it does not seem to be a realistic option for one who understands what alienation really is. For 'sins' are not just evil acts which men do; 'sin' is a condition into which all men are born, a condition from which they cannot naturally escape. But if that is the case then it does not seem just that men should be held responsible for what they themselves cannot help—that is, they should not be punished for being 'in sin' even if it is just to punish them for their particular 'sins'.

It will be helpful at this point to recapitulate what has been said about 'alienation' in the preceding chapters. The moral

situation, as I have been depicting it, is that there is an absolute
moral claim on all men, and that this claim takes the form of a
demand for a general responsive attitude and a commitment to
realizing, in oneself and others, certain distinctive virtues. But
though one may postulate such a moral demand it cannot in fact
be clearly and unambiguously apprehended; one can never be
quite certain that one knows what one ought to do; and many
men appear never to experience such a demand in any direct
way. Further, it is man's experience that he always falls short of
doing what he believes that he ought to do; and so there is a sense
in which he admits that it is not possible for him to do what is
demanded of him. It is never possible, for instance, for a man to
adopt fully and unreservedly the attitude of loving concern for all
other men and reverence to God throughout every moment of
his life. Yet this is what is demanded of him; and what is morally
demanded must be possible in some sense or it would not make
sense to speak of it as a moral demand—it would be without point.
For one could not have a place for the concept of 'demand' unless
one also had the concept of reflective, conscious agents who could
understand the possibility of alternative courses of action and could
be determined to choose by, among other things, verbal recommen-
dations. Without such a concept, such 'demands' would have no
relevance to what was done, they would have no part in human
activity and thus it would be senseless to speak of them as 'demands'
at all. Thus the notion of a 'moral demand' could arise only if, and
in so far as, one admits the existence of free and responsible
agents whose conduct can be determined by such a demand.

2. This does not show, however, that everything that is morally
demanded must be possible, or even that any moral demand is
completely realizable. It must be possible for men to do something
in response to such a demand, but not necessarily all that is
demanded or even precisely that which is demanded. Indeed there
is reason to think that certain moral demands, and those of the
deepest concern, cannot in principle be completely met. It seems
to be the case that when a man achieves one level of moral attainment he sees new demands lying before him. Or perhaps he sees
new extensions of the principle which he already fulfils over one
range of actions.

Thus, for instance, a man may perform all the duties of his

station; and then see the possibility of showing love in, for example, new developments of concern and sympathetic action. There are some duties which can be completely fulfilled—such as always to tell the truth. But there are others, and especially the attitudinal demands which are of most concern to the religious life, of which it is senseless to speak of a maximum possible fulfilment. Of such classes of duty it always appears to be true that there is an 'ought' which lies beyond whatever one can at the moment attain; it is as if one can never catch up with the ideal, for as one approaches one conception of it the conception itself changes and thus recedes to a new distance. The moral demand is infinitely recessive; one may say that any precisely formulated obligation can be attained but that all precise formulations can be, ought to be and will be transcended. So all precise obligations ought, in time, to be transcended—that is, one ought, in respect of these duties, always to aim beyond what one can now achieve.

But how does one know what one can at any moment of time achieve? Clearly this must be done by inductive observation, which can never provide more than probabilistic conclusions; and so all one can say is that one ought, for example, to be charitable to as great a degree as one can. It is as if the direction of obligation were defined by reference to a given goal but the degree of obligation was left unspecified. So the obligation, strictly speaking, is to aim at the ideal and to strive for it as hard as one can. One may conclude, then, that something must be possible for man in the way of meeting his obligations; if 'oughts' are to be applicable to man at all he must be conscious and rationally determinable in some way and to some degree. But what the individual can do towards meeting the generally stated obligation, and how far he can do it, cannot be decided either by empirical induction or by *a priori* deduction from the fact of obligation itself. Thus one feels constrained to an indefinite extent; and consequently one can never be sure one has done what one ought. One might call such attitudinal demands regulative rather than constitutive moral principles—they do not set out precisely what must be done; they regulate the conduct of one's life in a certain direction; consequently they always set an unattainable goal, a *focus imaginarius* of the moral life.

If this is a realistic account of the human situation in face of the attitudinal demands of morality, it is possible to gain some

understanding of how it is that Christians are able to say, both
that the existence of moral demands necessarily entails that the
realization of such demands in the world is possible (and, Christians
believe, will finally be actualized in the Kingdom of God), and
also that it is not possible for fallen men to fulfil the demands of
morality. For the world is so constituted that there is always
something one can do towards meeting the moral demand; and
yet this something is never felt by men to be enough to meet the
demand. Even to be constantly increasing in love is not the same
as to be constantly loving; and there is very rarely any question of
constant increase, in any case. More often there are intermittent
bursts of moral enthusiasm interspersed with long periods of
relapse into self-centredness or self-satisfaction; and there are
many times when the demanded attitude just cannot be aroused
at all simply because it has to be evoked without any clear apprehension of its object; neither an act of will nor a theoretical assent
can bring about a demanded attitude; and so, very often, the harder
one tries to adopt the attitude the less is it realized in one's life—
there is some sort of parallel here with the search for happiness,
which may with some truth be said to bring about what it desires
only when the search ceases.


3. It may be said that men should be satisfied with as much
progress as they are able to make; that even a little fitful love is
morally better than a world without love; and it may have to
suffice. But here it must be remembered that, the Christian
believes, God is the Creator, the one who constitutes the
possibilities which are open to men; and it may well be doubted
whether the pain and suffering which human selfishness brings
in its train compensates for the small amount of love which is
here being envisaged. Could an omnipotent Creator not have
made it possible for man to be loving at all times, freely and
naturally, instead of imposing upon him an incessant and arduous
warfare in which, at best, some small territory can be temporarily
won from the claims of self-interest and moral perversity? The
traditional Christian claim has been that God did indeed so
constitute the world that it was possible for men freely and
naturally to realize the moral demands made upon them. But it
was also possible for them to refuse and reject these demands;
and when they did so refuse the whole subsequent human race

became alienated from God; this is the 'Fall of Man'. Men born after the Fall are not able to obey the moral demand in the same way; and even a clear apprehension of the moral demand is not open to them. The difficult, partial and inconstant pursuit of an ever-receding ideal is the moral task of fallen man; it is impossible for him by his own efforts to achieve the moral vocation which he still obscurely feels and to find fulfilment in the realization of the moral values which claim his existence.

One can therefore distinguish, at least in theory, between those moral acts for which an individual is responsible—that is, only those which it is possible for him to perform—and those for which, though he does indeed fail in some sense to realize the full moral demand, he cannot be held accountable. This is a distinction which can only be made in theory, however; for even in one's own case one cannot be sure how much imperfection is culpable and how much necessitated by one's character and environment. It is no doubt because of such considerations that the Christian exhortation 'Judge not'[4] reminds us that we cannot presume to know just how far any person's moral responsibility extends.

The admission of this distinction seems to leave open the possibility that some men may successfully perform all those moral acts for which they can properly be held responsible—with the proviso that neither they nor any other human could be sure that they had done so. It seems to me that this possibility should simply be admitted; though one would expect it to be extremely rarely realized—if ever—because of the prevalence of evil acts and motives in the environment, the almost exclusive concern of social organizations with worldly status and security, and the virtual necessity of collaborating in the intrigues and deceptions of others if any moral purpose is to be brought about at all in the world. All these factors constitute temptations of such subtlety, strength and continual pressure that they must be almost irresistible to anyone who lacks a clear apprehension of the Good and who has in any case been surrounded by worldly influences since birth. One is consequently justified in the suspicion that no one (except, for Christians, Jesus) ever has been or ever will be morally perfect, even in that area of life in which perfection is possible. For it is not as though men were born into a morally neutral world and could proceed to choose from a position of complete impartiality. Each person is born into an already fallen world, and his character is formed by his social relationships with his family and other people so that from the very first he develops a natural inclination of the will towards the world and its concerns. Some element of succumbing to temptation is virtually inevitable in such a world, though not indeed absolutely necessary.

But whether or not men can be held responsible for any of their moral failures, it is certain that all men are in a 'state of sin', in the sense that they are alienated from the moral demand—they neither apprehend it clearly and precisely nor are able to realize its demands fully and constantly. The moral life is a warfare in which there are no decisive victories and, for natural man, no assurance of ultimate success. Under such conditions it is perhaps not surprising that men sometimes lose their morale or relax their efforts and that, except at times where a firm stand has to be taken (as when some great human liberty is threatened), they are for the most part content to take things as they come, not per- petrating great harm but not pursuing heroic virtue either. It is not surprising; but it is morally wrong; and it is a sign of the alienation of men from the moral ground of their being that they are able to acquiesce in a state of moral mediocrity in the midst of a world of enormous suffering and injustice.

Such alienation or estrangement from the ground of human being is what has been traditionally termed 'original sin'; and it is most important to distinguish this notion from the Augustinian concept of 'original guilt'. The latter notion is illustrated in this passage from Augustine's *City of God*: 'We are all in that one man [Adam], since we all were that one man who fell into sin . . . already the seminal nature was there from which we were to be propagated and this being vitiated by sin, and bound by the chain of death, and justly condemned, man could not be born of man in any other state.'[5] The original sin of man is here construed as being the actual sin of every man, mysteriously present 'seminally' in the first man. So when Adam freely rejected God we also did so 'in Adam'. Accordingly, as he was justly condemned to punish- ment and death, so also we are justly condemned; and this, of course, implies that we are not just born into a state of sin or estrangement from God but that we are born guilty before God, justly damnable, even before we perform any responsible actions in our earthly life.

I find this notion of an 'original guilt' before God morally abhorrent and quite incompatible with what the New Testament teaches of the loving nature of God. I cannot imagine a God of any moral character creating and sustaining a world of creatures which he can 'justly' consign to perdition; it would seem more just not to have created such a world in the first place. In order to preserve any doctrine of the goodness of God one must suppose that his decision to sustain a fallen world can only be founded upon his desire that it may find redemption and reconciliation; and at least two conditions are required for such a supposal to be maintained. First, one must have a sufficiently good reason for allowing a fallen world, with all the pain and sorrow that entails, to exist at all; and second, one must have some account of the way in which that world can be redeemed and reconciled to God.

4. In this book these topics must be discussed with necessary brevity and a consequent degree of crude oversimplification; but clearly something will have to be said about them if the three-fold theistic attitude is to be more fully explicated. The question I now wish to deal with, then, is that of what good reason a Creator could have for allowing a fallen world to exist, as it so evidently does. For even if pain and death are not conceived as just punishments for an original guilt they are still tragic imperfections in the world; and one must ask why the world is allowed to contain such imperfections, why all men should be born into such a world instead of into some primal paradise of bliss, and condemned to virtually inevitable moral failure instead of being given a totally unrestrained and thus more truly free moral choice.

There are two main lines of attempted explanation of this situation in Christian thought; but both of them agree in starting from the undeniable given fact of alienation; their task is to try to show the compatibility of alienation with the goodness and omnipotence of the Creator. One of them, by far the most prevalent in the history of Christian thought, I shall call the Augustinian view—following Professor John Hick's terminology in *Evil and the God of Love*.[6] On this view, man was originally created perfect in the knowledge and presence of God, but given the choice of accepting or rejecting fellowship with God. When he rejected it all mankind, as his progeny, was destined to be alienated from God; and even if one rejects Augustine's theory of original guilt, as I think one must, it remains true that alienation is a consequence of an original Fall away from the immediate presence of God.

This story is complicated by the presence of demonic beings who tempted the first man, who had themselves previously rejected God, and who now control the world, though limited by the Divine power.

The Augustinian view of the Fall has come to seem unrealistic to many people, partly because it speaks of a world of spiritual beings—which men tend to disbelieve in—and partly because the story of a Fall from grace seems incompatible with the biological account of the origin of man as a gradual evolution from more primitive forms of life. Professor Hick adduces other objections to the view, also. He writes, 'When we think of a created being thus living face to face with infinite plenitude of being, limitlessly dynamic life and power, and unfathomable goodness and love, there seems to be an absurdity in the idea of his seeing rebellion as a possibility, and hence in its even constituting a temptation to him'.[7] In similar vein he writes in *Faith and Knowledge*, 'A quite overwhelmingly unambiguous self-disclosure . . . would be received by a compelled and not a voluntary awareness'.[8] Again from that book, 'To know God is to know oneself as standing in a subordinate relationship to a higher being and to acknowledge the claims of that Being upon the whole range of one's life'.[9]

From this view that to apprehend God is necessarily and at the same time to acknowledge the claims of God, Hick infers that man must be placed at an 'epistemic distance' from God in order that a free personal relationship to him should be possible. Assuming that there is something ultimately good about an uncompelled personal relationship, and that such a thing is only possible where God is not directly known, it seems to follow that direct knowledge of God could never have been possible for man. The Augustinian view of the Fall is consequently rejected by Hick and replaced by what he calls the Irenaean view. Man in his original state is now conceived as, from the very first, at an epistemic distance from God, in a world 'in which the divine reality is not unambiguously manifest to him.'[10] He can only establish the requisite personal relation to God by a positive act of faith; his environment is necessarily quite ambiguous as between an atheous and a theistic interpretation; and self-centredness is such a natural possibility that the Fall, in the sense of an inclination towards the world, considered in and for itself, becomes virtually inevitable. 'When God summoned man out of the dust of the evolutionary process he did not place him in the immediate consciousness of his own presence but in a situation from which man could, if he would, freely enter into the divine Kingdom and presence.'[11] But it then becomes as good as inevitable that man should make 'the experiment of regarding the world as an independent order with its own inherent structure and laws'. Indeed, just such an experiment is the beginning of science; but it necessarily brings about a forfeiture of the vision of God and an 'immersion' in nature.

By such considerations Hick is eventually led to posit the necessity, and even the moral desirability, of the Fall. For man was so created that his mind 'was originally directed towards the absorbing task of mastering a largely hostile environment';[12] the Fall, man's concern with the world as an independent structure, necessarily precedes any attempt on man's part to establish that relationship with God which is the true purpose of his being. As Hick says, 'How can he [man] be expected to centre his life upon a Creator who is as yet unknown to him?'[13] And again, 'Man as he emerged from the evolutionary process already existed in the state of epistemic distance from God and of total involvement in the life of nature that constitutes his "fallenness".'[14] It is, on the Irenaean view, man's present task to transcend his fallen state by freely accepting God's offer of salvation from this inevitable self-centredness, in Christ. Man was created in the image of God; but it is his destiny—to be realized through his own free choice—to become conformed to the likeness of God.

The picture that Hick draws of the inevitability of alienation as a condition of individual self-consciousness, and of the eventual reconciliation of all men to God through his redemptive act, is a powerful and persuasive one. Nevertheless, I think that it is internally incoherent; and this can be brought out by a consideration of the notion of 'freedom' upon which Hick relies in constructing his account.

5. The most basic idea in Hick's development of the Irenaean view of the Fall is that it is good for God to create free beings, and that creatures cannot be free unless placed at an epistemic distance from God. Man must be free, not just in the weak sense that all or some of his acts proceed from his own character and are not externally compelled, but in the stronger sense that either of two or more alternatives may be chosen, and the choice cannot be

predicted in advance by any knowledge even of the agent's nature. For God is the Creator of the natures of all men; and if men were only free in that they did what their natures caused them to do, God would be directly responsible for all human acts. But what God desires is that men should love and devote themselves to him; and he could not value such love and devotion if it was the case that he had simply created beings such that it was in their nature to love him, of necessity. So, as Hick puts it, 'it would not be logically possible for God so to make men that they could be guaranteed freely to respond to himself in genuine trust and love'.[15] Thus man must be free, at least in relation to God; and such freedom consists in his capacity either to love and trust or to hate and reject God; and to do so in a way which is in principle unpredictable.

Ignoring for a moment the extremely anthropomorphic imagery which is here being used, and which is perhaps not a finally adequate account of the relation of creature to Creator, one may wonder what it is that determines different men to make their basic moral choice in different ways. But the rather depressing answer must be that we can never know; if we admit freedom at all then we cannot hope to understand it or explain it in terms of anything other than itself; for if it was explicable by reference to causes or reasons then it would no longer be freedom. Here we meet with one of the ultimate paradoxes which constantly bedevil human thought but which seems to be ineradicable from thought at its best. If freedom is explicable, it must be explained by giving its causes or reasons; but if there are reasons for an act, then that act can be said to be determined by those reasons. On the other hand, if we reject all suggested reasons or causes of an act, so that there is literally nothing to determine the choice which is made, then that choice becomes totally arbitrary; and an arbitrary choice is of no moral worth whatsoever; it is necessarily random and without criteria.

If we are to regard moral freedom as important, then, we must avoid saying first, that it is determined by antecedent causes, and second, that it is completely undetermined in any respect. Can we say, then, that it is determined by reasons accepted by the agent himself?[16] One may say this; but then the question can again be pressed one stage further back: why does the agent accept these reasons? Does he do so freely or is he determined by his mental make-up to accept them? To take a concrete example, suppose I say that I did a certain act because it was right; that is my reason. I could have acted differently, and then I would have acted, for example, in order to promote my own well-being. Whatever I did I would have had, or could have provided, a reason for it. The question is what, if anything, determines me to accept the reason 'Because it is right' or the reason 'Because it promotes my own well-being'? It is no use saying that a further reason determined me, because then an infinite regress is begun; and, again, if one says that nothing determined one, one is back to the thesis of a totally arbitrary choice. So one must say that this is just an ultimate human choice about what one is to do—act selfishly or altruistically (in this case). One cannot say why the choice that was made, was made—for that would be to suggest reasons or causes for it. Therefore freedom must, by its essential nature, be inexplicable.

6. But though one cannot ever say why an individual makes the moral choice that he does make, one can go some way towards showing why the possession of such freedom is a moral value and how its existence is an intelligible part of the structure of reality. The only way in which this can be done is by showing that the possession of freedom is a necessary condition of the possession of something which is good in itself, and for its own sake. For the Christian, this final good is the fulfilment of human nature in a relationship which can be least misleadingly characterized as one of 'love'. It may plausibly be said that one of the conditions of attaining such an end is the abandonment by the Self of its own interests and concerns in total devotion to value for its own sake. For this, in turn, to be possible there must of course be a Self with interests and concerns of its own which can be chosen for its own sake. But the fact remains that if the positive sense of 'freedom' is to be preserved, the decision that springs from it must still be wholly inexplicable. I do not think that Hick is quite reconciled to this situation, however; for he seems to regard it as a reason against the Augustinian view that Adam's choice against God would be 'unmotivated' or in some way irrational.

He writes, 'The creature's defection requires some motive or reason or apparent reason';[17] that is, there must be some assignable reason for the Fall of man. If all this means is that there must exist a Self which can be chosen for itself, that there must be alternatives of choice for a morally free being, so much is true. But Hick does not seem content to posit two alternatives, one moral and one immoral, and a simply inexplicable choice between them. In order, no doubt, to safeguard against mere randomness of choice, he wishes that one possible choice should somehow be more reasonable than the other, that it should be more natural for a reasonable being. I think that this desire on Hick's part for an account of moral choice in terms of reasonableness emerges at many points in his discussion.

In the first place there is his key doctrine that it would not be possible for creatures to be free if they had an immediate consciousness of God. For God is the Creator of all creatures, the total moral demand which claims all men, the response to which brings about the fulfilment of human being; and how could a mere creature even conceive of rejecting such a being? Rejection would be totally unreasonable and therefore unthinkable for a rational being. Here is the typical stress on what is reasonable. But one ought to ask why submission to the Divine will should be any more *reasonable* than refusal of it. If one accepts Hick's view of freedom as totally inexplicable choice, then it is no more reasonable to choose the good than to choose the bad; one is certainly moral and one not; but morality is not rationality; and from the point of view of rationality either choice is quite inexplicable. Indeed, if this were not the case one would in fact have rejected freedom, in the strong sense, in favour of some form of determinism—namely that human action could be ultimately explained or shown to be intelligible by reference to determining reasons for action.

Of course, Hick seems to recognize this fact; for he does hold precisely that freedom would not be possible for a being with immediate consciousness of God. But why should this be so? One may certainly wish to say that one could not apprehend God without at the same time acknowledging that he made a total moral demand on one's life; but the acknowledgement *that* a moral demand exists is not the same as the acknowledgement *of* that demand, in the sense of submission of one's own will to it. Hick himself writes, 'Belief in the reality of God, and a practical trust and obedience towards him, must be distinguished in thought',[18] even though he goes on to say that they always occur together in fact. But the distinction is one that must be made in fact as well; for if it is not made it becomes impossible to apprehend God as moral *demand*. That is, where there is no possibility of refusing to obey there cannot be any such thing as a demand; instead there will only be determinations to action. So it seems to follow from Hick's view that if and whenever any creature apprehends God adequately that creature becomes necessitated in its actions; it cannot even freely trust and obey God because there is no possibility of free action. One cannot trust and obey unless one could, possibly, distrust and disobey; and if no creature directly apprehending God could do the latter then no creature could do the former either. This is rather a pessimistic view for a Christian to take since it entails either that adequate knowledge of God will never be possible or that, when it is realized (in the Kingdom of God), free trust and obedience will cease to be possible. Hick believes that it will be possible for men to come more directly into the presence of God; how else can one interpret such statements as, 'God has made us for himself, and our whole being seeks its fulfilment in relation to him'?[19] But then, on his view, freedom becomes only a transitional stage on the way to necessity; and one must seriously wonder whether it has served any useful purpose in the economy of the Universe if men could simply have been necessitated to love God in the first place.

I think that Hick's equation of acknowledgement *that* moral demands exist with acknowledgement *of* them in one's conduct is just a confusion. But it is a highly respectable confusion, having been patented by Plato himself in the doctrine that to have knowledge of the Good is necessarily to be good.[20] It is plausible, but probably false in fact, to think that all men would always choose what they clearly saw to be good for them in the long run. But it is not at all so plausible to think that they would choose what they really saw to be good—not for them, personally, but just morally good—even if it harmed them in some way. In any case, even if one did think that men always would choose what they saw to be good, even if it harmed them, this doctrine would lead one, as it led Plato, to construe moral evil as mere intellectual ignorance. Men would only pursue evil because they lacked knowledge of what was good.

7. At this point, perhaps Hick would say that since moral freedom, the freedom to choose selfishness which is morally bad, is a moral good, therefore ignorance of the true Good is desirable as a means to its implementation. But this argument can very easily

be turned on its head; and it may be said that since ignorance is an evil and moral freedom can only derive from ignorance; and moreover, since evil brings so many miseries and disasters in its train, it would have been better not to have had moral freedom at all in any sense in which freedom does depend upon ignorance. On a Platonic view, I can see no moral purpose that is being served by the existence of such a freedom as man is alleged to have; if a man chooses evil only because he does not see what is really good, then the obvious thing to do is to show him what is really good and avoid actualizing evil at all.

A further and related point is that an account of the Fall which regards it as due to a mistake based upon an ignorance of what God really is can hardly count as a rejection of God and of obedience to him. One can only, after all, be said to reject that of which one is aware; and yet man's choice in favour of the world is made only because he is not fully aware of God. It seems to be very misleading to speak of this as 'rejection' of God in any meaningful sense. Hick supposes that all men really would desire God as the fulfilment of their own lives if only they could see him as he is. But in that case, why can they not see him as he is? Because, says Hick, it is important that they should be free to reject him. But all that can mean is that it is important that they should act mistakenly, through ignorance. I fail to see any importance in such a situation; but more relevantly, perhaps, this Platonic view negates the notion of 'freedom' as inexplicable choice, which Hick explicitly advocates, in favour of a thorough-going determinism. For the situation is that if men apprehended God they would be necessitated to act in a certain way (though not, as has been seen, to 'trust and obey' him, as Hick holds); because and in so far as they are ignorant of God they are necessitated to choose acts and things which are not truly good but which nevertheless seem best to them in their ignorance; and finally, when God once again reveals himself to men fully they will be necessitated to return to him in a state of final and universal blessedness. Now this is a possible view of the nature of the Universe—a view of it as a completely necessary process of creation, alienation and return to the One, which is found in paradigmatic form in the work of Plotinus.[21] But there is no place for freedom in that world-view; men are bound to choose what they believe to be good; and they believe to be good that which their intellects determine them so to believe. There are no inexplicable alternatives here; men are determined to choose in accordance with their nature and especially, on this view, their intelligence.

It seems to me, therefore, that Professor Hick is working with both of two incompatible world-views; in one of them 'freedom' is regarded as an ultimate and inexplicable choice; and the inevitable consequence of this is that the world must, so long as freedom remains in it, be at least partly inexplicable and unpredictable. In the other, 'freedom' becomes an intelligible part of one Divine plan, destined for inevitable fulfilment; for it is simply the capacity of men to be determined by what they think to be sufficient reasons. I think Hick is right in supposing that the former is the concept of 'freedom' required by Christian thought. But such freedom is not mere ignorance; it is an incomprehensible choice between alternatives, equally clearly apprehended. Such a choice could not be wholly free if one of the alternatives was wrongly or inadequately apprehended or if the other seemed the more natural and rational one to choose; the agent must be fully conscious of what is being rejected as well as of what is being accepted; and either choice must be equally inexplicable in terms of causes or reasons.

8. In order to preserve a Christian view of moral freedom, then, one must reject the Platonic theory that all men choose what they believe to be morally good; thus there is no motivation here for supposing a necessary 'hiddenness' of God. In fact there is a positive motivation for denying any such hiddenness, since that would limit in an unfair way the agent's knowledge of the alternatives of his choice.

There is yet one more defence of Platonism which could be advanced, however, and there is some reason to think that Hick might generally concur with it. This is that there is no ultimate distinction to be made between one's own good and the morally good. As Hick puts it, 'we all seek happiness as our final goal',[22] and he appears to mean by this that the morally good is identical with the final happiness of all men, and the morally evil is identical with their non-fulfilment and misery. If this is so then it is much more plausible to argue that no man would choose evil if he could foresee all the consequences of his choice in the way of personal unhappiness. So, as Kant argued, if men could obtain certain knowledge about God and the future life then they would certainly (if they were reasonable) be moral, but for the wrong reason—because they knew it would pay in the long run.[23] Therefore ignorance as to one's supernatural destiny is a necessary condition of true morality—doing right simply because it is right, whether or not it pays.

This theory does not, however, seem to be very convincing. It certainly seems that no man would wish to choose personal unhappiness when faced with an alternative of endless and unspeakable bliss. But this is not the choice which faces a moral agent in the Christian scheme. The agent has to choose between commitment to self-concern and commitment to objective value. The latter choice will indeed bring personal fulfilment in its train and the former will bring misery and disintegration. But it would be self-contradictory to aim at objective value because of the happiness it will bring—that would simply be a form of self-concern and would consequently preclude the possibility of true happiness. So even for a man who clearly sees his whole future destiny set out before him, only the pursuit of value for its own sake can bring happiness; the desire for personal happiness would necessarily, being a form of self-love, produce evil. There consequently seems to be no good reason why ignorance should be a condition of moral choice.

One may add to this the consideration, pointed out forcefully by Kant himself, that what would count as happiness for a fully moral agent—'true' happiness—would not be at all the same as what an immoral or imperfectly moral agent would term happiness. For what makes a man happy depends very largely upon his character.[24] So far from morality being definable in terms of happiness, the truth is that the measure and quality of happiness must be defined in terms of moral goodness. And this is an additional reason for rejecting the over-simple supposition that moral choice is a matter of opting for either one's own happiness or misery, apart from any distinctively and irreducibly moral considerations.

9. Thus there is no good reason here, either, for supposing that the hiddenness of God is a condition of man's moral freedom. Yet there is another line of reasoning upon which Hick relies for this supposition. That is to compare human knowledge of God

with encounter with some quite overwhelming personality: 'the
nearest analogy on the human level', he says, 'is the becoming
aware of another which is at the same time a falling in love with
that other'.[25] We would inevitably be involved with God and be
forced to worship such infinite worth; in the face of it our
personality would be crushed or even destroyed; or, if not that,
at least we would be unable even to conceive of evil. There is
here, I think, a notion which must be accepted by Christians in
some form. That is, there must be some explanation of the
strange hiddenness of God in our world, the obscurity and
ambiguity of the moral demand and our inability to meet it, and
the absence of decisive proof of God's existence which would
seem, in principle, so easy to provide.

Naturally, any attempted 'explanation' must be highly speculative
and can do little more than suggest stories which may come
somewhere near the truth. Nevertheless, it is possible to discern
the broad alternatives of explanation—in terms of an Augustinian
or Irenaean theory—and decide which is more compatible with
the goodness of a Creator God, even though the details of such
an account must remain quite opaque to us. Let us suppose, then,
that in the course of evolution, as man came to self-consciousness,
he was possessed of an immediate sense of the presence of God
as well as a knowledge of his own self-hood in a world of material
and organic beings. I can see no reason for thinking, as Hick does,
that man would be compelled to love and worship God as the
creator and goal of existence, the ground of the moral demand
and of his final fulfilment. All these suppositions that Hick makes
rest on the assumption that man has already decided for rather
than against God. But suppose, instead, that man decides against
God, that he rejects the moral demand. In a sense, of course, it
will be impossible for man to overcome the Divine omnipotence;
but on the other hand God does allow such rejection as man is
able to make. When Hick asks, 'How could he [man] plan to
reject the sovereignty of the divine omnipotence?'[26], the answer
is that, in one sense, he cannot reject it since it is God's omnipotence which creates the possibility of rejection; but in another
sense, and the one most relevant to the situation of human choice,
man can reject the Divine intention for his life. That is he can
freely reject God even though, in so doing, he cannot escape
from the sustaining power of God which alone holds him in
being. And when Hick asks, 'Why should he [man] ever desire

to reject the Lordship of the infinite Love in which, above all else, he rejoices?'[27], the answer is that it is again begging the question to think that man rejoices in the Divine love. We cannot indeed say why man should want to reject this love; but no more can we say why he should want to accept it. If X loves Y, nothing at all follows about the attitude of Y to X; so one cannot say that because God loves men therefore men must love God in return. If one says that one does not need to explain why one should accept love, that such acceptance is natural and not in need of explanation, then one is denying true freedom of decision by making one alternative more reasonable than the other, and one is thereby reducing morality to reasonableness or prudence. As long as freedom is retained, the 'why' question must be equally applicable—and equally unanswerable—in the case of both acceptance and rejection of love.

There is, I conclude, no absurdity in the notion of a creature existing in full consciousness of its Creator and yet free to reject the Creator's love for and demand upon its existence. There is no absurdity in the idea of its seeing rebellion as a possibility, for the simple reason that rebellion is a possibility within the providence of God, and a possibility the existence of which is a condition of moral freedom. What cannot be made into a condition of moral freedom is the actual (necessitated) choice of rejection by all men. It may be that since the Fall all men are born, necessarily, into a state of alienation; but this must be conceived as the consequence of the free choice of their ancestors, not as the condition of being morally free.

It may be a consequence in this way: suppose that when men first came to moral freedom they rejected devotion to God in favour of self-concern. Though God's love would be rejected, there could be no escape from its ubiquitous presence and un-limited power. Man would thus be in the frustrating situation of knowing his total dependence upon the very being whose claims he was rejecting. Sartre depicts the situation very well when he speaks of the sense of suffocation men would feel before the prying, all-seeing eyes of the Almighty;[28] nothing is outside his knowledge or beyond his power; and so at every point the pride which drives men to set up themselves at the centre of things is threatened and undermined.

One may thus think that a continued direct apprehension of God would render the existence of a creature who rejects this God unbearable—it might be as if someone whom one despised had an all-consuming, cloying and possessive love, and an unshakable presence from which one could never escape. The alienation and estrangement of the world from God might accordingly be better conceived as a protective device created by men to safeguard their personal inviolability, than as an original part of God's plan for man's growth towards freely chosen fellowship with himself. The latter interpretation gives God a direct responsibility for the evil and suffering consequent upon alienation which the former avoids; to regard evil as a possible consequence of freedom seems more consistent with God's goodness than to regard it as a necessary condition. But I think the most decisive consideration is that human ignorance of the being and nature of God, of the future destiny of the soul and of the working of spiritual forces within man and the natural world seem rather to reduce man's fully conscious freedom of choice to excusable ignorance, than decisively to place moral responsibility upon men themselves. So the Irenaean view actually undermines that notion of human freedom which it is designed to protect. A modified form of the Augustinian view, however, purged of some of the excessive stress on sex and guilt, can account for the situation of human ignorance and moral incapacity in terms of a protective mechanism for preserving the inviolability of the Self and for repressing knowledge of the future, inevitable consequences of one's present choices. It is, one might say, not God who alienates man but man who represses knowledge of God. And the choice between these two interpretations seems ultimately to be the choice of a Hegelian view of a necessary world-process of alienation and return, or a view of a world tragically alienated by free human choice, which God freely creates, sustains and redeems. There is, no doubt, a real option here. What one cannot do, but what I think Hick is attempting to do, is to combine the Plotinian-Hegelian view with belief in a really undetermined and unpredictable human freedom. It is the latter view which alone can justify the importance placed upon challenge and decision in the Christian life; in this sense, the freedom of man is one of the central coping-stones of Christian belief.

# XV

# THE WORK OF GRACE

1. In the preceding chapter sin was spoken of as a condition of estrangement from the moral demand which takes the form of a defence mechanism to preserve the inviolability of the self from the ubiquity of the Divine love. It was thus conceived as the result of a primal rejection by men of the Divine intention in creating them. While the reason for such rejection must remain incomprehensible if freedom is to be preserved, one may justify its possibility by the consideration that only that which can be kept for one's own can be freely given; if God required man's love as an uncompelled obedience, it was logically necessary to allow the possibility of disobedience. It is the measure of Divine omnipotence that it can create truly free creatures which are, in essential respects, beyond the control of the Creator.

Even if one accepts such a general line of explanation, however, one may wonder why all men are now born into an inevitable condition of alienation; for it may seem unjust that succeeding generations should suffer the effects of alienation without themselves having freely rejected the moral demand.

I shall assume that there is little moral difficulty with the doctrine of the suffering of those who freely choose evil. Once misleading pictures of a ruthless Judge meting out eternal torment for trivial misdemeanours are cleared away, I think it is both comprehensible and just that men should be free to choose a course of life which will naturally and inevitably lead to their own estrangement and isolation from the source of their very existence, with attendant consequences of suffering, pain and sorrow. For in this case suffering is freely chosen, in the sense that future ills are ignored for the sake of a present course of life which is recognized to be immoral.

But if one takes this view that suffering is not an arbitrary punishment for, but a necessary and natural consequence of, a way of life known to be immoral, then one is left with the moral problem of why these consequences should accrue to agents who have not shared in their antecedent causal conditions—that is, why the innocent, or at least those who being born 'in sin' have not yet freely chosen, should suffer also.

Now I think that this problem is sometimes made to seem even more intractable than it really is because of an over-simple conception of man's moral relationships. According to this conception each man receives just the due consequences of his own acts without consideration of the acts of others, so that the life of each individual obeys a moral law of cause and effect in isolation from the lives of all other individuals. Undoubtedly such a world would be a possible one for God to create; but the penalty of it would be the complete breakdown of all human relationships as we know them. And since the Christian belief is that the highest conceivable human good lies in the actualization of the possibilities of love inherent in the free encounter of persons in a common world, it is plain that such a world of isolated individuals, however just by mathematical standards, is incompatible with the Christian ethic.

In a world wherein the free encounter of person with person is held to constitute the highest value, the acts of each man must have far-reaching ramifications upon the lives of his neighbours. And in a world wherein it is a necessary condition of such freedom that individuals can choose a diminishment of their own personality and a refusal of loving relationships, the network of human relationships will be a complex interweaving of moral evil together with moral goodness; and the natural consequences of evil, in the form of suffering and sorrow, will be the common heritage of all men born into that social framework. Thus your hatred causes suffering to me; and my carelessness may result in your death. The innocent must suffer with the guilty when both are born into a world in which personal relationships, for good or evil, constitute the fundamental and inescapable characteristic of existence. The rain falls on the just and on the unjust alike and the sins of the fathers are visited on their children; for that is the essential condition of a world in which free personal relationships, entailing a shared environment in which each person's act affects all other persons in some degree, constitute the fundamental value.

However, it may still be thought that the suffering of the innocent, even if explicable in this way, represents a moral unfairness that a perfectly good and powerful God would not allow. One is left with the uneasy feeling that each man should, after all, receive the due deserts of his own actions, however much the Christian explanation rings true to the actual facts of life. Thus Buddhism and Hinduism insist on the law of Karma which apportions rewards and punishments throughout endless re-incarnations until at last every man has obtained just what he deserves. And some Christian writings also seem to suggest that special rewards in an after-life will compensate for undue suffering in this one. But I cannot see how an excess of pain at one time can be compensated for by an excess of pleasure at a later time. The thought of future happiness may make present pain more bearable, but its occurrence will not make one's suffering more fair. Thus I think that Biblical passages which speak of future rewards for present endurance are not to be taken as intended justifications of suffering, but rather as proclamations of a sure hope which will bring courage to the afflicted and disheartened—a very different thing.

One clue given by the Christian faith to the problem of innocent suffering is provided by its distinctive doctrine of Redemption. According to that doctrine, the greatest conceivable moral excellence is exhibited in the action of a perfectly innocent man who voluntarily underwent great and unmerited suffering in order that thereby men might be influenced by the demonstration of such a love to renounce their habitual self-concern and turn to accept the supreme personal relationship offered by God as the essential foundation of all positive human relationships. And it is in the fact that Christ need not have suffered, but chose to do so, that one can dimly discern a possible justification for God's toleration of innocent suffering. For the Christian contention is that love is the supreme moral excellence; and love may be summarily defined as complete devotion to the well-being of others. Since man was created by God to love, the only completely innocent man is one who loves completely and with the whole of his being; who is, as Bonhoeffer has put it, completely revealed and surrendered to others with no particle of selfishness remaining.[1] In Jesus Christ alone, it is claimed, there existed such a man; and consequently he alone was worthy of exemption from all suffering. He is the pattern of innocence and love; and consequently he is the exemplification of the startling truth that the perfectly good man will choose to enter into the suffering of this world freely and fully.

The reason for this, though not transparently clear to us, is that love, at least on the Christian understanding of it, is redemptive and costly. In being concerned solely with the good of others it seeks to lead them to the fullest expression of their possibilities and capabilities; and it does this even at the cost of its own security and comfortableness. When a mother loves her child wisely her whole concern will be for his ultimate well-being and the sacrifice of her own comforts for that end will be deemed worth while; for it is in sacrificial love that she finds the complete fulfilment of her own vocation. So we may suppose that the perfectly God-centred man will count his own sufferings as well worth while if by their means even one other person is released from the slavery of self-engrossment to begin to learn the way of love which is found in total abandonment to God.

Exactly how human suffering accomplishes its redemptive effect is not always clear to the human understanding; but the doctrine of the Communion of Saints is merely a theological formulation of the truth that every man's death diminishes one, and the joy of one's neighbour enriches one's life also. The perfectly good man, according to the Christian evaluation, is the man whose whole concern is for others. Why should such an innocent person suffer? The answer is that such a question, with its implications of concern for receiving one's own moral dues, simply cannot arise for the man who is wholly concerned for the good of others. Wherever suffering and evil exist, as long as there remains the merest possibility of a turning away from Self and towards relationship with God, the man who is motivated solely by love will find his vocation in working and sacrificing for that goal.

Jesus taught that the love of God is so unfailing that, even though all men reject it, it will reach to the uttermost possible limits of suffering in the hope that even one should turn again and repent. It is in this sense that the truly good man—who is the only perfectly innocent man—will choose to share in the sufferings of a world estranged from God, the source of its existence, rather than to accept the 'fair' reward of his morality and dwell in a perfect world which would necessarily have no point of relationship with the imperfect world of humanity.

In this way, granting the Christian evaluation of love as the supreme ethical value and the essential characterization of the Divine nature, I think one can discern plausible reasons why

God should tolerate the suffering of innocent persons. For if any person loves fully and truly he will choose to enter into a world where suffering is part of the natural order. In this way the freely offered acts of love of the righteous ensure that the human environment, however perverse, is never wholly without those possibilities of repentance and moral healing in which men find their hope and consolation. On this view, it is only the suffering of the innocent which prevents this world from being Hell.

Conversely, if any man chooses to escape a world in which unmerited suffering is part of the natural order so that he may receive only the due reward of his own righteousness, then he is lacking in love, in total abandonment to the needs of others. His lack of love is just the measure of his estrangement from God; and it is that freely chosen estrangement which withdraws the world from the governance of its Creator and entails suffering as the visible sign of the world's perversion and diminishment.

The case may perhaps be put bluntly thus: if any man is perfectly innocent, he will choose to participate in a world in which suffering plays an integral part. If he would not so choose, then that choice betrays a measure of self-concern, the inevitable consequence of which is estrangement from God, and consequent suffering. God allows suffering as a natural consequence of human self-concern; he allows innocent suffering for the opportunity it may bring for the expression of love which will go to any lengths to accomplish the wholeness implicit in human relationships.

One may still object to this statement on the ground that the principle of fair play—of due reward and punishment for every moral excellence and failing—must be an ultimate principle of ethics. To this the Christian must reply that it cannot be his ultimate moral principle, which is the principle of costly love. And this makes his God not a moral mathematician, calculating precise rewards and punishments, but the paradigm of innocent and redemptive suffering.

Perhaps I should point out, however, that I do not by any means consider these remarks to constitute a 'solution' to the problem of suffering. In many cases, especially those which concern the pain of children and animals, what I have said does not even seem very appropriate; and on the larger problem of suffering there is little constructive that could be said so briefly. My purpose has been a much more limited one, namely, to offer some general justification for the continued existence of an alienated world—given the existence of a loving God—which would not rely on the concept of retributive punishment for sins committed seminally 'in Adam'.

2. Thus the persistence of the world in a state of alienation from the moral demand is not to be regarded as an instance of God's just wrath, punishing succeeding generations of men because of the crime of one progenitor, and justifiably condemning them all to endless perdition. It is to be seen, however mysteriously, as the exemplification of the infinite concern of God for the final good of all his creatures, so that he sustains even a world which has rejected him in the hope of redeeming men to himself at however great a cost. It is at this point that the doctrines of the Incarnation and Atonement would have to be expounded in any adequate account of the Christian view of human destiny. But my concern in this volume is not so much with the moral justification of Christian doctrines—certainly a complex and delicate task in an age which has widely rejected as immoral the notions of guilt, retribution, penal substitution and sacrifice—as with the provision of an interpretation of the actual moral experience of Christians which may make clear the place of theological language in the everyday life of believers.

What is needed to complete this interpretation is an exposition of the third element in the theistic attitude, the one which is most distinctively Christian, which I propose to call the *charismatic* element in the Christian approach to the moral life. This element arises out of the acknowledgement of an absolute moral demand coupled with a recognition of one's alienation from that demand and, almost inevitably, of one's failure to live up to the demands one does recognize. It is in this situation, in which the fulfilment of a Divine purpose for human lives seems inevitably destined to be frustrated, that the Christian gospel of reconciliation is preached: and Christ is proclaimed to be the one who reconciles alienated man to the moral ground of his being. It would not, of course, be true to say that Christ overcomes alienation or abolishes it. After Christ, men remain estranged from God and unable still to meet his demands fully. What he does is to offer reconciliation from within the situation of alienation; he reveals the true nature of the moral demand, assures forgiveness of moral failures, and provides the power of a new life and the promise of future fulfilment.

There are two major features here which have been traditionally thought of as 'justification' and 'sanctification'. Christ justifies in that he assures forgiveness on condition of repentance; and he sanctifies in that, through the working of the Holy Spirit, he does make new life possible, in part at least. Both these features are of very great importance for the moral life of the Christian. For in the first place it is extremely difficult to retain a true sense of the absoluteness of the moral demand in the face of our continued failure to meet it. The sense that one has not done what one ought to have done can lead to extreme depression and neurosis—for the belief that one is a failure in what, above all things, it is most important to succeed in doing, is at best a depressing belief. Indeed, the confessions of many of the greatest spiritual teachers illustrate vividly the desperate agony of mind produced by the knowledge that one is not as one ought to be, that one stands perpetually and it seems inevitably condemned by ceaseless moral claims. The alternative seems to be to deceive oneself about the force of the moral demand and to adopt a more amenable morality for human frailty. But again the sense of anxiety is only repressed and produces its consequences at deeper though less conscious levels of personal life. For men who see their human situation clearly, then, the Christian would claim that there is no escape from the tragic awareness that one's own 'true', Divinely purposed being has become an impossibility; and what one will become must always be a distortion of one's true self, and thus there must be inevitably a lack of fulfilment as a man. Man thus rejects not only God but himself as Divinely intended; and the knowledge of such self-rejection, the negation of one's own being, brings despair.

It is this complex pattern of attitudes, which would have to be much more fully explored in any adequate phenomenology of moral experience, which has been characterized by many Christians as 'guilt' or 'a sense of sin'. The use of the term 'guilt' can, as I have remarked in the previous chapter, become misleading if it leads one to suppose that it can be alleviated by punishment either of oneself or, even worse, of some substituted victim. For the human sense of despair at man's 'fallen' condition is not so closely tied to individual responsibility as is the non-pathological sense of 'guilt' in human law; and in any case there does not seem to be any good reason to think that any sense of guilt can, or ought to be, removed by punishment.

Some philosophers have spoken of punishment as somehow remitting the sense of guilt and of removing it by paying the offender back for his crime.[2] Now it may be true that some criminals cease to feel guilty when they feel that they have paid for their offence; this may be a fact of human nature. But unless one holds a retributive view of punishment—that crime deserves punishment just because it is wrong and for no other reason—it will not make much sense to speak of 'paying for' an offence by being punished. So one cannot connect the notion of 'guilt' with that of a price to be paid for wrong done. What, then, is the rationale of guilt if it cannot be assuaged by punishment and if it cannot bring about any undoing of the wrong already done? It must be said that there does not seem to be any point at all in feeling guilt for its own sake; it can do no possible good and it causes distress, if it is sincere, to the guilty party. Should one then dismiss it as a pathological feeling, to be eschewed by all reasonable men? We may draw back from this suggestion because we feel that a man who does not feel shame or guilt for his wrongs is less than human, does not see the harm he has caused, and is unlikely to amend his ways in future. It is this last clause which makes clear the proper function of guilt in the moral life. If a man is to amend his life for the better he must sincerely repent of what he has done and resolve not to do it again. But repentance is not possible unless one knows that one has done something wrong, which one was free to do or not to do. And it is this belief which is the necessary condition of feeling guilt—indeed, it may not improperly be said to be itself the feeling of guilt, if one is thinking of the nature rather than of the emotional depth of guilt. In this way guilt can be seen to be reasonable when and only when it leads to repentance. And this shows why punishment cannot really be said to remit guilt; for one cannot bring about repentance by simply punishing a man. One must therefore reject those crude accounts of Christian doctrine which speak of man's original guilt being remitted by punishment; and which go on to say that Christ has been justly punished in our place so that he has taken away our guilt and enabled God to forgive us.[3]

Almost everything is ethically wrong about these accounts. As I have suggested, man has no 'original guilt' in the sense implied; and guilt is not remittable by punishment. Furthermore, it seems a contradiction even of the perverted notion of justice being employed by the theory itself to say that one man may justly suffer for another's wrongs, as though it did not really matter who paid the penalty for what offences as long as some penalty was exacted somewhere. Finally, it says little for the love of God that he is alleged to be unable to forgive men until they, or others, have paid for their offences. It hardly seems to be 'forgiveness' to insist on the payment of the due penalty first; certainly, a criminal would think it an odd use of the word if a judge said, 'I forgive you for your crime, but you must still serve twenty years'. The Christian may argue, with some force, that forgiveness is not just remission of penalty but the establishment of a free and unconstrained personal relationship in which the forgiver does not allow the forgivee's act to impair the quality of their relationship.[4] But then there is even less reason to think that punishment should be any sort of condition for forgiveness; for would the infinitely loving God not be always prepared to offer himself to man without conditions? Thus what I have called the crude account of justification stands condemned as unintelligible and immoral.

3. But the doctrine of justification does not fall with that interpretation of it; it remains firmly grounded in the fact of alienation, in the consequent sense of moral despair, and in the impossibility of overcoming—as opposed to repressing—despair by a true repentance and renunciation of all self-concern. Certainly one may say that contrition is possible to man; but if repentance is held to incorporate a real element of self-reformation there must be a sense in which one must deny the possibility of real repentance, since men are fated always to be to some extent at the mercy of their worldly concerns. Now although a Christian, believing in the love of God, must affirm that God will always and unconditionally forgive men, there is little point in saying this if men still cannot overcome the despair of self-rejection in themselves. Nor can this despair be overcome merely by the consideration that God offers free personal relationship to us; for what causes the despair is that we have so constituted our own being that we cannot attain the personal fulfilment which can result only from total obedience to the moral demand. What God offers us is worthless if we are unable to respond to the offer. It is for this reason that the Divine forgiveness should not be considered as

simply a characteristic of God, much less as his acceptance of a substitutionary penalty, but rather as an actual reconstituting of the being of man.

This reconstituting is first and fully effected in the life of Jesus, the man who is not estranged from God; and it is effected thereafter in the lives of all those who acknowledge Jesus as Lord. It is not, of course, fully effected; and to that extent Divine forgiveness remains a promise more than a present reality; it promises that despite one's present estrangement and past self-diminishments the Divine intention, and accordingly one's true fulfilment, will be realized in man at last. One must still suffer the constant warfare and frequent defeat of life within the context of an estranged world; but the assurance of 'forgiveness' is that one will not be finally defeated by one's failures and incapacities, that these will not finally stand in the way of a complete fulfilment of God's purpose as long as repentance lasts.

The Christian view is that man cannot overcome alienation but God can; and in the Incarnation he entered into the human situation and transformed it from within; by the perfection of his love, shown in the perfectly obedient life of Jesus, he showed himself able to reconcile any condition of alienation to its true ground; in Paul's words, 'He hath made him to be sin for us, who knew no sin.'[5] God reclaims men from within their own situation, in the life and death of Jesus. But how can this work of reconciliation apply to believers at all times and places?

The Christian faith is that Christ's work did not end with his death on the cross but that he still lives out his life of perfect obedience in the world, in the lives of those who will acknowledge him and accept him into their lives. It is this aspect of the indwelling of Christ in the believer which is the characteristic emphasis of the Christian life. Whereas secular moralists must hold that it is 'I', the willing centre of my personal being and action, who must act morally, who am obliged by and able to respond to the moral demand, the typical Christian claim is that 'I' am a 'fallen' being with an inherent disposition of the will towards the world and its concerns, and consequently unable of myself to fulfill the Divine Intention. The escape from this impasse lies in the renunciation of 'self', allowing God himself to become the 'ground of my loving'. This is a decision, but not a decision to fulfil the moral law; rather it is a decision to let God do in us what he wills. It is the acceptance of moral failure and, as Tillich has put it, my acceptance of God's acceptance of it.[6] And it is the renunciation of reliance on my own moral efforts alone. For the Christian concept of morality is essentially bound up not just with *my* possible action but with an action of God, wrought in or available to us in living the moral life.

It is the Christian claim that if we only repent of our condition of sin and turn to Christ with complete trust he will live in and through us, transforming our attitude to the world and enabling God to be loved for himself through us. What is impossible for us can only be done by God; but the proclamation of redemption is that he can and will do it through us. In that way we can become conformed to the moral demand by associating ourselves, as it were, with the perfect Divine love which dwells in us. As Nicolas of Cusa wrote, 'Thou, my God, who art Love, art Love that loveth.'[7]

4. The secularist may well make a two-fold protest at this point. First, he may reject the notion of another person acting 'in' us, as though two agents could inhabit the same body and even the same mind; and second, he may protest that, in any case, only my acts can be relevant to my moral worth; anything God did in me could not properly be considered as my act at all and therefore could not be considered as enabling *me* to be conformed to the moral demand.[8]

To the first objection, I would have thought that there should be little difficulty in the notion that the sources of human action are extremely obscure and often seem to arise at levels below that of conscious attentive willing. And what is being said by the Christian is that what cannot be brought about by a conscious act of will—the pure attitude of love for God—can be brought about by some other source which seems to exist within the personality, though not at a conscious level.

Naturally, it is much more difficult to say what that source is; and it is here that one must remember that one's interpretation of the experience of 'rebirth' will depend upon the whole context of one's beliefs about human nature and destiny. As far as Christians are concerned I have already argued, in Chapter XIII, that this experience of regeneration cannot be divorced from the whole context of beliefs which are founded upon the authority of Jesus. The interpretation of it as a reconciliation to a moral ground of one's being, and as an act of God himself through the Holy Spirit, depends upon acceptance of Jesus' claim to an authoritative experience of the moral demand. It is only within this context that one is able to say that the felt experience of new life is that of God loving himself through man.

As for the second objection, it seems to rely upon the concept of 'desert' that I have already been concerned to reject. That is, it implies that there should be some appropriate reward or penalty for each act which I responsibly perform; so personal fulfilment is regarded as a reward for conformity to the moral demand. Then, if such conformity was held to be due only to the act of God in me, that is, not to be my own responsible act, I would not deserve the reward of fulfilment—that would be like me being rewarded for someone else's action and it would be morally unjust.

I have suggested, however, that alienation is not to be considered as a 'punishment' for wrong-doing but rather as an inevitable result of the rejection of the Divine purpose for oneself. Similarly, fulfilment should not be considered as a 'reward' for goodness but as the natural consequence of performing one's true function as a man. The human situation, then, is that all men are born into a condition of alienation; and in this situation they find that they are unable to perform the function morally demanded of them. This means that, in this world, fulfilment is indeed not possible. But the Christian gospel is that it has become possible, now in part and after earthly life completely, because God himself has acted to redeem men from their situation. Of course, it is essential to human freedom that men should be able to reject God's redemptive act, just as some of them at least rejected his creative purpose for them. But to accept that act is to confess that human fulfilment is no longer attainable only through total obedience to the demands of morality; it is to rely unconditionally upon the immanence of Christ in us and his promise for our future. Salvation by faith, not by moral success, is the essence of the Christian life.[9]

Is it then immoral, or conducive to moral laxity as is often claimed by its opponents, to suggest that everything is allowable since everything is forgiven? There could hardly be a greater misunderstanding of the Christian faith than this. There would be no necessity for redemption if the moral demands made upon man did not remain absolutely binding and therefore calling for the utmost effort to fulfil them. It is only when man has exerted his utmost effort and still failed that he is driven to accept his own inability to fulfil the Divine intention, and thus to fall back on the offer of grace through the indwelling of Christ. His faith is not a mere calling on the name of Jesus; it is founded on the total commitment to moral goodness, the sure reliance on Christ's declaration of Divine forgiveness, the assent to Christ's indwelling which requires sincere repentance as its condition, and the hope of future fulfilment of God's purpose which Christ promised. These are the conditions of faith; and thus, though an ethic of 'justification by faith' is incompatible with any ethic which insists on due rewards for moral success, it is quite consonant with, and in fact requires, a total devotion to moral effort coupled with a realistic assessment of one's own moral condition and a sincere assent to the Divine intention which is expressed by the dedication of one's own life to Christ, to let him work in us as he may. Justification by faith is thus not an alternative to moral endeavour; it is a supplement to the moral life without which all endeavour would be doomed to ultimate frustration.

But in saying that it is a supplement I do not wish to suggest that it is a sort of after-thought to the Christian life. Growth in the Christian life consists in the ever-more complete manifestation of the love of Christ in us, in an ever more perfect ability to subordinate our conscious willing to the natural outworking of the love which springs from a regenerate heart. This is the movement from the first state of justification in which Christ is first present, releasing us from bondage to the world, to the final state of sanctification in which our will is solely and simply one continued *fiat* to the working of the Divine love within us. In this last state moral struggle and inconstancy disappears from human life and the human will is perfected in acceptance of God's purpose. But such a state does not seem possible in this life; and so, as things are, the will must learn submission through struggle and hardship. In this arduous warfare the interior life of the Christian will be quite different from that of the secular moralist. For whereas the latter must simply aim at the realization of goodness by a conscious direction of will, the Christian must aim at it by learning to submit his conscious will to the indwelling power of Christ. Whereas the one approach must focus on achievement, the other must focus on obedience to one who can achieve in him.

It is for these reasons that the Christian endeavour is one of being conformed to the image of Christ rather than of achieving moral goodness *simpliciter*. The Christian ethic can appropriately be called charismatic in that it offers a new power for living the moral life. If this power is intermittent, obscure, and often altogether absent, this is a measure of the obedience which men have yet to learn. Nevertheless, the ultimate triumph of God's redemptive action in human lives is foreshadowed in these fitful beginnings; and thus it is that, in a situation of constant moral failure, the Christian affirmation should be not just an heroic commitment to further moral striving but a learning of greater obedience to a work of grace wrought in the believer, a thankful acknowledgement of 'Christ in me, the hope of glory'.[10]

# XVI

# HEAVEN AND HELL

1. The structure of what I have called 'the theistic attitude', the total attitude which Christians are called to adopt, should now be apparent. It has a threefold structure; first, of worship for the creative ground of all values; second, of contrition for one's complicity in an estranged world; and third, of thanksgiving for the redemption which is available through Christ and of commitment to the fulfilling of his redemptive work in others and in ourselves. This is also the structure of prayer, which is reflected in the pattern both of the Church's liturgy and of private devotion; and since the attitude is a total one, to be adopted at all moments of the Christian life, it can be seen how one should properly speak of the Christian life as a life of prayer. The special times which may be set aside for prayer are only moments for remembering and reinforcing in ourselves the attitude which should always and everywhere be ours. But, as was made clear in the preceding chapter, the theistic attitude can only be brought about by the work of grace, the real indwelling of Christ in our lives, which entails the learning of perfect obedience to him and abandonment of the self on our part.

Whilst this may certainly be a goal of human striving, it is vastly implausible to suppose that such a state of self-abandonment can be achieved at once and without effort by any human being. Though individuals vary very much in the sorts of effort they can successfully make in this sphere and in the natural endowments with which they begin the process, it may be said with certainty that there is no man who must not begin from some condition of selfishness and struggle painfully thereafter to overcome it. In this sense each man is born into a fallen world as a fallen being. He is there given a redemptive vocation to reconcile the world to God through a free assent to and co-operation with God's own work of reconciling grace. It is each man's vocation to redeem; but this includes the redemption of himself through the acceptance of the power of grace.

But, it may be reasserted, one cannot hold a man responsible for that over which he has no control. If he is born with a natural unclarity of moral vision and a natural inclination of the will towards self and the world, and if his best moral efforts are fated to leave him still below the standard set by the moral demand, then surely he cannot be blamed or punished for those failures which he cannot help. The answer to such a protest is simply that what it says is correct. The only reason why some Christians have felt compelled to deny it is that wishing to assert the justice of God they have assumed that he would reward the morally deserving and punish the wicked. They have consequently interpreted Heaven as a reward for good conduct on earth and Hell as a punishment for bad. And since Christ came to redeem men from Hell it must be true that, since all men stand in need of redemption, all of them must really be wicked. Such a course of argument leads to insuperable moral problems, and secular moralists are entirely right to reject the attempted Christian solutions to them.

One protest commonly made is that the endless torments of Hell seem rather a severe punishment for a mere seventy years of often rather innocuous wrong-doing. Sometimes this is answered by saying that sin is an offence against God, not just against men, and it is therefore infinitely grave. It was Newman who, with a typical lack of proportion, remarked that one lustful thought was as grave an affront to the dignity of God as genocide.[1] Even if one could stomach this remarkable thought one might wonder if men really have any awareness of the gravity of their misdeeds, whether they realize that, in doing wrong, they are in fact rejecting and rebelling against an infinite and Holy God. Even if that is what they are doing, can one hold those who have no awareness of the fact blameworthy? Moreover, on this doctrine all men, whether they know it or not and however moral they try to be, have rejected God and continue to do so. Thus a man (and I think it probable that there are some) who spends all his life in search of God, who does everything in his power to do right, who lets no opportunity for the exercise of virtue pass by him— that man must be considered to have offended God and to deserve eternal punishment as much as any murderer who ever lived.

2. These are difficulties in the doctrine of Hell; but the greatest objection of all is to the basic conception of punishment upon

which it is based. One may wonder whether sin deserves as much punishment as Hell is said to provide; but a much more serious doubt would be whether it is ever morally right to punish wrong-doing at all. I am not concerned with the question of whether one should punish offenders in order to reform them or to deter themselves or others from future offences, but with the question of whether one should ever punish retributively—that is, because a wrong has been done, and for no other reason. If Hell is a punishment it must be a retributive one; since it is conceived to be eternal it can hardly reform; it would be an outstandingly inefficient deterrent to others; and if its only object was to deter the offenders from harming the innocent there would be no need for the existence of the traditional torments in Hell—for deterrence it is sufficient to ensure physical isolation, which might in itself be quite pleasant. Hell then, as it is traditionally conceived, is a retribution imposed by God, the just Judge, because wrongs have been committed in the past.[2]

There are very good grounds, implicit in the New Testament itself, for thinking that retribution far from being just is grossly immoral. In the New Testament we are exhorted to forgive our brother indefinitely (whether or not he repents, presumably);[3] we are told that God purposes only the good of mankind, that he loves the world so much that he would 'give his Son' for it, and that he is like a Father to men.[4] How then does the imposition of a retributive punishment do good or show love to anyone? It cannot help the one who has been harmed; for the past cannot be undone. And it is not, of course, meant to help the offender; it is meant to make him suffer. All it does, therefore, is to increase the amount of suffering in the world without having any beneficial effects whatsoever. But, one may say, suffering should be increased in this case in the interests of 'fairness'; offenders must be paid back. We may certainly think it is 'unfair' that the innocent should suffer through another's crime; if anyone is to suffer we may think that it should be the offender. But, once the deed has been done, no one else need suffer; the question is not *which* person should suffer but should anyone else (even the offender) suffer *in addition to* his victim?

I would think that when the position is stated like this, posing as alternatives either an increase of suffering in the world or a maintenance of the status quo, few could doubt that the latter alternative is the more moral. And yet a feeling of uneasiness remains which is perhaps not solely due to a primitive desire for vengeance remaining unregenerate even in the Christian. The uneasiness arises from considering the imaginative spectacle of a world in which the wicked flourish and the good suffer torments and deprivation. It is not so much that one wishes to increase the amount of suffering in the world by making everyone suffer equally, but that one feels there must be a deeper connection between virtue and happiness, which is somehow obscured in this fallen world.

It may seem that there is something abhorrent in the thought of a world in which men, with great difficulty and self-sacrifice, are completely virtuous but only at the cost of renouncing or opposing all their dearest inclinations. Kant himself, the apostle of duty, calls the ethics which is content with such an ideal, 'misanthropical ethics';[5] and it has led many philosophers to propound, by reaction, that it is one's duty simply to aim at the happiness either of oneself or of all men equitably.

3. I think that what has gone wrong here is the erection of a fundamental dichotomy between happiness (construed as the satisfaction of all one's inclinations) and virtue (construed as obedience to the Moral Law)—a dichotomy which Kant first introduced into Western philosophy in this stark formulation. For what this dichotomy postulates is the division of human nature into two tragically divided camps—the inclinations, which bring happiness; and the Conscience, or Practical Reason, which simply demands obedience. It is true that, having made this division, Kant uses all his ingenuity to reunite the two, to the extent of bringing in God as the *deus ex machina* who resolves the tragic conflict.[6] But the division should not have been made in that way in the first instance. For, as has been suggested, what is binding on man is not the negation but the fulfilment of his nature. Strangely enough, Kant also believes that morality is the fulfilment of human nature, *qua* rational agent: but it still seems to him that such fulfilment cannot be guaranteed to bring happiness in its train. Now there is a sense in which this is a plain fact—the sense in which, for example, a man's obedience to what he sees as his duty brings upon him great worldly misfortune. Such cases will have to be carefully considered. But if for a moment they are ignored, and if one asks what the condition will be of the man who obeys the moral demand and so fulfils his nature, being just what he ought to be, does it not seem clear that it will

*ipso facto* be a condition which can be appropriately characterized as 'happiness'?

For happiness is not a property which can be added to or taken from a man, whatever his actions and dispositions may happen to be. It is, as Aristotle said, the contentment which comes of performing one's function well.[7] It is not true that the satisfaction of one's inclinations will *ipso facto* make one happy; a man may have all the worldly goods and every opportunity of satisfying inclinations for which he wishes and yet be profoundly unhappy. And conversely, a man may be happy in the most adverse conditions of poverty and illness. That does not, of course, show that such a state is desirable; but it does show that happiness cannot simply be regarded as the satisfaction of whatever inclinations one may happen to have. And though it is almost impossible to give a definition of 'happiness', it does typically seem to include a belief about oneself, in addition to mere feeling-states—the belief that things are going with one as well as they could be—or a general contentment with one's lot, whatever it is. The attainment of happiness may even require one to eschew certain inclinations—as an obvious instance, a strong inclination to promiscuous sexual relations might be incompatible with the attainment of happiness, at least in most societies. Others will no doubt have to be modified and restrained; and so, even at the level of induction from experience, the man who seeks happiness will be wise to seek to adapt his inclinations to his situation and aim at an enduring position of respectability rather than a riotous indulgence of his passions. It is significant that Epicurus, who has given his name in popular thought to a policy of licence and libertinism, in fact recommended the most austere actions as the most sure way to find happiness.[8]

Not only is happiness almost certainly incompatible with the satisfaction of all one's inclinations; the situation is further complicated by the fact, noted with blatant inconsistency by J. S. Mill, that many of one's inclinations ought not to be satisfied. As Mill put it, there is a hierarchy of 'pleasures', such that a small amount of a 'higher' pleasure is more worth having than a large amount of a 'lower' pleasure.[9] So there are, one might say, different *kinds* of happiness which result from different kinds of activities; the moral happiness which results from fulfilling the moral Ideal is of a different quality from the happiness resulting from a good meal. But though this may be so it is not true, as some moral philosophers have supposed, that morality can be recommended to men simply on the ground that it will make them happier (on the qualitative scale) than immoral men. For the obvious reply is that if a man already is immoral it is precisely the lower kinds of happiness which will appeal to him most. As Schopenhauer aptly put it, 'every man is at home only in the atmosphere suitable to him'.[10] So even if there is a morally superior, intrinsically satisfying form of happiness, it will be so only for the man who already is moral.

Some people may find the distinction between the intention of the moral agent (to do what is right simply because it is right) and the consequences of right action (the production of a superior kind of happiness) difficult to keep clearly in mind. But it is of vital importance for the Christian system of ethics, which has often been accused of being immoral in that it tempts men to do good *in order to* attain the reward of eternal happiness. What must always be borne in mind is that the man who does good only *in order to* attain his own happiness stands condemned by the Christian code; he will not attain the end he seeks. But the man who does good for its own sake and not in order to attain any ulterior consequences will, in the fulfilment of his nature, find a superior sort of happiness. One might put this situation in a rather crude picture and say that Hell is full of people who are engaged in acts of heroic virtue, trying to get to Heaven; while Heaven is full of people who are not particularly concerned with being there. Of course this picture, while it makes a point, is crude. In the first place, those who are concerned to implement the moral Ideal must be concerned with the possibility of such implementation and so, in a sense, with their continued existence as manifestations of the Ideal. And the simple man's desire for heaven is perhaps not as reprehensible as it may at first appear; for while it is certainly not the highest moral response, nevertheless, if the desire is for a sort of happiness which requires hard self-discipline and resoluteness of intention for its attainment— even though it errs in taking the end for the means—it shows that a discrimination between the various kinds of happiness has been made. And the increasing clarity with which 'superior' happiness is seen, and the closeness of its relation to the fulfilment of man's final end, may induce the man who begins by desiring only happiness finally to cultivate that moral disposition which alone can make superior happiness fully attractive to him.

Mill combined a discrimination of kinds of happiness with the belief that the happiness of all was the end of moral action. But once it is seen that the superior happiness is that which ensues from man's fulfilment of his final end, the end becomes the virtuous life of all men. Yet of course this is beyond one man's power to will; and thus it seems that the general happiness cannot be a proper end of human action—and this Kant did see. All one can do is to pursue virtue in oneself and seek to encourage it in others: the man who is happy in this way will find that his way of life has so modified his inclinations that he no longer counts those which he is unable to satisfy as worthy of being satisfied. There can be no question, then, of man's nature, *qua* fulfilled moral agent, being at odds with his nature, *qua* being of unsatisfied inclinations; if his nature is indeed fulfilled, and in so far as it is, no inclinations will be unsatisfied which it is proper to satisfy. One may say Kant knew this in making his distinction of human nature before and after the Fall.[11] It is only after the Fall, he holds, that inclinations are in opposition to and take precedence over the moral law.

That is emphatically not to suggest, however, that there is no conflict between the demands of morality and security and success in the world. That conflict most certainly does exist, and is tragic; but it is not a conflict between two parts of man's proper nature. Happiness is to be found in the fulfilment of man's proper nature, and therefore in obedience to the demands of the moral Ideal. There is no question here of happiness being a superadded quality given as a reward for virtue; it is in itself a quality of virtue which is consequent only on virtue being what it is.

The conflict between duty and self-realization is not, properly speaking, a conflict between reason and inclinations; it is a conflict within morality itself. For the world is so constituted that one's performance of what is right actually *precludes* the fulfilment of one's nature. For example, in order to save the lives of my fellows I may have to sacrifice my own life; this is undoubtedly the right thing to do; but it can hardly be said that it is conducive to my self-development; indeed it terminates my self! It is because of cases of this sort that moralities of self-realization have been condemned as basically selfish—whereas, it is said, true morality is concerned above all with equality and impartiality between men.[12]

The virtues of self-sacrifice are necessary virtues in our world;

but there is nothing good about self-sacrifice in itself: it would be absurd to have a world in which it was morally right for everyone to sacrifice himself just for the sake of it. The sacrifice must be in order to further a greater end—and that end, for the Christian, is ultimately the fulfilment of human nature, somewhere and by someone. There is conflict present in the human moral situation; but it is not primarily a conflict between duty and happiness; it is a conflict between the demand to fulfil oneself and the impossibility of attaining fulfilment in specific worldly situations; a conflict between self-realization and impartiality. This is a conflict between two duties, not between duty and inclination.

Not only is there a conflict between the demands of self-realization and impartiality, however; it is also the case that, because of man's condition of estrangement, complete self-fulfilment is in any case impossible in the world. Even for the man who believes himself to be redeemed by Christ, the realization of the complete life of prayer in which supreme human fulfilment lies remains a goal to be hoped for rather than a state which may be attained in the present. To that extent one cannot say that happiness is ever completely possible for men on earth.

And finally, as long as pain and suffering remain in the world the happiness which naturally accrues to the virtuous man must be limited by his proneness to natural disasters and ailments and by the consequences of the thoughtless or evil acts of other men. Accordingly, although one may plausibly say that happiness and virtue are not two quite distinct elements of human life, but that happiness lies in the consciousness of fulfilling one's end as a man; nevertheless one must concede that, in the present world, true happiness is never attainable, that it must often actually be renounced, and that it remains subject to the contingencies of an alienated world. It is because of such considerations that the man who believes in the origin of the world from a necessary moral creator will feel constrained to postulate a life beyond this one in which the work of grace, imperfectly exemplified in men, can be completed; and it is the truth of such a postulate to which the resurrection of Jesus testifies.

4. So religious morality is *teleological* in that it sees the human self as a being which grows towards happiness in fulfilment of its own capacities, or towards deprivation in an ever-shrinking

concentration on selfish needs and desires. The Christian pictures of Heaven and Hell are poetic expressions of a reality which manifests the limiting possibilities of human life. It is not that Heaven is a reward for good deeds (or even for sincere faith, which would merely turn Christian faith into another sort of 'work' deserving its appropriate reward) or that Hell is a retribution for bad deeds. As long as such notions of 'desert' are retained in Christian thinking, just so long it will be impossible to arrive at a true understanding of what 'justification by faith' is. For the whole point of the gospel is that what God offers us in Christ cannot be correlated in any positive way with our moral successes. And to attempt to explain this by holding that it is Jesus' moral success which deserves the reward we can receive is merely to renounce the principle of desert without admitting the fact. Once one person can justly receive the reward for another person's actions the principle of desert has been completely undermined. Some theologians, seeing this, have felt driven to say that God is not just, or that he is 'supra-just' (which amounts to the same thing). Such desperate measures are not needed, however, if one simply states that 'justice', as a principle of fair play, does not require the notion of 'desert' at all. And it is precisely the import of the Christian doctrine of the atonement that the concept of 'desert', of what is 'due' to one, collapses in the face of the paradigm of self-sacrificial love which is found in Jesus.

If one accepts Heaven and Hell as limiting possibilities of tendencies which are present in less extreme and more ambivalent form in earthly life, then one can gain some idea of their nature by extrapolating from these tendencies to what we can conceive as their extreme limit. Though one will not thereby be able to give a description of the future life, as though it was something verified by observation, what one may do is to picture imaginatively the final limit of the human inclinations to self-centred and value-centred being respectively, and to suppose that these represent the final states of free creatures who make such moral choices as are available to them in this life. Thus the beginning of a man's eternal life is to be found in his present response to the demands made upon him in his situation. To speak of Heaven and Hell is to make clear the ultimate implications of his present response; so it is not only to speak of some distant and problematic future; it is to illuminate the present situation of human choice in its basic polarity of self or objective value. On the other hand, one must not fall into the mistake of thinking that talk of Heaven and Hell is nothing but a symbolic way of stressing certain features of the human situation on earth. Such talk does attempt to express, how inadequately we do not know, a future and real fulfilment of human being in obedience to the moral demand which is not possible on earth; and as a necessary corollary of human freedom it must also express, as a real possibility, the final diminishment of human being which springs from ultimate rejection of the moral demand.

Such a conception will have a subtle but all-pervasive effect on the way in which the moral life is conceived. The secular moralist often argues that if a thing is right then it ought to be done whether or not a future fulfilment of human life exists; and moreover, if something is done with the thought of achieving such fulfilment, the act becomes not moral but self-interested and thus merely prudential. But the situation is not as simple as it is thus made to sound; and to try to show this I will take an analogy from the study of music. The mastery of a musical instrument is something which does bring a great deal of pleasure to the performer as well as to others; but it may well be said to be valuable in and for itself to possess such a skill. Here there exists that integral relation between virtue and happiness which lies in the fact that happiness springs from doing well something which is intrinsically good. But such mastery is not easily accomplished; it requires years of difficult and concentrated effort with many frustrations and periods of boredom or even active loathing. The hopeful performer, if he is wise, will endure these trials for the sake of the greater good which only they can bring about. If some great teacher now assures him that he is incapable of ever achieving the mastery he desires, it is difficult to say what his reaction might be, but it is almost certain that his attitude towards his performing will change. He may still hold that he ought to play as well as he possibly can; though as he grows older the temptation to despair and a certain relaxation of effort will grow stronger. He may feel that since there is no goal that he can achieve he will remain content with a more mediocre standard. Or he may give up altogether in disgust and disillusionment.

The analogy with moral experience is plain. Christians believe that earthly life is a training for a future fulfilment 'in Heaven', and they conceive all their duties as tasks involved in attaining this supreme goal. It would be quite fallacious to argue that any teleological morality—any morality which aims at a final goal—is a merely prudential morality. For if the goal itself is ethically valuable and morally binding then of course the fact that all one's earthly duties aim at a goal beyond themselves does not render their performance prudential. But it is true that duties which are regarded in this teleological way must be seen quite differently from duties which are simply accepted as binding in and for themselves alone. The secularist—who denies any final supra-terrestrial goal—cannot take a teleological view of those things which seem to him duties. And if this is so then it is possible and even probable that he will actually take a different view from the Christian of what his duties are. Certainly for both secular and Christian moralists there is much suffering to be prevented and much pleasure it is possible to provide for others in the world, Heaven or no Heaven. The difficulty comes with the Christian emphasis on an objective and authoritative attitudinal ideal of human life. A secularist may adopt such an ideal; he may even hold it to be categorically binding on him; but his view lacks any metaphysical framework which could make it an intelligible part of the universe. The idea that one attitude to existence is the proper one for man as such seems to be closely tied to the idea that there is a natural end of human life, which implies the existence of final causality. For one is not just saying that this attitude is the one a purely rational man would choose, or that it is necessary as a means to social harmony or individual happiness; one is saying something rather different— that the obligation to cultivate this attitude, normative though it is, is yet somehow implicit in the nature of things themselves. Saying that it is man's 'function' as man is saying not only that one ought to achieve it but also that it is the possibility which is the 'natural' development of things as they are. An analysis which imputes this sort of normative value to the processes of natural development implies the existence of a final causality which can stipulate this value as the final end of things. Accordingly, if one rejects the concept of an 'end for man as such' it becomes irrational to insist that one attitude to life is proper for man as such; since without appeal to human happiness or convenience as an ultimate norm there is no rational basis for making such a claim. And how could a secularist, who thinks of human life as having emerged as an ephemeral phenomenon in a blind and ethically neutral

R

universe, find any place for the concept of a final causality in nature?

One may, of course, reject any attempt to seek intelligibility in this sphere, to make our interpretation of moral experience consistent with a metaphysical view of the nature of the world; and one may insist that the moral demand must just be unquestioningly accepted for what it seems to be. But the increased knowledge of the human mind brought by psychoanalysts shows this to be a dangerous procedure; it can be shown with a fair degree of probability that many of the things people feel to be moral demands can be traced to neuroses or disorders contracted in infancy; and so it seems important to check one's moral beliefs for rationality in the context of all one's other beliefs. Perhaps one may not query *that* one has a certain moral intuition; but one may ask oneself whether it might not be a delusion.

Naturally, an ethical obligation cannot be contradicted by any particular matter of fact. But it would not be reasonable to think that what one conceived one's obligations to be was quite irrelevant to the facts, in a general way. It seems to me that a man who does not believe in God or a future life ought certainly to relieve suffering; but I do not think he would be reasonable to view personality, both in himself and in others, as a Christian does. It might be reasonable for him to 'respect' personality, in the sense of leaving people free to do as they please within the limits of social harmony, or even in the stronger sense of empathizing with them in their concerns and sorrows. But it would seem unreasonable for him to be ultimately concerned with the fulfilment of a moral ideal in himself and others which is inordinately difficult even to aim at and impossible to achieve. Would it not be reasonable for him to regard such a felt demand as irrational, and something to be eschewed in a world so unfitted to realize it?

I must here confess that this may be just my psychological reaction to the thought of such a depressing Universe; for it is a matter of what one does, or would under certain conditions, regard as reasonable or unreasonable. But perhaps I am on stronger ground in affirming that the Christian notion of a personal ideal is intimately bound up with the concept of 'function'; and that this concept can have no intelligible place in a Universe in which final causality is either denied or deemed impossible of complete realization. In these ways, and perhaps in others too, the Christian and the secular conceptions of the moral life must differ. And this difference will be emphasized by the Christian's claim to experience a power of Divine grace which serves as a confirmation of the hope that is in him and establishes him in his vocation to seek a fulfilment which is not of this world. I think that Christians might therefore quite reasonably say that they would not undertake the sort of life they have undertaken if they did not believe in a fuller fruition of love beyond earthly inconstancies and disappointments (though they might well commit themselves to a rather different conception of morality). But they might add that it is their experience of an absolute moral demand to seek perfection which is one of their strongest reasons for postulating the existence of Heaven (together with considerations based on the goodness and creative power of God, the death and resurrection of Jesus, and the interior work of grace). This can be so because, as Kant suggested, in the absence of possible disproofs of God and a future life, and in connection with an acceptance of a philosophical view which opposes materialism, the experience of such a demand is sufficient to move the mind to a positive assent to beliefs which might otherwise have been entirely problematic for speculative reasoning.[13]

5. One may picture Heaven, then, as an ultimate limit of that fulfilment of human being which is found in an unconditional response to the moral demand, a losing of the Self which in its desireless acknowledgement of the value which claims it becomes, for the first time, aware of the fullness of being which it receives. But when one speaks of an ultimate limit this does not imply that at some point of time the human Self will rest complete and satiated without further activity or growth. If one has a true idea of the infinity of God one can see that there is an endless number of new worlds and experiences to undergo, a literally infinite number of things to learn and understand and enjoy. One can progress for ever, as one's soul requires, without at any point being able to say that at last one knows the fullness of the richness of God's being. While one cannot comprehend such an endless progress of the soul, one can see that such an infinite growth into an unfathomable love is a natural consequence of the infinite being of God; and it is the Christian hope of 'eternal life'.

There is another side to the picture, however, which must be admitted if human freedom is accepted as a basic postulate.

While Jesus spoke of the Kingdom of Divine Love which is freely available to all men, he also warned solemnly, on not a few occasions, that men would be excluded from his Kingdom unless they repented and turned in faith to him.[14] Those warnings are quite unmistakeably present in the New Testament, and it needs an unduly strained exegesis to excise them. But that does not mean that one must accept the crude and morally abhorrent interpretation which some Christians have put upon them in the past: namely, that unless men explicitly avow Jesus as Lord they will be justly consigned to perdition. Such an interpretation calls for a complete denial of that charity which Jesus taught was the supreme moral value. It is often coupled with a complete lack of loving concern and understanding for the delicate psychological balance of the human mind, and a cultivation of fear, intolerance and repression rather than genuine love. It is a cruel and immature thing to prey on human fears, guilt and uncertainties just to obtain a supposed 'convert' to a faith which preaches a fundamentally immoral God.

Yet Jesus does teach that there is a Hell; and is this not incompatible with the love of God for men? If one does not consider Hell as a retributive punishment for bad behaviour but as an evocative picture of the state to which one's present motivations and inclinations will inevitably lead if one acquiesces in them, and thus a revelation of what one's present condition really is, then one must see Hell as a necessary pole of the basic duality involved in human choice. To attain Heaven is to renounce one's self-concern; but what can be renounced can also be retained and coveted. This is the path to Hell, to make oneself the centre of the world and to try to make everything else subserve one's own ends. For if things exist only as means to one's enjoyment they lose their value; they become material for consumption, to satisfy an ever-unfulfilled appetite. We cannot hold them in reverence, we can only use them; and in using them we are not satisfied but our desire grows stronger than ever. The desiring Self seeks to draw the world into its own essential nothingness—nothing, for it is only an eternal grasping, the incomplete and unfilled. It contains nothing; for whatever it grasps it throws away as soon as it has served its use; it keeps nothing and has no being of its own. Such a Self is pure want which is satisfied by no object but which seeks to destroy the being of everything outside itself. It is forced to continue in being by its own relentless desire, but it is endlessly self-annihilating and self-torturing. Yet as long as it refuses to be drawn outside itself—which can finally be done only by repentance and acceptance of the power of grace—it must condemn itself to this form of existence. Thus the fact of human freedom is grounded in man's capacity either to regard his being as want and the world as a tool or instrument to satisfy this want; or to regard his being as a gift and privilege and the world as a sacrament of value and goodness. This is the fundamental choice implicit in existence as man; and just because it is a choice Hell must always be a possibility of the human situation.

Despite my sympathy with those who feel a sense of moral revulsion at the Christian doctrine of Hell I nevertheless believe that, if one is to hold the human personality as of absolute value because of its possibilities of love and happiness, one must admit that human freedom may be used to cause hatred and suffering. And though morally it seems just that the possibility of a trans-formation of life should always be open to men, even 'in Hell', one cannot avoid the logical possibility that they may finally refuse to repent. The Christian doctrine is that Jesus gave himself to the uttermost in an attempt to redeem men from Hell; and one cannot but suppose that he will continue to do so for eternity if need be. The only thing he cannot do is to deprive man of his freedom to refuse him. So I cannot be confident that universalism is true—the belief now held by many Christians that all men will eventually be saved and so God's purpose will not ultimately be thwarted. As Professor Hick argues, 'We must thus affirm in faith that there will in the final accounting be no personal life that is unperfected . . . for if there are finally wasted lives and finally unredeemed sufferings, either God is not perfect in love or he is not sovereign in rule over his creation.'[15] Hick concedes that 'it remains theoretically possible that he will fail'; but still maintains that it is a moral or practical certainty that his infinite concern and resourcefulness will finally enable all men to find their fulfilment in his love. While I wish that one could be certain of such an outcome to the human drama, it seems that such certainty can only be bought at the price of undermining the reality of human freedom and of confusing a commitment to the Good, which realizes happiness, with a commitment to the Good *for the sake* of happiness. For one could only be sure that all men would ultimately turn to God either if their freedom was not ultimate or if one could point out that such a turning would be more reasonable; that is, that it would be for their own good, and not just more moral. Does this mean then, as Hick claims, that the Divine purpose may finally be thwarted? In the sense that the world may not be as he intends, yes. But there seems to be no logical difference between a *final* thwarting of God's will and a merely temporary thwarting of it. The latter must be conceded by all theists; but that entails that God is not sovereign over his creation in the sense that his will is always done in it. From the point of view of logic God's omnipotence is therefore undermined equally much—or equally little—by one small disobedience as by the final disobedience of all men. So Hick's postulate of a *final* triumph of God's purpose does not in any way remedy or recompense for the fact that it has been thwarted by men. In other words, no considerations of God's omnipotence can have any force in support of the thesis of universalism. In any case there is a more important sense in which God's will is not thwarted, either temporarily or finally, by man's disobedience, and this is that man can only realize those possibilities which God permits; so God remains sovereign, in the only sense in which he could logically be sovereign over a being which he created to be free.

6. I conclude then that if repentance is indeed necessary for salvation, and if men really are free, God must never compromise their freedom by forcing them to repent; so they may, for all we can see, refuse to do so. Of course, this is a distressing possibility; a belief in Hell is by no means a comforting one; but two things may help to make it compatible with God's love. First, the souls in Hell have made themselves what they are, and could escape if they desired; but they prefer the torment of the existence they have both to the offer of repentance and to complete non-existence.

Second, we may perhaps best conceive them, as C. S. Lewis does in *The Great Divorce*, as men who have been so engrossed with themselves that their personalities have gradually shrivelled and grown totally self-enclosed until in the end they wither away as personalities.[16] They thus cease to be persons at all, in any true sense, and become pathetic bundles of obsessions and unquenchable desires with neither ability nor desire to communicate or to be helped by others. They exist in complete isolation, resisting every attempt to reach them as an unwarranted interference with their no longer human consciousnesses; clinging

to their own existence yet forever cut off from anything that can
be called happiness. We might conceive that such beings are so
de-humanized as to be even beyond compassion. This may seem
harsh; but this is probably because we still tend to think of them
as victims of harsh circumstance than as beings who have their
desires met, though at unending cost to themselves, and because
we rarely meet examples of unmitigated evil in everyday life.
Perhaps an analogy can be found in some of the phenomena
reported by psychical research. Most often the apparitions which
are recorded perform singularly pointless and trivial tasks; they
walk up and down staircases, peer through key-holes, rap on
tables and send down messages saying how good the cigars are.
We sometimes call such things 'wraiths' or 'phantoms'; and this
brings out the point that, if they exist, they are little more than
disintegrating remnants of human personalities, the faded remains
of persons hardly recognizable as men. Add to this the characteristics of such men as Eichmann or Torquemada, men who
kill and maim without reason. If souls in Hell are of this nature,
compassion would be as inappropriate for them as tolerant
reasonableness would be to an unbalanced and armed psychopath.
We could feel no reactive attitude to them, no attitude which
would assume the possibility of communicating with them as
persons: and we might acknowledge the power and justice of
God in letting them be what they have chosen, however incomprehensibly it may now seem to us, to be.

The Christian ethic is thus completed by putting before men
a solemn and momentous vision of the ultimate nature of the
moral choices which form the context of their everyday living.
It is not self-interest which would choose Heaven, thus pictured,
nor fear which would eschew Hell; such motivations would, in
ways I have suggested, be self-defeating. Nevertheless, such a
teleological conception of human destiny provides moral experience
with a depth, a profundity and an intensity which the bare
secularist proclamations of obligation cannot match. This is no
argument for the truth of the Christian conception; and if the
secularist is right it may be that one must just renounce such a
sense of intensity as illusory. The Christian claim must be that
his is a conception which coheres intelligibly with a generally
theistic view of the moral life, that it is testified to by the teaching
of Jesus and his apostles, and that it is sustained in his own life
by the experimental realization of a new life in God through the

work of grace, which generates in him a hope for the fulfilment of the Divine promise of eternal life. It is therefore an ethical commitment which is based on metaphysical considerations no more or less certain than any general view of the world and man's place in it must be, given the limitations of human knowledge. And so it can stand in its own right as a claim to authoritative truth which can challenge man's understanding of his human, and particularly his moral, experience. At that point, the Christian believes, the work of reason must give way to the work of grace.

# XVII

## CONCLUSION

1. I began this book by posing the general question, whether or not morality depends upon religion. It should now be apparent that this question is too generally phrased to be capable of a precise answer. All one can say is that some moralities are not religious and some are. But it may be denied that there can be any such thing as a 'religious morality'; and it may be asserted that religious beliefs are quite distinct from moral beliefs, that they can have at best only the effect of psychological incentives to act morally, and that they seem in some ways inimical to a truly moral attitude. These objections to the idea of a religious morality were canvassed in Chapter I where, in the person of the Devil's Advocate, I argued that religion founds morality on fear of punishment or hope of personal reward; that religious beliefs are logically less certain than moral beliefs since they could, in principle, be falsified; that religion is itself immoral since it requires belief without sufficient evidence or preparedness to falsify its assertions; and that in any case religion can add nothing substantive to the ethical principles of, for example, non-theistic humanism.

I have subsequently tried to answer these objections by saying that:

(*a*) Religion does not found morality on considerations of reward and punishment; and, indeed, Christianity replaces the notion of 'desert' by the principle of sacrificial love (Chapters XIV–XVI).

(*b*) Religion is fundamentally concerned with the factual ground of moral obligations and the general structure of the human situation in the light of this ground. It is therefore not accurate to say that religious belief is less certain than moral belief, since what it propounds is a particular doctrine of the basis of moral beliefs. The search for empirical evidence is as inappropriate here as in the case of particular moral principles; though the search for empirical confirmation of or coherence with one's beliefs is not. As for the possibility of falsification, there are ways of falsifying religious beliefs—by considerations of inconsistency, inadequacy to experience or lack of pragmatic value—though they are not straightforward or clearly decisive (Chapter XIII). But this possibility does not make religious belief less certain than moral belief; the two are so closely bound together that beliefs about what one is obliged to do (a moral belief) naturally correlate with beliefs about how obligation is to be construed (that is, whether religiously or not). And it is impossible to say that either form of belief is logically presupposed to the other; rather they are logically interdependent. When this relation between morality and its metaphysical ground, with which religion is concerned, is clearly perceived, one will no longer be disposed to think that moral beliefs can be more certain than beliefs about the basis of morality or that the canons of religious belief should be assimilated to those of empirical enquiry rather than to those of a morality which reflects upon its own nature.

(c) Thus the question of whether religion adds anything substantive to a non-religious morality (apart from the 'extra duty' of worshipping God) can be answered in the affirmative, though the differences are those of attitude and emphasis rather than of clearly defined alternative and competing sets of moral principles. Suppose, for instance, that a humanist takes as his supreme moral principle the maxim, 'Respect humanity in others and oneself as of supreme worth.' Of course this very general maxim could be interpreted in a number of ways. 'Respect' might mean 'revere as supremely valuable' or simply 'do not interfere with'; it may mean 'sympathetically identify' or just 'aim at the happiness of'. Again, 'humanity'—as the object of respect—may mean anything from the empirical data of personality to some more abstract conception of a metaphysically free rational agent. Now is it possible that, in all this variety of interpretations, the humanist may hit on precisely the same one as the Christian? I do not think so. For the Christian concern for others must be an integral part of the wider attitude of worship, contrition and thanksgiving which governs his life. He will therefore see other persons as beings whose destiny is to grow in the fulfilment of their natures by a perfecting of their response to the moral demand, who require the power of grace and renewal to establish them in a life of responsive love, and who are promised a final realization of the work begun in them by the redemptive act of

God in Christ. He will be concerned for them as he is concerned for the bringing about of the Divine purpose in the creation of the world; just as he will be concerned for himself not in a selfish and grasping way but as an instrument of God's purpose, a being called to perfection, that he might be a worthy temple of the Holy Spirit.

A man whose sole concern is for himself is an egoist; but a man whose sole concern is for others—if this means devoting himself to the satisfaction of their needs and desires, whatever their nature—is, the Christian would say, misguided. There is no more virtue in increasing the bondage of others to the clamant insistence of their desires than in doing the same for oneself; and there is a great deal of danger in it. What man must be concerned for is the perfecting and liberating of human nature for the unstinted love of God in himself and others. So it may be that a humanist and a Christian may practice charity in the same ways—securing the physical welfare of others and sympathizing with their troubles—but the interior attitude which governs these acts will differ, as will the end to which they are directed. For the humanist this empirical individual with which he deals is all there is; and the end of his actions must be achievable within the confines of one short life. For the Christian, on the other hand, man is a being called to an eternal destiny; and the end of his actions is a fulfilment which he himself cannot bring about. Thus even if both humanist and Christian agree in advocating love for one's neighbour, what they conceive their neighbour to be and what they consider the end to which their love is directed to be, will necessarily differ in accordance with their differing general attitudes to the nature of the moral life. In particular, the humanist system of ethics is unlikely to contain the five elements—of being objective, authoritative, attitudinal, teleological and charismatic—which I claim distinguish Christian ethics, though it may possess some of these elements. And thus there are real underlying differences between a humanist and a Christian conception of the moral life which will remain, however much they may overtly subscribe to identical moral principles such as 'love for one's fellow men'.

2. In Chapter II these general differences were presented systematically in terms of different answers to five basic types of ethical

question—the meaning of moral terms, the epistemology of morals, the general principles of morality, the metaphysical context of morals, and the means of achieving goodness. The five elements of ethics outlined in the previous paragraph are necessary conditions and, taken together, sufficient conditions, of Christian morality; and they locate the distinctiveness of the Christian interpretation of the moral life.

3. The first element, of *objectivity*, was outlined in Chapters III and IV; I argued that any subjectivist view undermines the seriousness with which men take morality, and that the attempt to find a criterion of 'moral truth' by means of the notion of 'universalizable prescriptivism' does not succeed in escaping this charge. For it ultimately depends on an ethical postulate of impartiality, and it cannot, on the theory, be said to be *true* that men ought to be impartial. But this is just what is ultimately important in ethics. Nor can naturalistic views provide an adequate account of ethical objectivity; for the contingency of all 'natural', empirical facts is incompatible with the necessity ascribed to moral truths by the committed moral agent.

In Chapter IV I construed the objective referents of 'ought' statements—that which determines their truth, if true—as non-empirical claims, the apprehension of which is necessarily an acknowledgement of them *as* claims, though not a commitment to implementing them. I further analysed these claims as quasi-conceptual, universal and exemplary in nature. That is, the fact that claims bind men to specific sorts of act means that they must have a conceptual content, since they bind men generally to types of action and not just to particular acts on particular occasions; and since, as obligations, they must necessarily be possible to implement, they must be conceived either as themselves constituting the general possibilities of human being or as providing exemplary schemata of such possibilities. I argued that it is a natural consequence of this view to form the concept of an infinite creative ground of the universe whose unlimited creative power can ensure that omniscience which is requisite to apply the hypothetical schemata on every appropriate occasion.

4. In Chapters V and VI I argued that Christian ethics was *attitudinal* in nature, binding men to realize certain virtues of

character which constitute a fulfilment of their distinctive natures. The various values which claim men are unified and given form by the exemplary ideal of Jesus Christ, who exemplified the perfect attitudinal response to the unitary ground of all ethical claims and reveals its nature to others. In Chapter VII I defended the Christian concept of obligation as 'obedience to the will of God' against the objections of Professor Maclagan, equating 'God' with the unitary ground of moral values which imposes a moral purpose on the lives of men. One can speak of 'God's will' in one sense as that objective moral purpose, and in a stronger sense as the teleological causality of the moral Ideal on the world. And one can speak of God as personal, in that personalistic analogies are appropriate descriptions of the moral demand, though not in any way which leads one to think of him as a person in the human sense of a free moral agent. Further ways of speaking of God as personal are provided by revelation, which prescribes regulative models for the direction of the will in devotion and action. These models complement but are not derived from the concept of 'God' founded in moral experience. Finally, one must conceive the being of God as necessary in its existence and nature and as necessarily affecting the nature and destiny of any possible world.

5. The third element of Christian morality, its *authoritative* character, was then developed, beginning, in Chapter VIII, with a general defence of the legitimacy of speaking of moral knowledge. I held that though moral beliefs may be expected to differ in accordance with differences in intellect, temperament, role and culture; and though human apprehension of moral values suffers from ambiguity, relativity to the situation and perversion; nevertheless one can properly speak of a development in moral apprehension in accordance with general criteria of impartiality, coherence and universality. Thus one may proceed to revise and extend one's moral knowledge in accordance with these criteria without ever claiming final and complete knowledge.

Within this general epistemology of a partial and developing knowledge, Jesus may be conceived as one who uniquely discerns and responds to the moral demand as it really is. Thus his life is the exemplary ideal for Christians—it shows each value in its true character as part of one total responsive attitude, and gives form and direction, as a regulative ideal, to each man's vocation.

The concept of 'vocation' is central to Christian ethics; and it calls for the notions of a particular will of God for his creatures and of a knowing, responsive element in the Divine Being, since human responses to the original moral demand generate new particular demands. In his general nature, then, God is a necessary infinite being; but in his particular relations with the world one can properly speak of a developing 'knowledge' and 'will' which is modified by the permitted acts of his creatures.

In Chapter IX I held that, though every man is called to his appropriate vocation, all are also called to adopt a general theistic attitude to the ground of moral values itself. This attitude arises out of a perception of certain universal elements of the human situation as it stands in relation to its moral ground. These elements are authoritatively characterized by Jesus; and they form a three-fold pattern of (a) response to the Creator and Goal of the world; (b) apprehension of human alienation; and (c) acknowledgement of the promise of reconciliation.

In Chapter X I defended the view that there can be authorities in matters of morality since moral knowledge requires training and skill, appropriate experience and temperament. In this respect the claim of Jesus to a unique authority is the essential foundation of any concept of revelation; and it can be rendered intelligible by the supposition of the preservation from sin, or alienation, of Jesus. Christian revelation must thus be founded on the experience of Jesus, and the predicates he ascribed to God derive from that unique experience and have the function of specifying a particular theistic attitude.

In Chapter XI I examined this notion of religious experience and propounded a revised form of the Thomist doctrine of the analogy of proportionality; namely, that such experience could be characterized negatively by saying what it was not; and positively by using analogies drawn from other contexts which would specify a particular attitude to God; but which would be qualified so as to avoid the implication that they are literally descriptive of the being of God. In other words, language about God does not describe his nature (because no concepts are adequate to express his uniqueness); it indicates what the appropriate attitudinal relation to him is. The assurance of such appropriateness is the authoritative experience of Jesus; the predicates the Christian ascribes to God thus derive from the experience of Jesus and specify the attitude which it is proper for all men to adopt to the moral demand. In this respect my view differs from the similar interpretation of Bishop I. T. Ramsey who holds that religious language springs from some experience of the individual believer and has the function of evoking some specific experience in him or in others.

In Chapter XII I analysed more closely the nature of the attitude which is specified by Christian characterizations of God, and articulated it in a three-fold division of worship, contrition and thanksgiving—the appropriate responsive attitudes of fallen and redeemed creatures to their infinite ground and goal. In support of my general analysis of religious language I argued that attitudes require to be specified by their objects; and that the religious object is unique in being total, in that it provides a characterizing description of, without being identical with, each and every experience, and must therefore be conceived as a transcendent existent. The fundamental Christian characterization of God as 'love' was seen to epitomize the three-fold response of the theistic attitude.

In Chapter XIII I maintained that a doctrine of the unique revelatory authority of Jesus could only be sustained by asserting his preservation from 'original sin' and his possession of miraculous powers, which might be calculated to give him a reasonable assurance of his belief in his vocation to be the reconciler of men to God. Thus miracles are to be accepted by the Christian not as evidence for the truth of his beliefs but as conditions of accepting the claimed uniqueness of Jesus.

It is further necessary to enquire what the essential core of Christian revelation is, and what elements of belief might be regarded as transitory or unessential. In answer to this question I held that the essential core of revealed Christian faith is a conceptual structure of authoritative images which symbolize or express the human situation in the light of its moral ground and goal—the images of Creation, the Fall, Atonement and Redemption. In assessing the plausibility of such a structure, one may bring to bear considerations of conceptual consistency, coherence and adequacy; of insight into the human condition; of historical context and of pragmatic value in the lives of others and of oneself. But, in the final analysis, all reflection can do is bring one to the point where the challenge of Christ to human lives seems clear and intelligible, and leave that challenge to have its own effect on the individual who thus hears it.

So, in Chapters VIII–XIII, I sought to defend the reliance of Christian morality upon the unique authority of one man, Jesus, by showing how uniqueness could be attributed to him, and how his experience could become authoritative for all men because only he sees what God really demands of his creatures.

6. The last three chapters of this book have been brief and, to some extent, suggestive rather than explicit in what they say. Plainly, much more needs to be said on the topics of sin, incarnation, atonement and redemption, but to say it at all adequately will require another volume. What I have chiefly sought to do at this time is to attack the doctrine of 'desert' and the scheme of guilt, punishment and substitutionary atonement that goes with it. For although this doctrine enters into many traditional expositions of Christian doctrine I believe it to be fundamentally opposed to the basic Christian value of 'redemptive love' which does not count the cost.

So, in Chapter XIV, I developed in outline a view of 'original sin' as a condition of alienation from the moral demand into which all men are born, for which they cannot be held personally responsible, and which I construed as an ego-protecting device consequent on the primal disobedience of men. In this connection I opposed Professor Hick's thesis of an Irenaean theodicy as inconsistent with the view of human freedom he also wishes to defend.

In Chapter XV I expounded the fourth element of Christian morality, its *charismatic* quality. The Christian must make a decision of will, but it is not to fulfil the moral demands made upon him—which is impossible—but to render himself obedient to the indwelling power of grace, to co-operate with a work of God wrought in him. In this way, and in this way alone, his 'guilt' (his rejection of himself as Divinely purposed) can be overcome by an assurance of Divine 'forgiveness' which reconstitutes his Self so that the Divine intention will be realized in him despite his alienated condition. So the Christian is given a redemptive vocation in the world, both for himself and others, and what he must learn is not obedience to the rigorous demands of the moral law but obedience to the charismatic working of the Spirit, renewing and sustaining his attitude from within.

7. Finally, in Chapter XVI, in speaking of the *teleological* element in Christian ethics, I rejected the juridical notions of Heaven and Hell as rewards and punishments for good or bad conduct, and interpreted 'Heaven' as the natural fulfilment of human personality in free conformity to the Divine intention, and 'Hell' as the natural diminishment of personal being which results from a free rejection of the Divine purpose for that being. The choice between them is a choice between that which is of value in and for itself—God— and the self-centred enrichment of the creature; this is the basic moral choice involved in human existence; and it is this choice which makes true person-hood a possibility. In this sense, of course, it must be seen that God is not and cannot be a 'person'; for he is not free to be other than he is, the supreme source of all value. Thus only created beings are capable of being persons, vested with moral freedom in relation to their Creator to accept or reject his purpose for them. How such freedom is possible is necessarily incomprehensible to us; one can only say that it is a fundamental condition of there being persons as we know them, and thus that it is involved in the decision to create this world. The Christian view is that man's use of his own freedom must be teleologically conceived as leading either to his own final fulfilment or to his final diminishment in the limiting situations of Heaven and Hell.

8. My conclusion is, therefore, that there is a distinctively Christian conception of the nature of morality which is essential to Christianity and which necessarily differs from any non-Christian conception. It is not the case that Christians take the same view of morality as non-Christians, differing only in that they add 'duties to God' to their list of moral principles. Rather, the whole framework of the practice of the moral life will be different for a Christian and for a secular thinker. The Christian morality depends on specific factual assertions—that there is a God whose nature is Holy Love; that there is a continuance of life after death which can be one of growth into the fulfilment of an adequate response to the reality of God begun, however imperfectly or even unconsciously, on earth; and that there is a power of grace and renewal which can reorient our basic human attitudes and establish us in the life of responsive love, here and now. But these assertions are themselves matters of evaluation

s

rather than of empirical investigation. They are integral parts of an overall conception of the moral life as being objective, teleological, attitudinal, authoritative and charismatic; and in the formation of such a conception the factual and evaluative elements cannot be sharply distinguished.

A Christian system of ethics does not simply add new duties (to God) to an established list of duties; nor does it simply give a distinctive set of duties (like 'agape'). It provides a different way of conceiving the nature of morality, what the moral life is, what it is to be moral. It differs not as to particular duties or their scope but as to what ethics is. For the Christian the moral life is an exploration into God: it is not something he can share with the humanist, as though he could say, 'I agree with you in morals, but I believe in God.' He may agree on many specific principles of action; but when it comes to saying what morality is, the Christian gives his own distinctive account. In this book I have not attempted to show how particular duties towards oneself and others derive from the general theistic attitude, though of course they do; nor have I been concerned to deal with particular problems in practical ethics. I have tried to develop the Christian view of the metaphysical basis of morality, and thus of what morality is, and to show how 'revelation' may intelligibly be said to supplement and fulfil the natural theistic understanding of morality by developing a more precise characterization of the human situation in relation to the moral demand, which is founded on authoritative experience.

Thus one may first form the notion of the moral demand itself, the necessary ground of the exemplary universal concepts which determine the truth of moral propositions. When seen in relation to the human situation in the world this gives rise to the three-fold scheme of demand, alienation and reconciliation, which typifies the moral situation of man in very general terms. Revelation specifies further a characterization of 'God' which gives a particular interpretation of this scheme, and specifies appropriate human attitudes in the light of it on the basis of an authoritative experience of the demand. Finally, this complex of attitudes, which is directed to the totality of experience, gives rise to particular social and personal duties which express God's particular will. For the Christian all duties are 'forms of the love of God' for, though all are determined by specific moral facts, all derive from the fundamental fact which is God himself to whom all duties are ultimately owed, and are limited and partial aspects of the one total ideal attitude which he, in his own being, demands of man and which is exemplified in and revealed by Jesus. Thus God is both the ground and ultimate object of all human duties, and finite creatures are properly valued for themselves only when they are seen as grounded in the being of God; for, according to Christian belief, only then does one see them as they really are.

It is in the apprehension of a unitary ground of moral claims upon one, the acceptance of the claims of an authoritative experient of this demand, the experience of the indwelling power of the Spirit, and the trust that the work begun in one will at last be brought to fulfilment, that one might come to adopt a Christian conception of the moral life. And when it is formed the subsequent course of the Christian's life is a constant exploration and testing of this interpretation of his existence, in which moral commitment cannot be divorced from the purely speculative criteria of rationality available to him. In this sense his life and the way it is illuminated by the conceptual scheme he has accepted, remains a continued experiment in the reality and love of God; an experiment in which he must be himself an integral and incalculable component. It is the Christian belief that the experiment must be made; it is the Christian hope that its outcome will be the decisive confirmation of a reality which must now remain elusive and obscure.

One must concede, finally, that this hope may be vain and that the Christian view of morality may be radically misleading. Although I have tried to present the Christian position as sympathetically as possible, my interest has been primarily an analytic one—to state the basic features of Christian morality whether such a morality is eventually found to be acceptable or not. I have not taken it as my task to judge on that issue but to state some of the consequences and presuppositions of adopting a certain view of the nature of morality, and to make clear that it is a view of morality which is at stake, not a mere difference in ethical principles or a theological addendum to one common received non-theistic view of the moral life.

# NOTES

CHAPTER I

1. John Locke, *A Letter Concerning Toleration, 1689*, in *The Works of John Locke* (T. Tegg, 1823), Vol. 6, p. 47: Promises, covenants, and oaths, which are the bonds of human society, can have no hold upon an atheist.'

2. Matt. 7, 16. (All Biblical references are from the Authorized Version).

3. Cf. Kant, *Fundamental Principles of the Metaphysic of Ethics*, trans. T. K. Abbott (Longmans, 1959), 1st section.

4. Thomas Hobbes, *Leviathan* (J. M. Dent: Everyman, 1957), Pt 1, Ch. 13; p. 65.

5. Relevant sources are R. B. Braithwaite, *An Empiricist's View of the Nature of Religious Belief* (Cambridge University Press, 1955), and Paul van Buren, *The Secular Meaning of the Gospel* (S.C.M. Press, 1963).

6. Braithwaite, *op. cit.*, p. 32.

7. For a powerful exposition of objections to theistic morality see Richard Robinson, *An Atheist's Values* (Oxford University Press, 1964).

CHAPTER II

1. Cf. Kant, *Critique of Practical Reason*, trans. L. W. Beck (Liberal Arts Press, 1956), pp. 52-9.

CHAPTER III

1. Cf. R. M. Hare, *The Language of Morals* (Oxford University Press, 1952), and *Freedom and Reason* (Oxford University Press, 1963).

2. Kant, *Critique of Practical Reason*, Analytic, Ch. 1.

3. D. H. Monro, *Empiricism and Ethics* (Cambridge University Press, 1967), esp. Ch. 4.

4. 'Existence, Transcendence and God' in *Religious Studies*, April, 1968; 'Myth and Fact in Christianity' in *Scottish Journal of Theology*, November, 1967; 'Christian Ethics and the Being of God' in *S.J.T.*, March 1969.

5. Cf. R. S. Downie and E. Telfer, *Respect for Persons*, (Allen & Unwin, 1969), Ch. 5, pp. 120 ff. The authors defend objectivism in ethics on three grounds, which they term rationality (moral beliefs cannot be thought of as arbitrary), moral disagreement (disputes are about the truth) and moral seriousness (it is ultimately important to find and commit oneself to correct moral beliefs).

6. Kant, *Fundamental Principles* . . . , Preface, p. 4.

7. Cf. P. Nowell-Smith, *Ethics* (Penguin, 1954), Ch. 3, esp. p. 47.

8. See again Nowell-Smith, *op. cit.*, Ch. 3.

CHAPTER IV

1. Kant, 'Perpetual Peace', trans. L. W. Beck, in *On History*, ed. Beck (Liberal Arts Press, 1957), Appendix 1, p. 126.

2. D. Hume, *Treatise on Human Nature* (A. & C. Black, 1854). Bk 3, Pt 1, p. 231.

3. Cf. Phillipa Foot, *Moral Beliefs* (Proceedings of the Aristotelian Society, 1958–9); 'Moral Arguments' in *Mind*, 1958; *Goodness and Choice* (P.A.S. Supplementary Vol., 1961). A naturalist account is also proposed by G. J. Warnock in *Contemporary Moral Philosophy* (Macmillan, 1967), Ch. 6.

4. G. E. M. Anscombe, 'Modern Moral Philosophy' in *Philosophy*, January, 1958, p. 1.

5. This criticism is made by Nowell-Smith in *Ethics*, p. 39, and by Warnock, *op. cit.*, pp. 15–17.

6. Cf. R. M. Hare, *Language of Morals*, Ch. 1.

7. Sir W. D. Ross, *Foundations of Ethics* (Oxford University Press, 1939), Ch. 8 and p. 320.

8. Kant, *Critique of Practical Reason*, Analytic, Ch. 3, p. 89.

9. Kant, *Critique of Pure Reason*, trans. N. Kemp-Smith (Macmillan, 1929), B. 72, p. 90.

10. Cf. Charles Hartshorne, *Man's Vision of God* and *Divine Relativity* (Arcon, 1964); *The Logic of Perfection* (Open Court).

CHAPTER V

1. Matt. 5–7. What I have in mind is that in the Beatitudes one finds the exemplary pattern of the ideal human life. But for most Christians this is an asymptotic goal to be aimed at, not a set of rules for actual living (cf. my Ch. IX).

2. Thomas Aquinas, *Summae Theologicae* trans. H. McCabe (Blackfriars, 1964), 1a2ae, 94, Arts 1–6.

3. Cf. Mill's distinction of qualitative pleasures in *Utilitarianism* (J. M. Dent: Everyman, 1960), Ch. 2, p. 7: 'Some *kinds* of pleasure are more desirable and more valuable than others.' He implies that one ought to value some (mental) pleasures more highly than others.

4. Kant, *Fundamental Principles . . .* , pp. 15–19.

5. A good exposition of these contrasting views can be found in H. Thielicke, *Theological Ethics*, trans. W. H. Lazareth (A. & C. Black, 1966), Vol. 1, esp. Ch. 11.

6. J. Calvin, *The Institutes of the Christian Religion*, trans. F. L. Battles (S.C.M. Press, 1961), p. 949: 'Whatever he wills, by the very fact that he wills it, must be considered righteous.'

7. Plato, *Euthyphro*, trans. B. Jowett, in *Dialogues of Plato* (Oxford University Press, 1871), Vol. 1, p. 310.

8. W. G. Maclagan, *The Theological Frontier of Ethics* (Allen & Unwin, 1961), p. 64.

CHAPTER VI

1. Aristotle, *Metaphysics*, Bk 12, Ch. 7, 1072b, 4 in *The Basic Works of Aristotle*, trans. W. D. Ross (Random House, 1941).

2. Augustine, 'On the Morals of the Catholic Church', 15; in *Basic Writings of St Augustine*, ed. W. J. Oates (Random House, 1948), Vol. 1, p. 331.

3. For an exposition of the Confucian ethic, cf. *The Analects of Confucius*, trans. A. Waley (London, 1938).

4. Kant, *Fundamental Principles* . . . , p. 10.

5. Aristotle, *De Anima*, Bk 3, Ch. 4, 429a, 27 in *The Basic Works of Aristotle*, trans. J. A. Smith (Random House, 1941).

CHAPTER VII

1. W. G. Maclagan, *op. cit.*, p. 94.

2. *ibid.*, p. 68.

3. *ibid.*, p. 171.

4. Wittgenstein, *Philosophical Investigations*, trans. G. E. M. Anscombe (Blackwell, 1963), p. 32, para. 66. Wittgenstein uses 'game' as an example of a word with multiple criteria of application.

5. W. G. Maclagan, *op. cit.*, p. 177.

6. *ibid.*, p. 89.

7. *ibid.*, p. 94.

8. N. Bohr, *Essays 1958–62 on Atomic Physics and Human Knowledge* (Interscience, 1963), pp. 1–8. Cf also I. G. Barbour, *Issues in Science and Religion* (S.C.M. Press, 1966), pp. 282 ff.

9 Kant, *Critique of Judgement*, trans. J. C. Meredith (Oxford University Press, 1961), pp. 17–74.

10 In this regard, cf. I. T. Ramsey, *Models and Mystery* (Oxford University Press, 1964).

11. Cf. C. Hartshorne, as at Ch. IV, note 10, above

12. A. Farrer, *Faith and Speculation* (A. & C. Black, 1967), Ch. 7, esp. p. 118.

13. A. Farrer, *Finite and Infinite* (Westminster, 1943).

14. D. Hume, *Dialogues Concerning Natural Religion*, ed. Kemp-Smith (Nelson, 1935), Pt 9, esp. p. 189.

15. Aquinas, *op. cit.*, Vol. 3, Q. 12, Art, 1.

16. J. N. Findlay, 'Can God's Existence be Disproved?' in *New Essays in Philosophical Theology*, ed. Flew and MacIntyre (S.C.M. Press, 1955). The retractation is in *The Transcendence of the Cave* (Allen & Unwin 1967), Ch. 4.

17. Relevant discussions of God and morality can be found in H. D. Lewis, *Morals and Revelation* (Allen & Unwin, 1951), and *Morals and the New Theology* (Gollancz, 1947); H. Rashdall, *Theory of Good and Evil* (Oxford University Press, 1907), Vol. 2; W. R. Sorley, *Moral Values and the Idea of God* (Cambridge University Press, 1918); E. Brunner, *The Divine Imperative*, trans. O. Wyon (Lutterworth, 1937).

CHAPTER VIII

1. Cf. Plato, *Republic*, trans. F. M. Cornford (Oxford University Press, 1941), Pt 3.

2. A good exposition of this sort of argument is P. F. Strawson, 'Ethical Intuitionism' in *Philosophy*, January, 1949.

3. Cf. 1. Samuel, 15, 18. Some would say that Samuel was in this case mistaken; nevertheless it seems clear that to a large extent the moral virtues required of the Israelites just were different from the virtues required of us in our different situation.

4. Westermarck, *Ethical Relativity* (Routledge & Kegan Paul, 1932), p. 197.

5. Cf. F. Boas, *Anthropology and Modern Life* (Allen & Unwin, 1929); J. Dewey, 'Anthropology and Ethics' in *The Social Sciences and Their Interrelations*, eds. Ogburn and Goldenwiser (Houghton Mifflin, 1927).

6. There are numerous discussions of this dispute in moral philosophy. One classic discussion is to be found in A. C. Ewing, *The Morality of Punishment* (Kegan Paul, 1929).

7. For a defence of the notion of 'development' in morality see M. Ginsberg, *On the Diversity of Morals* (Heinemann, 1956).

8. An interesting attempt to draw the line and reconcile the opposing intuitions is made by W. G. Maclagan in 'Punishment and Retribution' *Philosophy*, July, 1939, pp. 292–4: 'If I deliberately wronged another person and he knew it, I should judge that he was failing in his duty if he took account of that wrong otherwise than as part of the conditions under which he was, so far as possible, to bring good into the world; but at the same time I should feel that I did not deserve that the wrong should be responded to only in that way' (p. 294).

CHAPTER IX

1. Aristotle, *Nicomachean Ethics*, trans. D. P. Chase (J. M. Dart: Everyman, 1911), Bk 10, 1179a; and Aquinas, *op. cit.*, 2a2ae; Q. 182.

2. J. Calvin, *op. cit.*, Bk 4, Ch. 13, 11; pp. 1265 ff.

3. R. M. Hare, *Freedom and Reason*, Chs 2 and 3.

4. Cf. W. Kneale, 'Objectivity in Morals' in *Philosophy*, April, 1950.

5. Cf. H. Rashdall, *Theory of Good and Evil* (Oxford University Press, 1907), Bk 2, Vol. 2, Ch. 4, for a discussion of the concept of 'vocation'.

6. Cf. Matt. 10, 41–2; 16, 27; Luke 22, 24–30; 1 Cor. 3, 8.

7. Plato, *Republic*, Ch. 12.

8. Luke 12, 48.

9. Eph. 2, 1–6.

CHAPTER X

1. Plato, *Republic*, Ch. 23.

2. Cf. A. J. Ayer, *The Problem of Knowledge* (Macmillan, 1956), Ch. 1, esp. p. 34.

3. Sir David Ross, *Foundations of Ethics*, p. 320.

4. Gen. 22.

5. S. Kierkegaard, *Fear and Trembling* (Princeton University Press, 1941), Problem 1.

6. 1 Sam. 15, 8.

7. See, for instance, J. Hick, *Faith and Knowledge*, 2nd edn (Macmillan, 1966), Chs 1 and 10.

8. Cf. G. E. Moore, 'William James' "Pragmatism"' in *Philosophical Studies* (Routledge & Kegan Paul, 1922).

9. For a general discussion of authority and autonomy, cf. Rashdall, *op. cit.*, Bk 2, Vol. 2, Ch. 5.

CHAPTER XI

1. Hick, *op. cit.*, Ch. 10.

2. A classical account of theistic experience is Rudolf Otto, *The Idea of the Holy*, trans. John Harvey (Penguin, 1917), esp. Ch. 4.

3. J. Hick, *Evil and the God of Love* (Macmillan, 1966), p. 314.

4. Aquinas, *Summa Contra Gentiles*, Bk 1, 28–34, trans. A. C. Pegis, quoted in J. Hick, *Classical and Contemporary Readings in the Philosophy of Religion* (Prentice–Hall, 1964), pp. 44 ff.

5. Aquinas, p. 46.

6. *ibid.*, p. 46.

7. *ibid.*, p. 47.

8. *ibid.*, p. 48.

9. *ibid.*, p. 49.

10. *ibid.*, p. 51.

11. A good account is in Descartes, 'Third Meditation', in *Discourse on Method* trans A. Wollaston. (Penguin, 1960).

12. I. T. Ramsey, *Religious Language* (S.C.M. Press, 1957).

13. *ibid.*, p. 47.

14. *ibid.*, p. 36.

15. *ibid.*, p. 70.

16. *ibid.*, p. 47.

17. *ibid.*, p. 46.

18. I. T. Ramsey, *Christian Discourse* (Oxford University Press, 1965), p. 82.

CHAPTER XII

1. Nowell-Smith, *Ethics*, p. 112, talks of pro- and con-attitudes as if there are only two attitudes, of desire and aversion.

2. P. van Buren, *The Secular Meaning of the Gospel* (S.C.M. Press), p. 101.

3. G. Ryle, *The Concept of Mind* (Hutchinson, 1949), p. 89.

4. Discussions of attitudes which state a substantially similar view are in A. Kenny, *Action, Emotion and the Will* (Routledge & Kegan Paul, 1963); and P. Geach, *Mental Acts* (Routledge & Kegan Paul, 1957).

5. Schleiermacher, *The Christian Faith*, 1, para. 4, trans. in N. Smart, *Historical Selections in the Philosophy of Religion* (S.C.M. Press, 1962), p. 307.

6. J. Cook Wilson, 'The Existence of God' in *Statement and Inference*, ed. A. S. L. Farquharson (Oxford University Press, 1926), Vol. 2, paras 565 ff.

7. Kant, *Critique of Practical Reason*, Analytic, Ch. 3.

CHAPTER XIII

1. R. B. Braithwaite, *An Empiricist's View of the Nature of Religious Belief* (Cambridge University Press, 1955).

2. J. A. T. Robinson, *Honest to God* (S.C.M. Press, 1963), p. 75.

3. F. Ferre, *Language, Logic and God* (Eyre & Spottiswoode 1961), Ch. 12, pp. 162 ff., sets out a similar list of criteria.

4. J. Wisdom, 'Gods' in *Logic and Language*, 1st Series, ed. Flew (Blackwell, 1963).

5. *ibid.*, p. 189.

6. *ibid.*, p. 195.

7. *ibid.*, p. 199.

8. Karl Barth often speaks like this, though one must remember that dialectic is essential to his way of thinking, so that this is a half-truth for him. Cf. *Church Dogmatics*, (T. & T. Clark, 1936), Vol. 1, Ch. 1, section 6.

9. Wisdom would not allow such talk of a 'transcendent reality'; insight, for him, would be *solely* into patterns *within* experience. Nevertheless his analysis of 'insight' is equally valid as an account of the way in which men try to assess the relation of human existence to a transcendent moral demand, granted the existence of such a demand.

10. Matt. 22, 42.

11. Heb. 4, 15.

12. Hume, *An Enquiry Concerning Human Understanding*, ed. Selby-Bigge (Oxford University Press, 1955), Section 10, 'On Miracles'. Hume also thought that miracles were *a priori* impossible—a remarkable contention for a philosopher who doubted all other *a priori* knowledge!

13. Cf. A. Farrer, *Faith and Speculation*, p. 130.

14. Farrer, *The Glass of Vision* (Westminster, 1948), gives an illuminating treatment of imagery in Christian doctrine.

15. Hick, *Evil and the God of Love*, pp. 322 ff.


CHAPTER XIV

1. R. Bultmann, 'New Testament and Mythology' in Bartsch, *Kerygma and Myth* (S.P.C.K. Press, 1953), p. 7.

2. Gal. 3, 22.

3. 1 John 1, 8.

4. Matt. 7, 1

5. Augustine, *City of God*, trans. M. Dods, G. Wilson and J. Smith (Random House, 1950), Bk 13, Ch. 14.

6. Hick, *Evil and the God of Love*.

7. *ibid.*, p. 314.

8. Hick, *Faith and Knowledge*, p. 139.

9. *ibid.*, p. 143.

10. Hick, *Evil and the God of Love*, p. 315.

11. *ibid.*, p. 319.

12. *ibid.*, p. 322.

13. *ibid.*, p. 322.

14. *ibid.*, p. 323.

15. *ibid.*, p. 310.

16. Such a view is espoused by Flew in 'Divine Omnipotence and Human Freedom' in *New Essays in Philosophical Theology*. But this is what Kant called 'the freedom of a turnspit'—one's ultimate reasons are determined by one's own character, for which one is not responsible.

17. Hick, *Evil and the God of Love*, p. 314.

18. Hick, *Faith and Knowledge*, p. 144.

19. Hick, *Evil and the God of Love*, p. 380.

20. Plato, *Republic*, Pt 3.

21. Cf. Plotinus, *Enneads*, trans. S. MacKenna (Faber, 1962). For a similar modern view see J. N. Findlay, *The Transcendence of the Cave* (Allen & Unwin, 1967).

22. Hick, *Faith and Knowledge*, p. 254.

23. Kant, *Critique of Practical Reason*, Dialectic, Ch. 2, 9.

24. *ibid.*, Analytic, Theorem 4, Remark 2.

25. Hick, *Faith and Knowledge*, p. 133.

26. Hick, *Evil and the God of Love*, p. 314.

27. *ibid.*

28. J. P. Sartre, *Being and Nothingness*, trans. Hazel Barnes (Methuen, 1957), Pt 3, Ch. 1, 4. For Sartre, of course, God as the omniscient, omnipresent Other would deprive man of his Self-hood altogether, which is more than I am claiming.

CHAPTER XV

1. Bonhoeffer, *Sanctorum Communio* (Collins, 1963), p. 118 ff.

2. e.g. Bradley, *Ethical Studies*, (Oxford University Press, 1927), p. 27.

3. Anselm, *Cur Deus Homo?* (John Grant, 1909), Bk 2, Ch. 19.

4. Cf. R. S. Downie, 'Forgiveness' in *Philosophical Quarterly*, April, 1964.

5. 2 Cor. 5, 21.

6. P. Tillich, *The Shaking of the Foundations* (S.C.M. Press, 1949), p. 163.

7. Nicolas of Cusa, *The Vision of God*, trans. E. G. Salter (J. M. Dent, London, 1928), Ch. 17.

8. W. G. Maclagan, *The Theological Frontier* . . . , pp. 110 ff.

9. Cf. Rom. 3, 28.

10. Cf. Col. 1,27.

CHAPTER XVI

1. J. H. Newman, *On Anglican Difficulties* (James Duffy, 1857), letter 8, p. 190.

2. Cf. Aquinas, *Summæ Theologicæ*, 3, Supp. Qu., 94; 'The punishment of the damned will cause it [the joy of the blessed] indirectly.'

3. Eph. 4, 32.

4. John, 3, 16.

5. Kant, *Lectures on Ethics*, trans. Louis Infield (Harper Torchbooks, 1963), p. 77.

6. Kant, *Critique of Practical Reason*. The contrast is made in the Analytic, Theorems 1–4; the reconciliation in the Dialectic, 2, 5.

7. Aristotle, *Nicomachean Ethics*, Bk 1, 1102a.

8. Epicurus, *The Extant Remains*, trans. and ed. C. Bailey (Oxford University Press, 1926).

9. Mill, *Utilitarianism*, Ch. 2.

10. Schopenhauer, *The World as Will and Idea*, trans. Haldane, R. B. and Kemp, ed. W. Durant (Simon & Schuster, 1928), p. 190.

11. Kant, *Religion Within the Limits of Reason Alone*, trans. T. M. Greene and H. Hudson (Harper Torchbooks, 1960), Bk 1, sections 3 and 4.

12. e.g. J. L. Stocks, *Morality and Purpose* (Routledge & Kegan Paul, 1969), p. 29.

13. Kant, *Critique of Practical Reason*, Analytic, 1, 2.

14. Cf. Matt. 5, 29; 25, 41; John 15, 6; Luke 16, 23.

15. Hick, *Evil and the God of Love*, p. 376.

16. C. S. Lewis, *The Great Divorce* (Geoffrey Bles, 1946).

# INDEX OF NAMES

# INDEX OF SUBJECTS

T

GEORGE ALLEN & UNWIN LTD

*Head office:*
*40 Museum Street, London, W.C.1*
*Telephone: 01-405 8577*

*Sales, Distribution and Accounts Departments*
*Park Lane, Hemel Hempstead, Herts.*
*Telephone: 0442 3244*

*Athens: 7 Stadiou Street, Athens 125*
*Auckland: P.O. Box 36013, Northcote Central, N.4*
*Barbados: P.O. Box 222, Bridgetown*
*Beirut: Deeb Building, Jeanne d'Arc Street*
*Bombay: 103/5 Fort Street, Bombay 1*
*Calcutta: 285J Bepin Behari Ganguli Street, Calcutta 12*
*Cape Town: 68 Shortmarket Street*
*Dacca: Alico Building, 18 Motijheel, Dacca 2*
*Delhi: 1/18D Asaf Ali Road, New Delhi 1*
*Hong Kong: 105 Wing on Mansion, 26 Hankow Road, Kowloon*
*Ibadan: P.O. Box 62*
*Karachi: Karachi Chambers, McLeod Road*
*Lahore: 22 Falettis' Hotel, Egerston Road*
*Madras: 2/18 Mount Road, Madras 6*
*Manila: P.O. Box 157, Quezon City D-505*
*Mexico: Villalongin 32, Mexico 5, D.F.*
*Nairobi: P.O. Box 30583*
*Rio de Janeiro: Caixa Postal 2537-Zc-00*
*Singapore: 36c Prinsep Street, Singapore 7*
*Sydney, N.S.W.: Bradbury House, 55 York Street*
*Tokyo: C.P.O. Box 1728, Tokyo 100-91*
*Toronto: 145 Adelaide Street West, Toronto 1*

THE MUIRHEAD LIBRARY OF PHILOSOPHY

## PHILOSOPHY AND RELIGION

AXEL HÄGERSTRÖM

During the first half of the twentieth century an anti-metaphysical philosophy grew up at Uppsala University in Sweden. The founder of the movement was Axel Hägerström, although the development of its distinctive ideas was the composite achievement of a number of extremely capable philosophers, not the least of whom was Adolf Phalen.

The Uppsala philosophy had a profound impact on Swedish thought, which has become almost universally anti-metaphysical in the twentieth century. American and British positivism, however, was all but oblivious to the Scandinavian movement. This failure of communication was especially unfortunate from the Anglo-American side, for the approach of the Swedish positivists was much more judicious than that of the Vienna circle. The Swedish philosophers might have shown how positivism could avoid the mistakes which have brought it into general disrepute.

Philosophical discussion has been returning to the problem of metaphysics, albeit now with more of an historical interest. The present volume represents a perhaps belated attempt to introduce into this discussion the distinctive ideas and approaches of the Swedish school, the consideration of which is so long overdue.

The essays included in this volume are among Axel Hägerström's most important writings and when added to the essays previously published in *Inquiries into the Nature of Law and Morals*, afford an adequate and comprehensive summary of his philosophy. The general trend of this philosophy is indicated by the motto which Hägerström chose in declaring his views: 'Moreover I propose that metaphysics must be destroyed.'

## PHILOSOPHY AND ILLUSION

MORRIS LAZEROWITZ

The main object of this book of essays, as of its two predecessors, is to improve our understanding of technical philosophy. The central enigma of philosophy, which has caused deep disquiet in many thinking people, is that nothing in it ever gets settled; rival philosophical views and their arguments remain suspended in thin air, without finding a secure resting-place. The essays may be considered as contributions towards answering a question raised by Hans Reichenbach: 'Why must philosophers forgo a generally accepted philosophy?' The explanatory hypothesis that the author puts forward about the peculiar linguistic character of philosophical views and arguments will be recognized as having its roots in Ludwig Wittgenstein's later thought. Some readers of Wittgenstein distinguish between the 'false philosophy' in his work and other parts of it which they find more congenial to their own thinking. Wittgenstein's 'false philosophy' falls into what Professor Lazerowitz calls 'Metaphilosophy' and it holds out promise of an enlightening answer to Reichenbach's question. The essays of this book have the unity of a single orientation, the development of an hypothesis which will give us insight into the workings of philosophy. A number of basic issues are treated in the light of this hypothesis; issues centring on empiricism and rationalism, direct and indirect perception, the reality of time, induction, the existence of propositions, causation, the internality of relations.

# ACTION

## SIR MALCOLM KNOX

This study of moral experience is based on Gifford Lectures delivered in Aberdeen. It begins by describing the way in which the action of human beings rises from being instinctive to being chosen. Moral problems arise when man has to choose. At different times men act for pleasure, or to obey a rule, or to obtain some benefit, or to do their duty. All these reasons are considered in the book, and it is argued that tfley all have their place in such different levels of experience as play, law, economics, politics and personal relationships. Special consideration is given to the nature of action as such. The book ends with an examination of the relation between morality and religion. The wide range of the author's argument and his numerous concrete examples present a challenge to the contemporary linguistic philosophy which he rejects.

The author has spent half of his working life in teaching philosophy at Oxford and St Andrews, and the other half in business and university administration. Thus he discusses moral problems from a wealth of different experience, rather than on a purely theoretical level. His forthright statement of his views should serve as an introduction to moral philosophy for undergraduates, and should interest general readers for whom, rather than for professional philosophers, this book is intended.

## THE GIFFORD LECTURES. 1964–65

# THE DISCIPLINE OF THE CAVE

## J. N. FINDLAY, MA.A., Ph.D., F.B.A.
Professor of Philosophy in the University of London (King's College)

These lectures are the first series of a course of Gifford Lectures whose second series was given in December 1965 – January 1966, and entitled *The Transcendence of the Cave*. The second series continues the theme of the first series and is essential to its complete understanding.

The lectures make use of the Platonic image of the Cave to emphasize the fact that men feel their familiar experience to be full of many and strange restrictions, and to involve puzzles and discrepancies which they do not even see the possibility of solving and removing. Deep-set philosophical perplexities of this sort can be seen as arising out of the misunderstanding and meaningless abuse of ordinary ways of thinking and speaking. But they can equally be seen, in the Platonic phrase, as 'drawing up towards being', providing an apagogical proof of the 'absurdity' of ordinary thought, speech and experience except as modified and supplemented in ways which may point altogether beyond it. What may be called a mystical and otherworldly element, and a graded series of experiences in which it is enjoyed, may therefore need to be introduced into, or rendered explicit in, all our experience, action and diction, not as some gratuitous modification or addition, but in order to give viable sense to the most commonplace human utterances and activities, such as perceiving and manipulating environmental objects, conversing with other conscious beings, doing scientific experiments, etc. The presuppositions of such a manner of reasoning, of course, involve much fundamental criticism and revision of contemporary conceptions of language, logic and meaning and of their relation to experience and to the teaching of the use of words.

The method of the lectures involves some use of a method akin to the descriptive, phenomenological method of Husserl, as well as a method akin to the dialectical, revisionary method of Hegel. The lectures also draw for inspiration on Platonist, Neoplatonist, Scholastic, Buddhist and other sources.

THE MUIRHEAD LIBRARY OF PHILOSOPHY

# NON-LINGUISTIC PHILOSOPHY

## A. C. EWING

The positivist school of philosophy has been widely criticized for its excessive attention to language and for the narrow limits it imposes on philosophy. This book
challenges the school in two ways: it attacks particular views and arguments put
forward by the positivists, and it tries to create a philosophy which goes beyond
the limits set by them. Article 1 attacks the verification principle, which denies
factual meaning to anything outside the realm of natural science; 2 defends intuition; 3 and 9 criticize attempts to evade the difficulties presented by the metaphysical sceptic; 4 and 8 oppose the arguments which tend to reduce the mind to
something not distinct from the body; 5 attempts an intensional as opposed to an
extensional treatment of the best known type of argument in logic; 6 defends real
necessity in causation and arrives at a mode of justifying induction which is alien
to the positivist school; 7 deals with Kant's earlier objections to metaphysics; 10
defends a theory of truth opposed to the semantic and verificationist theories; 11
criticizes an attempt by linguistic philosophers to discredit one side in the free-will
controversy; 12 challenges an account of religion which does not commit it to any
metaphysical view; and 13 and 14 seek to present the metaphysical claims of religion
in a reasonably defensible form.

# REASON AND SCEPTICISM

## MICHAEL A. SLOTE

This work rebuts Wittgensteinian and Phenomenalist attempts to overcome epistemological scepticism, and provides powerful new arguments for the *scientific*
reasonableness of belief in an external world.

Professor Slote argues that belief in an external (physical) world, in the general
veridicalness of perception and memory, in other minds, and in (temporarily) unobserved objects can be justified by means of general principles of scientific
methodology. He rebuts recent arguments to the effect that attempts to overcome
various forms of epistemological scepticism are jejune and misguided.

Professor Slote's major achievement, however, is to provide detailed and powerful
new arguments against scepticism, about the external world, other minds, etc. He
argues that it is reasonable to accept the 'hypothesis' of an external world that is and
has been pretty much as it seems to be, and to have been as the best scientific explanation of the existence of our present sense experiences and memory impressions.
A new form of the 'argument from analogy' is employed to establish the existence
of other minds and unobserved objects, and is defended from various objections.
And sceptical challenges to scientific methodology—among them Goodman's *New
Riddle of Induction*, are examined and answered.

Finally Professor Slote discusses scepticism about the existence of God and
illuminates certain previously ignored *rational* but *non-scientific* grounds for belief
in a deity. The grounds are weaker than those that can be provided for belief in an
external world, etc., but they still *may* be strong enough so that belief in some sort
of deity is not altogether unreasonable.

# THE PROBLEMS OF PERCEPTION

R. J. HURST

This book offers a comprehensive survey of the problems of perception, paying special attention to those set by the causal processes involved in perceiving, by the subjective conditioning of what is perceived, and by the occurrence of hallucinations. After a critical examination of the main current attempts at a solution, including those made by recent 'linguistic' or 'analytical' philosophy, there is developed an original explanatory theory based on a restatement of the Double Aspect Theory of the relation of mind and body.

Although intended primarily for students and teachers of philosophy, the book should appeal also to the intelligent layman: psychologists and neurologists should find of particular interest its discussions of the philosophical questions their studies raise.

# LECTURES ON PHILOSOPHY

G. E. MOORE

EDITED BY CASIMIR LEWY

G. E. Moore lectured at Cambridge every year from 1911 until his retirement in 1939. These lectures were often attended by philosophers from different parts of the world, and they were one of the chief means by which he extended his influence on the philosophical thought of his time. Dr Lewy has now edited a selection from some of these lectures. They discuss problems in epistemology, in philosophical logic and in the methodology of philosophy. They contain ideas which Moore did not publish elsewhere, and they should be of unusual interest to students of analytic philosophy.

# PHILOSOPHY OF WHITEHEAD

W. MAYS, PH.D.

Whitehead stands out among modern philosophers by his depth of vision and wide range of interests. This book effectively demonstrates that his thought has a much greater consistency and precision than is usually assumed. The author convincingly argues that the key to the understanding of Whitehead's philosophical system is to be found rather in his earlier philosophy of science than in traditional philosophy. He contends that logical, mathematical and physical ideas, as well as descriptions of direct experience, play an essential role in Whitehead's later thought. On the one hand, this book gives a critical exposition of the main concepts of Whitehead's philosophy as seen in their scientific perspective. On the other, it clarifies his treatment of specific philosophical problems, such as the nature of sense-perception, causality, free-will and the body-mind problem. In this way the author throws a new light on those features of Whitehead's system which have puzzled philosophers for three decades.

## KANT'S FIRST CRITIQUE

### H. W. CASSIRER

This book is one of the few published in this country which deals fully with the whole of Kant's Critique of Pure Reason. The author engages in a detailed investigation of the text of the Aesthetic and Analytic, and pays the same close attention to the Dialectic which seeks to establish the fallaciousness of all arguments purporting to lead us beyond sense-experience. The work is throughout both expository and critical in character. The criticism is directed against certain tenets which Kant himself believed to be of crucial importance. For example, it is shown that the argument of the so-called Metaphysical Deduction of the categories is invalid, and that there are insuperable difficulties in Kant's view that supersensible things-in-themselves must be supposed to lie behind the objects which the mind encounters in experience.

If the author has nonetheless thought it worth while to offer another discussion of Kant's theory of knowledge, this is because he is convinced that, despite its weaknesses, it contains a very great deal which is of permanent value and importance. The book is throughout written in simple and straightforward language, all matters which could be of interest only to Kantian specialists having been rigorously excluded. It is hoped that this procedure will enable the general reader to form his own judgement of the author's thesis that the Kantian method of approaching problems of philosophy offers considerable advantages over the method of out-and-out empiricism which is in vogue at the present day.

## SOME MAIN PROBLEMS OF PHILOSOPHY

### G. E. MOORE

These lectures, though written forty years ago, are of more than historical interest. In them Professor Moore presents two typical, philosophical problems—that of the external world and that of what it is for a thing to be of a certain kind. With the directness and love of clarity for which he is famous he tries to make his exploration no harder than it must be. But anyone who accompanies him will soon realize that philosophy is no picnic, and will have before him a lively example of those qualities which are, at all times, called for in those who seek philosophic truth.

## PHILOSOPHY IN AMERICA

### EDITED BY MAX BLACK

A collection of fourteen original essays on a variety of philosophical topics by some of the most talented younger American philosophers, specially commissioned for this volume, with a preface by the editor.

Previous anthologies of British and American philosophy in the Muirhead Library have consisted of contributions by philosophers of established reputation. By choosing now to present to a wider public the work of young philosophers still on their way to 'the top', the editor hopes to enable the common reader as well as the specialist to become acquainted with some of the best of the lively and penetrating work of philosophical investigation of a young generation.

The contributors were chosen by the editor after consultation with a large number of prominent American philosophers. Each contributor was left free to choose his own topic and to handle it as he thought best.